The Best AMERICAN SPORTS WRITING 2002

GUEST EDITORS OF
THE BEST AMERICAN SPORTS WRITING

1991 DAVID HALBERSTAM
1992 THOMAS MCGUANE
1993 FRANK DEFORD
1994 TOM BOSWELL
1995 DAN JENKINS
1996 JOHN FEINSTEIN
1997 GEORGE PLIMPTON
1998 BILL LITTLEFIELD
1999 RICHARD FORD
2000 DICK SCHAAP
2001 BUD COLLINS
2002 RICK REILLY

The Best AMERICAN SPORTS WRITING™ 2002

Edited and with an Introduction
by Rick Reilly

Glenn Stout, *Series Editor*

HOUGHTON MIFFLIN COMPANY
BOSTON • NEW YORK 2002

Visit our Web site: www.houghtonmifflinbooks.com.

ISSN 1056-8034
ISBN 0-618-08627-7
ISBN 0-618-08628-5 (pbk.)

Printed in the United States of America

DOC 10 9 8 7 6 5 4 3 2 1

Contents

Foreword

THE READERS of this book are a unique constituency. For many, I suspect that *The Best American Sports Writing* makes a more or less regular appearance in their hands sometime between Labor Day and Christmas. It is something of a no-brainer for certain fans of sports and writing, an instant gift happily received. The annual migration of this book from bookstore to bookshelf can be calculated almost to the day, as if inspired by discreet and distant urgings buried deep in the DNA, a kind of seasonal response to diminishing light.

This kind of anticipation, like waiting for the first good snow, creates an exacting level of expectation in many readers. Over time they have developed a great sense of ownership over the final product, as well they should. After all, books cease to belong to the author — or in this case, the editors — as soon as readers turn to the first page. Their experience is all that matters, and when they start reading, the book becomes more theirs than its creators'.

Many writers, particularly those in daily journalism, know exactly what I mean. The *Los Angeles Times*'s Bill Plaschke, whose story "Her Blue Haven" leads off this collection, makes use of a similar situation as the basis for his story; regular readers of our work feel they have a stake in each and every word. They take us seriously, even when we don't always take ourselves that way.

That doesn't mean that the readers of the books in this series are so slavishly devoted that they are above criticism. Quite the opposite. The readers of this series who contact me are rarely shy about expressing themselves. My name on the book jacket gives them that right. Over the years they have made it clear to me that although they enjoy the fluctuations of the menu each year, at the end of the meal they want to feel satisfyingly full. A book like this requires the investment of several hours of readers' time, and it is their right to feel they have used that time well.

Fortunately, most do, at least among those who contact me. Of those who do complain, most are concerned with a kind of scorekeeping, as in, "There were too many newspaper stories," or not enough newspaper stories, or too much football, or not enough hockey. Or too many famous writers, columns, men, women, curse words, adjectives, consonants, etc., etc., etc. — or not enough of those same items. One reader even calculated the annual cost per page of his purchase since the beginning of the series. For the record, we are holding our own against inflation.

I tend to measure how well I do my job by the way these complaints inevitably even out over the year. Most couch their criticism between compliments anyway, and when readers argue from the opposite sides of the same fence, I figure I must be doing something right.

Each year I invite readers to take part in this series, to send me stories they think might merit inclusion in the book. And they do, often with an eye at least as accurate and discerning as my own. For some reason, authors remain somewhat reticent about submitting their own material, and despite my repeated efforts, some editors I contact each year asking for submissions, particularly in the newspaper field, don't always do so.

Fortunately, the readers take up the slack. Several sent me Plaschke's story, and there is at least one other story that made its way into this volume that I would not have seen had a reader not clipped it, stuck it in an envelope, and sent it off to me. So keep it up.

In addition to those complaints and suggestions, a few missives stand out each year for one reason or another. One reader writes me each and every year asking when the book will be published and where he can find it. And every year I write back and say, "September," and, "Your local bookstore." I assume he is successful. He never asks where to find last year's edition.

Last September 17 I received an e-mail from a reader in New

York City. In that strange time, in the wake of the 9/11 carnage, I think many of us everywhere found it difficult to focus and concentrate, particularly on something made so instantly trivial as sports. I felt this myself, for I was working on another project and was forced to write or consider the words "New York" over and over again. For weeks the name of that city felt and sounded different, as if heard for the first time and describing a brand-new place, and each time it caused a momentary and uncomfortable pause from which there seemed no escape. At the same time I was rapidly inundated by sports reportage from all over the country that touched on the horror of that day and found myself lost in the mind-numbing litany of tragedy piled upon tragedy. While I was fortunate in that everyone I loved and cared about in the city survived, still, the buildings had fallen and their shadows never seemed to lift.

And then I received this:

> . . . As I struggled to cope with what was going on around me, I kept looking for a way to "take a break" — living in NYC has made it very difficult to do this — everything from the smoke in your hair to the constant wail of sirens, to the naked skyline is an ever-present reminder.
>
> I tried to read, watch movies, talk with friends about other stuff, but nothing worked. . . . I sat around unable to think or feel. And then on Wednesday afternoon I shuffled over to my bookshelf, one last attempt to find some satisfying distraction. As I scanned the shelves a large black and gold volume popped out at me — *The Best American Sports Writing of the Century* . . . the subject matter interesting but removed from reality, the quality of writing poignant but not too deep. . . . I found some solace in the stories, in the words. . . .

And so did I, in his. I don't repeat this story because it was sent to me, but because I believe it was directed to the writers of each and every volume in this series. It is easy for the authors who commit themselves to these and other pages each day and year of their lives to grow cynical, to feel that too many words fall still and silent and stupid, unheard, immaterial, and insignificant. We work, after all, in what others occasionally deride as "the toy department." But I think that this e-mail provides the best and only justification for what any of us do. Words can win awards and sometimes inspire change, they can cause us to laugh and cry or to fall asleep or turn the page. But they can also matter and mean more, perhaps briefly, in the hands of those we serve. None of us can tell precisely why or when that will be, apart from those brief moments when the reader tells us. And as any writer can tell you, perhaps the most important part of what we do is learning to listen well. So to the readers of this book, and the writers who are responsible for it each year, thank you.

My task each year is simple. I read as much as possible in hundreds of sports and general interest publications in search of work that I feel might merit inclusion in this book. I try to avoid missing anything, so each year I contact the editors and sports editors of hundreds of magazines, asking for either submissions or complimentary subscriptions. I also contact sports editors of a like number of newspapers and ask them to submit material.

But as I indicated earlier, I also welcome submissions from interested readers and writers. And writers, hear this: *you are more than welcome to submit your own material.* My only concern is for the final product. I don't much care how material comes to me, only that I see it in the first place.

Just after the first of the year I forward those stories that I find myself wanting to read again and again — usually about seventy-five — to our guest editor, who makes the final selection. That task fell this year to the estimable Rick Reilly, who supplemented my picks with some of his own.

As you read this, I am several knees deep in stories under consideration for *The Best American Sports Writing 2003* and always welcome more. Each nonfiction story must have been published in 2002 in a newspaper, magazine, or online publication in either the United States or Canada, and it must be column-length or longer. Reprints are not eligible. All submissions must be received by me by February 1, 2003.

All submissions must include the name of the author, the date of publication, and the publication name and address. Photocopies, tear sheets, or clean copies are fine — reductions to 8½-by-11 are best. Newspaper stories should be mounted on paper, if possible, since loose clips stuffed in envelopes often suffer in transit. Owing to the volume of material I receive, no submissions will be either returned or acknowledged. Neither is it appropriate for me to make any comments about any individual submission.

Publications that want to make absolutely certain that I see their material are advised to send a complimentary subscription to the following address. This is not, and never has been, a requirement, but with a subscription I can survey material over the course of the year rather than in a deluge each January.

Submissions and subscriptions should be sent to this precise address:

Glenn Stout
Series Editor
The Best American Sports Writing
PO Box 381
Uxbridge, MA 01569

I may also be contacted by e-mail at BASWeditor@cs.com, but please note that no submissions will be accepted electronically, either pasted in or as an attachment.

Earlier editions of this book can be ordered through most book dealers or online sources. An index of stories through the year 2000 is available on glennstout.net.

Thanks again to Eamon Dolan and Emily Little of Houghton Mifflin for their trust and help each year, and to Rick Reilly for his active involvement. Siobhan and Saorla again managed to hold their own against the endless onslaught of paper. Readers Scott Chait and Ed Page, among others, made significant contributions to this volume as well. And thanks again to the writers for allowing me to shape their book.

GLENN STOUT

Introduction

THE ONLY JOB I've been able to hold on to is sports writing. I've flopped at everything else. I've been fired more than ceramic pottery and Billy Martin put together.

I was fired from my first job at fourteen. Lady didn't like the way I chewed my gum. Got fired from a rental-equipment place at sixteen. Thought the boss said, "Fill these jackhammers with fifteen parts oil, one part gas," but it turns out it was the other way around. Got fired from a gas station at eighteen. Left a guy's oil cap off and it fell down into his fan belt and the station had to pay $435 to fix it for him. Got fired as a bank teller at nineteen. Lost $500 one day. Still don't know where it went.

But knock on wood, sports writing hasn't 86'ed me yet. Started doing it for a living at twenty. That's twenty-five years ago now. If there is ever a nuclear winter and sports writing is no longer needed, I'm toast.

I'm not saying I'm good, but I think I know what good is. Good is the stuff we've chosen for this book. Good is not easy. College kids write me all the time asking how to make their writing better. I always hate answering that letter. You send them tips and you come off like a know-it-all. You ignore it and you come off like a jerk.

But editing this book has made me think about it. Two chewed chair legs and three pots of coffee later, I finally came up with ten simple strategies that I know will work no matter the subject, length, or deadline. And so, I present now, for your shredding pleasure . . . the Reilly Rules.

1. Never Write a Sentence You've Already Read.

That was said by Oscar Wilde, but it's still the best way to make words jump off the page and squirt grapefruit juice in the reader's face. Why write: "He beat the crap out of the guy" when it's so much more fun to write: "He turned the guy into six feet of lumps"?

You ever notice the way cops talk on the eleven o'clock news? On TV, the cop will go all *Dragnet* on you: "We apprehended the alleged suspect after a prolonged pursuit." But then you hear the same cop down at Dunkin' Donuts and he's going, "Man, we chased this fruitcake everywhere! Guy thought he was Secretariat!"

The best writing sounds like that. It sounds like a guy talking to you over a fence. The *Los Angeles Times*'s Jim Murray, the greatest sportswriter who ever lived, wrote like that. Murray put simple words in an order nobody had seen before.

Murray once wrote in the *Los Angeles Times* that John Wooden was "as square as a pan of cornbread." Boog Powell was "just slightly larger than the Istanbul Hilton." USC's sweep left was "as unstoppable as a woman's tears." And, "Willie Mays' glove is the place where triples go to die."

Steve Rushin of *Sports Illustrated* writes like that. He would sell his sister to the Iraqis before he'd write a boring sentence. In his piece "Cold Comfort," he describes what it felt like the moment the radio told him his elementary school was closed on account of too much snow.

"Instantly, it's Mardi Gras and V-E Day and the Lindbergh parade all in one, and the flakes falling outside look like ticker tape."

Guy makes me sprain my grin.

Blackie Sherrod of the *Dallas Morning News* once described rogue quarterback Bobby Layne's arrest for drunk driving this way:

"Layne . . . stopped off to indulge in some heavy research with scholarly friends. Late that evening, Bobby was driving to his hotel, innocently enough, when he was sideswiped by several empty cars lurking at curbside."

Ever read *that* before?

2. Get 'Em in the Tent.

Murray used to say, "They'll never see the circus if you can't get 'em in the tent." Translated: Without a good lead, they'll never appreciate your death-defying twinkle-toe transition in the twenty-third paragraph. Maybe that's why he once led off a column on the safety hazards at the Indianapolis 500 with: "Gentlemen, start your coffins!"

Have you ever been zapping around on the remote, going from one show to the next? And then something comes on that you just can't zap because you *have* to know what's going to happen next? That's what a great lead does. In this fragmented world, readers are looking for the tiniest excuse to turn the page, put you down, and get out of their chair. There's no city ordinance that says they *have* to read you.

So you have to make it impossible for them not to go on to the second graph. Take, for instance, Tom Scocca's boxing lead from "Blood Sport."

"Idly, last week, I watched Beethavean Scottland get beaten into a coma."

Or *Outside*'s Steve Friedman's lead from "'It's Gonna Suck to Be You'":

"The first time he tried it, the vomiting started after sixty-seven miles. . . ."

How are you *not* going to keep reading?

3. Say What You Think.

Wholesale tin-eared butchery sports writing goes like this:

"Monolith Tech and Conglomerate University waged a real war on Saturday.

"'That was a real war out there,' said Monolith head coach Bruiser Smith."

Bad sportswriters have this thing about pens and pads. They *have* to use them — to exhaustion. So if they take the time to talk to a coach or a player or a fan, then they're damn sure going to use it. But do you realize that some of the greatest sportswriters in history — Damon Runyon, Ring Lardner, Grantland Rice — quoted almost nobody? They said what *they* felt, knowing they could say it better, funnier, and pithier than any lummox in shoulder pads.

What good is it to quote five people saying Bubba is fast when you can say it by yourself with just, "Bubba is faster than rent money"?

Check out the way Dan Neil sums up a night of demolition derby in his hilarious "Big Night in Bithlo" from *Car and Driver:*

"As the last toxic fumes from the jet-car bus burning waft over the crowd, the armadillos poke their heads out from their burrows, and the crowd heads toward their pickup trucks, this edition of Crash-O-Rama seems an unqualified success, and by that I mean a complete disaster."

Not a quote in sight.

4. It Sucks Before You Start.

You wrote a piece that sucked. The reason it sucked is not the way you wrote it. It's that when you finally sat down to write it, you didn't have any good stuff. Unless you're Dave Barry or Dan Jenkins or David Copperfield, you're not going to make Pulitzers out of puke.

Sports Illustrated's Gary Smith, the I. M. Pei of profilers, has a rule. He's not done researching a subject until he's interviewed at least fifty people. That's why he only does four a year. And that's also why those four are often the most unforgettable of the year. They are meticulous in their depth of reporting, nearly preposterous. And yet he throws around quotes the way Don Rickles threw around compliments. He prods and searches and hunts until he knows a story so well he can tell it himself, in his own crisp, penetrating prose.

It's not a hunt for detail. It's the hunt for the *right* detail. The *Philadelphia Daily News*'s Mark Kram, Jr., in his "Joe's Gift," describes how a boy put up a wall between himself and his grief at the drowning death of his older brother, Harry:

"He began to systematically erase Harry from the premises: he sold his bicycle, gave away his books, beanbag chair, and other belongings, and set fire to his clothes."

That is *great* reporting. You come up with stuff like that, you can't help but write well.

(One other thing. The *Washington Post*'s Michael Leahy, who was given the Michael Jordan beat in 2001, is known as a very accurate reporter. In "Transition Game" he describes a scene in the locker room just before Jordan's first comeback game in a Washington Wizard uniform:

"Another writer, who had predicted his comeback amid much disdain, sidled up, patted his arm, and said, 'I didn't get any apology letters.'"

"'Don't expect any either,' Jordan said, unwilling to give this man a morsel tonight either. 'You ought to know that.'"

I know that's accurate. I was the writer he was writing about.)

5. The Interview Never Ends.

This is just a quickie, but so many writers shut down their ears when the formal interview ends. Don't. Keep your eyes and ears open and the invisible ink flowing even after the subject shakes your hand and says goodbye. Follow him out. Watch him drive off. You never know what might happen.

When I was covering golf for *Sports Illustrated,* I invented "trunking," which means following the winner from the eighteenth green, through his press conference, through his winner's dinner, through whatever happens, out to the parking lot, until he puts his clubs in the trunk, slams it, and tells you to get lost. I got more good stuff doing that, and *SI* golf reporters still do it. In fact, that's how *SI* managed to quote Vijay Singh winning the 2000 Masters, going out to the parking lot, slamming the trunk, and declaring: "This place can kiss my black ass!"

6. Forget Cereal Boxes.

We all get in ruts, where we believe the only sports worth writing about are the big four: baseball, football, basketball, and hockey — the basic stuff that shows up on the Wheaties box.

But more often than not, the best dramas, funniest scenes, most interesting characters, are places where we forget to go. One look through this book will tell you that. There's a compelling story about bullfighting, a fascinating profile of a blind mountain climber, and an eye-gouging look at backyard wrestling.

Sometimes you might even find a great sports writing story when you look at . . . sports writing. Or haven't you read *Los Angeles Times* columnist Bill Plaschke's "Her Blue Haven"?

7. Death to Overwriting!

The quickest freeway to Bushdom, Hackville, Crap City, is to overwrite. Don't.

Just . . . don't.

When President Kennedy died, Jimmy Breslin interviewed the gravedigger. That's underwriting. That's poignancy. That says more than a thousand overwrought paragraphs about "the nation's heavy-hearted grief." When Frank Deford came to the key moment in his classic profile of "The Toughest Coach Who Ever Lived" back in the 1980s, he did it like a knife going through left-out margarine:

"[Coach] chatted with [his daughter] and told her how much he missed and loved her, and then he handed the phone to Virginia and went to finish dressing for the Lions Club meeting. In the bathroom, Bull Cyclone had just slapped some cologne on his face when he dropped dead without a sound."

You can't be graver than death, louder than bombs, more Catholic than the pope. So don't try. Go the other way.

8. Adjectives and Adverbs Sorta Suck, Really.

If I can avoid using an adjective, I will. If I can avoid writing, "He was a lucky sort of guy," and write instead, "He was the kind of guy who could drop a quarter in a pay phone and have it pay 20 to 1," then I've not only made it fun for me and the guy in the Barcalounger in Peoria, but I stand a good chance of not being fired for the week.

When *ESPN Magazine*'s Gene Wojciechowski, as pure a writer as is working today, wants to show that the late Al McGuire was "trusting," he notes that McGuire would throw his car keys on the seat of his unlocked car. When he wants to show he was "quirky," he remembers how McGuire would shop in the oddest places for tin toy soldiers. For "rebellious" he quotes McGuire himself, saying, "I only comb my hair if there are four people in the room, and if there are four people, I'm getting paid." But not once does Wojciechowski write, "Al McGuire was a trusting, quirky, rebellious sort of a guy." And aren't you glad?

And don't even *talk* to me about adverbs. I hate adverbs. I would rather be coated in chicken drippings and dropped in a leopard den than use adverbs. If you can't find a better way to say "hungrily" or "proudly," you need to find a new line of work, preferably nowhere near words.

9. Look Around, Stupid.

Not to be insulting, but sometimes the best stuff is right in front of us. The only trick is seeing it. When *Orlando Sentinel* columnist

Mike Bianchi attended Dale Earnhart's funeral, he did something odd. He didn't write about Earnhart. Or Earnhart's family. Or Earnhart's legacy. He wrote about the other drivers sitting in the church that day, staring into a box they knew could contain *them* next week.

One time the writer John McNulty was profiling sensational Triple Crown winner Native Dancer, owned by the glamorous Vanderbilts. And McNulty pulled off one of the most delicious Look Arounds I've ever read. In fact, he closed his piece with it:

"As Native Dancer passed each stall where a Vanderbilt horse was being groomed, work stopped for a few moments. 'There he go,' one groom said, pausing to work on his horse, and it was nice to hear him say, 'You a good horse, too.'"

10. Ignore All Rules.

After all, you probably have real talent and will end up making Hemingway look like a guy who writes owner's manuals for Japanese televisions and will show up someday and take *my* job.

And I *refuse* to go back to the jackhammer refueling industry.

RICK REILLY

BILL PLASCHKE

Her Blue Haven

FROM THE LOS ANGELES TIMES

Bill Plaschke predicted doom for the Dodgers in 2001. . . . Plaschke criticized. . . . Plaschke forgot. . . . Plaschke compared unfairly. . . . The Dodgers need encouragement, not negativity. . . .

That was part of a 1,200-word screed e-mailed to me last December, a holiday package filled with colorful rips. It was not much different from other nasty letters I receive, with two exceptions. This note contained more details than the usual "You're an idiot." It included on-base percentages and catchers' defensive statistics. It was written by someone who knew the Dodgers as well as I thought I did.

And this note was signed. The writer's name was Sarah Morris. She typed it at the bottom.

Most people hide behind tough words out of embarrassment or fear, but Sarah Morris was different. She had not only challenged me to a fight, but had done so with no strings or shadows.

I thought it was cute. I wrote her back. I told her I was impressed and ready for battle.

Little did I know that this would be the start of a most unusual relationship, which eight months later is being recounted from a most unusual place. I am writing this from the floor, Sarah Morris having knocked me flat with a punch I never saw coming.

May I ask you a question? For two years I have been running my own Web site about the Dodgers. I write game reports and editorials. How did you become a baseball editorialist? That is my deam.

This was Sarah's second e-mail, and it figured. Every time I smile at someone, they ask me for a job.

Her own Web site? That also figured. Everybody has a Web site. The Dodgers guess there are more than two dozen Web sites devoted to kissing the almighty blue.

So my expert wasn't really an expert, but rather a computer nerd looking for work. I didn't need any more pen pals with agendas.

But about that last line. I chewed my lower lip about it. The part about "my deam."

Maybe Sarah Morris was just a lousy typist. But maybe she was truly searching for something, yet was only one letter from finding it. Aren't all of us sometimes like that?

It was worth one more response. I wrote back, asking her to explain.

I am thirty years old. . . . Because I have a physical handicap, it took me five years to complete my AA degree at Pasadena City College. . . . During the season I average 55 hours a week writing five to seven game reports, one or two editorials, researching and listening and/or watching the games.

Physical handicap. I paused again. I was in no mood to discuss a physical handicap, whatever it was.

I have had these discussions before, discussions often becoming long, teary stories about overcoming obstacles.

Courageous people make me jealous. They make me cry. But at some point, they have also made me numb.

Then I read the part about her working fifty-five hours a week. Goodness. This woman didn't only follow the Dodgers, she covered them like a newspaper reporter.

But for whom? Sarah called her Web site *Dodger Place.* I searched for it, and found nothing. I checked all the Dodger search links, and found nothing.

Then I reread her e-mail and discovered an address buried at the bottom: http://members.tripod.com/spunkydodgers.

I clicked there. It wasn't fancy, rather like a chalkboard, with block letters and big type.

There was a section of "News from a Fan." Another section of "Views by a Fan." But she covered the team with the seriousness of a writer.

The stories, while basic, were complete. Sarah's knowledge was evident.

But still, I wondered, how could anybody find it? Is anybody reading?

Nobody ever signs my guestbook.

Does anybody correspond?

I get one letter a month.

I read the Web site closer and realized that she does indeed receive about one letter a month — always from the same person.

So here was a physically handicapped woman, covering the Dodgers as extensively as any reporter in the country, yet writing for an obscure Web site with an impossible address, with a readership of about two.

That "deam" was missing a lot more than an *r,* I thought.

The days passed, winter moved toward spring, and I had more questions.

Sarah Morris always had answers.

I started my own Web site in hopes of finding a job, but I have had no luck yet. I have gone to the Commission of Rehabilitation seeking help, but they say I'm too handicapped to be employed. I disagree.

So what if my maximum typing speed is eight words per minute because I use a head pointer to type? My brain works fine. I have dedication to my work. That is what makes people successful.

I don't know how to look for a job.

A head pointer? I remember seeing one of those on a late-night commercial for a hospital for paralyzed people.

It looked frightening. But her stories didn't look frightening. They looked, well, normal.

Now I find out she wrote them with her head?

I asked her how long it took her to compose one of her usual 1,200-word filings.

3–4 hours.

While pondering that the average person can bang out a 1,200-word e-mail in about thirty minutes, I did something I've never before done with an Internet stranger.

I asked Sarah Morris to call me.

I wanted to talk about the Dodgers. I wanted to talk about her stories.

But, well, yeah, I mostly wanted to talk about why someone would cover a team off television, typing with her head for an invisible readership.

I have a speech disability making it impossible to use the phone.

That proved it. My first impression obviously had been correct. This was an elaborate hoax.

She didn't want to talk to me because, of course, she didn't exist.

I thought to myself, "This is why I never answer all my mail. This is why I will never go near a chatroom."

The Internet has become more about mythology than technology, people inventing outrageous lives to compensate for ordinary realities.

So, I was an unwitting actor in a strange little play. This woman writer was probably a forty-five-year-old male plumber.

I decided to end the correspondence.

Then I received another e-mail.

The first sentence read, *"There are some facts you might want to know. . . ."*

In words with an inflection that leaped off the screen, Sarah Morris spoke.

My disability is cerebral palsy. . . . It affects motor control. . . . I have excessive movement, meaning when my brain tells my hands to hit a key, I would move my legs, hit the table, and six other keys in the process.

This was only the beginning.

When my mom explained my handicap, she told me I could accomplish anything that I wanted to if I worked three times as hard as other people.

She wrote that she became a Dodger fan while growing up in Pasadena. In her sophomore year at Blair High, a junior varsity baseball coach, Mike Sellers, asked her to be the team statistician. Her special ed teacher discouraged it, but she did it anyway, sitting next to the bleachers with an electric typewriter and a head pointer.

We had a game on a rainy day. The rain fell in the typewriter, making it unusable, so Mom wrote the stats when I told her. I earned two letters that I am proud of still.

She wrote that her involvement in baseball had kept her in school — despite poor grades and hours of neck-straining homework.

Baseball gave me something to work for. . . . I could do something that other kids couldn't. . . . Baseball saved me from becoming another statistic. That is when I decided I wanted to do something for the sport that has done so much for me.

And about that speech disability?

When I went to nursery school, teachers treated me dumb. This made me mad, but I got over it. I hate the meaning of "dumb" in the phrase "deaf and dumb." My speech disability is the most frustrating.

Okay, so I believed her. Sort of. It still sounded odd.

Who could do something like this? I figured she must be privileged. Who, in her supposed condition, could cover a baseball team without the best equipment and help?

I figured she had an elaborate setup somewhere. I was curious about it. I figured she couldn't live too far from Pasadena. I would drive over one day and we would chat.

I live in Anderson, Texas. It's about 75 miles from Houston.

Texas? She didn't explain. I didn't ask. But that seemed like a long flight to see a little rich girl bang on an expensive keyboard.

By now, it was spring training, and she was ranting about Gary Sheffield, and I was hanging out in Vero Beach, and I would have forgotten the whole thing.

Except Sarah Morris began sending me her stories. Every day, another story. Game stories, feature stories, some with missing words, others with typographical errors, but all with obvious effort.

Then, fate. The Lakers were involved in a playoff series in San Antonio, I had one free day, and she lived about three hours away.

I wrote her, asking if I could drive over to see her. She agreed, but much too quickly for my suspicious tastes, writing me with detailed directions involving farm roads and streets with no name.

I read the directions and again thought, this was weird. This could be dangerous. I wanted to back out.

Turns out, I wasn't the only one.

I'm so nervous about tomorrow. I'm nothing special but a woman with disabilities. I don't know what makes a good journalism story. I don't know if I am it.

I pulled out of my San Antonio hotel on a warm May morning and drove east across the stark Texas landscape. I followed Sarah's directions off the interstate and onto a desolate two-lane highway.

The road stretched through miles of scraggly fields, interrupted only by occasional feed stores, small white churches, and blinking red lights.

I rolled into the small intersection that is Anderson, then took a right turn, down a narrow crumbling road, high weeds thwacking against the car's window.

After several miles, I turned down another crumbling road, pulling up in front of a rusted gate, which I had been instructed to open.

Now, on a winding dirt road dotted with potholes the size of small animals, I bounced for nearly a mile past grazing cows. Through the dust, I spotted what looked like an old toolshed.

But it wasn't a shed. It was a house, a decaying shanty covered by a tin roof and surrounded by weeds and junk.

I slowed and stared. Could this be right?

Then I saw, amid a clump of weeds near the front door, a rusted wheelchair.

P.S. We have dogs.

Do they ever. A couple of creatures with matted hair emerged from some bushes and surrounded the car, scratching and howling.

Finally, an older woman in an old T-shirt and skirt emerged from the front door and shooed the dogs away.

"I'm Sarah's mother," said Lois Morris, grabbing my smooth hand with a worn one. "She's waiting for you inside."

I walked out of the sunlight, opened a torn screen door, and moved into the shadows, where an eighty-seven-pound figure was curled up in a creaky wheelchair.

Her limbs twisted. Her head rolled. We could not hug. We could not even shake hands. She could only stare at me and smile.

But that smile! It cut through the gloom of the cracked wooden floor, the torn couch, the broken, cobwebbed windows.

A clutter of books and boxes filled the small rooms. There was a rabbit living in a cage next to an old refrigerator. From somewhere outside the house, you could hear the squeaking of rats.

Eventually I could bear to look at nothing else, so I stared at that smile, and it was so clear, so certain, it even cut through most of my doubts.

But still, even then, I wondered.

This is Sarah Morris?

She began shaking in her chair, emitting sounds. I thought she was coughing. She was, instead, speaking.

Her mother interpreted. Every sound was a different word or phrase.

"Huh (I) . . . huh-huh (want to show) . . . huh (you) . . . huh (something)."

Her mother rolled her through a path that cut through the piles of junk, up to an old desk on cinder blocks.

On the desk was a computer. Next to it was a TV. Nearby was a Dodger bobble-head doll of uncertain identity.

Her mother fastened a head pointer around her daughter's temples, its chin-strap stained dark brown from spilled Dr. Pepper. Sarah then began carefully leaning over the computer and pecking.

On the monitor appeared the *Dodger Place* Web site. Sarah used her pointer to call up a story. Peck by peck, she began adding to that story. It was her trademark typeface, her trademark Dodger fan prose, something involving Paul Lo Duca, about whom she later wrote:

> . . . Offensively, Lo Duca has been remarkable. Entering Friday's game, Lo Duca has batted .382 with five home runs and seventeen RBI. Last Tuesday Jim Tracy moved Lo Duca into the leadoff position. Since then, the Dodgers have won six and lost two. Lo Duca has an on-base percentage of .412. On Memorial Day Lo Duca had six hits, becoming the first Dodger to do so since Willie Davis on May 24, 1973. . . .

She looked up and giggled. I looked down in wonder — and shame.

This was indeed Sarah Morris. The great Sarah Morris.

She began making more sounds, bouncing in her chair. Lois asked me to sit on a dusty chair. There were some things that needed explaining.

Times photographer Anacleto Rapping, who had been there earlier in the day, and I had been Sarah's first visitors since she moved here with her mother and younger sister from Pasadena nearly six years ago.

This shack was an inheritance from Sarah's grandmother. When Sarah's parents divorced, her mother, with no other prospects, settled here.

The adjustment from life in Southern California to the middle of scrubby field more than thirty miles from the nearest supermarket was painful. Sarah was uprooted from a town of relative tolerance and accessibility to a place of many stares.

The place was so remote, when her mother had once dropped Sarah, helping her out of bed, and called 911, the emergency crew couldn't find the place.

"But the hardest thing for Sarah was leaving her Dodgers," Lois said.

So, she didn't. She used her disability money, and loans, to buy the computer, the television, and the satellite dish that allows her to watch or listen to every game.

She doesn't have any nearby friends, and it's exhausting to spend the five hours required for shopping trips to the nearest Wal-Mart, so the Dodgers fill the void.

They challenge her on bad days, embrace her on good days, stay awake with her while she covers an extra-inning game at 2:00 A.M.

She covers so much baseball, she maintains the eerie schedule of a player, rarely awaking before 10:00 A.M., often eating dinner at midnight.

Through the cluttered house, the path for not only her wheelchair, but for the entire direction of her life, leads from her bedroom to the kitchen to the Dodgers.

The air-conditioning sometimes breaks, turning the house into a steam bath. Lois totaled their aging van last year when she hit a black cow on a starless night, then missed so much work that they barely had enough money for food.

Yet, Sarah spends nine hours, carefully constructing an analysis of Gary Sheffield, or two hours writing about a one-run victory in Colorado.

I asked what her Dodger Web page represented to her.

Freedom.

I asked how she feels when working.

Happy. Useful.

I had contacted Sarah Morris months earlier, looking for a fight. I realized now, watching her strain into the thick air of this dark room to type words that perhaps no other soul will read, that I had found that fight.

Only, it wasn't with Sarah. It was with myself. It is the same fight the sports world experiences daily in these times of cynicism and conspiracy theories.

The fight to believe. The fight to trust that athletics can still create heroes without rap sheets, virtue without chemicals, nobility with grace.

It is about the battle to return to the days when sports did not detract from life, but added to it, with its awesome power to enlighten and include.

In a place far from such doubt, with a mind filled with wonder, Sarah Morris brought me back.

I had not wanted to walk into those shadows. But two hours later, I did not want to leave.

Yet I did, because there was an airplane waiting, and an NBA playoff series to cover, big things, nonsense things.

Sarah asked her mother to wheel her outside. She was rolled to the edge of the weeds. I grasped one of her trembling hands. She grasped back with her smile.

I climbed into the car and rattled down the dirt road. Through the rear-view mirror, through the rising dust, I could see the back of Sarah Morris' bobbing head as she was wheeled back to that cinder-blocked desk.

For she, too, had a game to cover.

If you see Karros, please tell him to watch his knees in 1999. He used to bend them more than now.

Sarah sent me that e-mail recently. It was about the same time she'd sent me an e-mail saying she had finally saved enough money to begin attending a college about forty-five minutes down the road in pursuit of her "deam."

I didn't get a chance to pass along her note to the slumping Karros, but it didn't matter.

A day later, he had a game-winning hit. The next game, a home run. The game after that, another homer.

If you watched him closely, you could see that he indeed was bending his knees again.

Eight months ago I wouldn't have believed it, but I could swear each leg formed the shape of an *r.*

FRANK DEFORD

Almost a Hero

FROM SPORTS ILLUSTRATED

AT HOME, the very old man sits by the window and looks out into the woods. It is another new day, of which he has had more than 35,000. Some 35,000 times the sun has come up for him. He likes to say, "I was given a life, and I used it."

When the very old man and his wife bought the property near Hamburg in 1949, they left it in its natural state. They built the house in the middle of the land, so that the deer and the foxes, the starlings and the woodpeckers, would still feel at home. The scene is almost Disneyesque, reminiscent of Snow White, the animals coming up close to the house, looking at the very old man sitting inside watching them.

It surprises people, how small the house is. After all, the very old man is Max Schmeling, the former heavyweight champion of the world, who is both famous and wealthy. He could live in a mansion. He and Anny never had children, however, and now she is gone. They were married for fifty-four years, and she has been dead for fourteen. "I don't need a big villa," Schmeling has said. There is plenty of room for her photographs. In her heyday, she was beautiful. She was Anny Ondra, the movie star. She was beautiful and he was handsome, and the world they lived in was stunningly vivid.

His secretary reports that this is what Schmeling says of the past: "I have had a very eventful life. I have been shaped by two world wars, by success and defeat, and by the beautiful times life has to offer. But" — one can hear him sighing here — "I have also suffered deprivation." Max Schmeling is not smug. He presents all the contradictions of Everyman, only in him the paradoxes are writ much larger because of who he was and what was going on all around him when he was in his prime.

He has two old, familiar housekeepers, who take turns tending to him in the cozy house in the middle of the woods. He needs a nurse at night, too, because, as befits a man who was strong and independent, he is loath to use a cane, even though he sometimes gets dizzy and falls. He is frail but well enough, and his diabetes appears to be under control. The housekeeper who is on duty on Fridays fixes him potato pancakes. That is the small pleasure he most enjoys, potato pancakes for dinner on Fridays. He has had successful cataract surgery on both his eyes, so when he is not watching the birds frolic, he reads a great deal. Newspapers are delivered to the house every morning, as well as magazines about soccer, hunting, and boxing.

Most Americans of a certain age know for an absolute fact that, long ago, Max Schmeling was the dirty rotten Nazi who got lucky and beat Joe Louis, but then got his comeuppance when our good Joe demolished him in the rematch — sticking it to Hitler in the bargain. Schmeling, though, was never a Nazi. He was sometimes credulous and sometimes weak and often an example of what the road to hell is paved with.

Schmeling has, however, been candid about his life under Hitler, baldly admitting to the concessions he made, to his sins of omission, to expedience in the face of evil. Neither does he deny that he liked the Fuhrer's attention. Vanity makes a rare thing of valor. But never has Schmeling revealed his noblest act, which he performed on Kristallnacht, the Night of the Broken Glass. All he will say is to protest, "I only was doing the duty of a man."

Even now, after the 35,000 days, when there cannot be many more sunrises left for him, the response to a question about his part in Kristallnacht comes back from his secretary: "Mr. Schmeling says, 'Leave me alone. I can't do that anymore. Everything there is to say has been said about me. I am tired of repeating myself.' Mr. Schmeling has been there for the media for seventy-five years. He would like to be left in peace."

Indeed, for all his many friends, he permits few visitors. After all, everyone is younger than he is, and everyone wants to ask him about those remarkable times when he was a champion and his wife was a movie queen and the world was breaking apart. Still, he refuses to talk about that anymore. His memoirs are full and frank, though, the reports of his friends warm and revealing. Executives from his company in Hamburg come to the house in the woods, bringing papers for him to sign. His company bottles and distributes soft drinks. Max Schmeling, the dirty rotten Nazi of lore, made his fortune after the war from Coca-Cola. There is something wonderfully perverse about that, isn't there? It's, well, it's very American.

With his considerable wealth, Schmeling has become a philanthropist, so he has his foundation to attend to, giving millions to the poor. Also, each New Year's Day, he sends greetings to the hundreds of people he knows, and on his friends' birthdays the men get telegrams and the women flowers. But, really, he has nothing more to say about the twentieth century. His final statement was that with which he concluded a new epilogue, three years ago, to his 1977 memoirs, *Max Schmeling: An Autobiography:* "I was always there — I'm still there. My life is that of a German in the twentieth century; or perhaps more precisely, it was a German-American life. It was, in any case, a fulfilled life which was never boring and of which, I must admit, I am somewhat proud."

Somewhat. It's a funny word for a man to choose to place in his own valedictory, isn't it? However, it is such an honest, tempered word. It signals to us, more than anything, that you had to have been present when the Third Reich was aborning and then thriving and then crumbling. Then you never would be so sure again. There would always be a somewhat in your life.

Whatever he was before and whatever he's been since, Schmeling will be defined in America as the villain who went to New York City in June 1938 to take Joe Louis's championship back to Hitler. Schmeling was a man of the world, himself the heavyweight champion at the start of the decade. He had spent so much time in the U.S. — rarely fighting anywhere else from 1929 till the war — that as a spiritual German-American he viewed New York as a "second home." Attractive and congenial, Schmeling had many American friends and was quite well received here. In 1936, when he handed Louis his first defeat, knocking him out in the twelfth round of a nontitle bout, much of the crowd in Yankee Stadium had even swung round to the German's side.

Ah, but that was the crux of it. In 1936 the rest of the world was not altogether sure about Hitler, and Schmeling was a German. By 1938, what the Third Reich stood for was clear. Schmeling was no longer a German. He must be a Nazi. When his liner, *Bremen,* docked in New York more than a month before the fight, pickets lined the shore. Schmeling had to be escorted off and sneaked up side streets to his hotel.

He was everywhere reviled, cursed to his face, with mocking Heil Hitler salutes thrown before him. When he did not cooperate by delivering pro-Nazi statements, inflammatory quotes were attributed to him. Yankee Stadium would be packed to the facade for the rematch, and in a nation of 130 million, 70 million listened on the radio. When Louis pulverized Schmeling in barely two minutes, America rejoiced. And Schmeling was left forever as the carcass on the canvas, vilified in our history.

Schmeling had known so well the other extreme. He was a hero to Germany before Hitler — he was the first great German boxer, the first German to win a world championship. That was in 1930, when he upset Jack Sharkey at Yankee Stadium before a crowd of 80,000. The same desperate longing for pride that Hitler would so cunningly exploit in a defeated, ashamed people could be seen first, in a much smaller way, in the adoration of Schmeling. Curiously, too, in counterpoint to what would soon come, Germany was never so free and open as it was in the 1920s. Berlin was, we know, a cabaret. When Schmeling went there from Hamburg, he was astonished — "a city of enormous energy," he would write, with "a hectic lust for life."

As he succeeded in the fight game, the café society of the capital welcomed him. Although barely schooled, never more than a laborer before he found the ring, Schmeling was no pug. His new friends were actors and artists, dancers and writers. He wore the finest tailored suits, bought at David Lewin's Prince of Wales shop in Berlin; he appeared evenings in black tie, or even in white tie and tails. He took out movie stars. He starred in movies. When sound came in, he even sang in movies.

Art, sports, and sex merged in Berlin, and suddenly, repressions cast aside, the human body was worshiped. Schmeling, dark and broodingly handsome (he was a dead ringer for the smaller Jack Dempsey), possessed a classically gorgeous male form, so he was more than the nation's preeminent athlete. He was a matinee idol, an Aryan god, in demand to pose nude for sculpture. He was very much a part of this new, liberated Germany, this avant-garde clique that thumbed its nose at hidebound Teutonic stiffness.

Schmeling's friend, the dancer Anita Berber, was chastised for dancing too brazenly onstage. Her response to the critics was to dance even more erotically. Then, convoyed by two elegant young escorts, Berber dramatically sashayed into the dining room of the exquisite Hotel Adlon to order three bottles of Veuve Clicquot. As soon as the waiter poured, Berber arose, unclasped the diamond broach on her expensive fur coat, and let the coat fall to the floor, revealing that she wore nothing whatsoever beneath. Then, standing there naked in the middle of a room aghast, she calmly raised her glass, toasting her companions.

That was Berlin before Hitler, the city where Schmeling shifted about in the most cosmopolitan, most daring circles, where he returned from New York a world champion, where he fell in love with Anny and married her. In this elite artistic environment, a number of people were Jewish. So were many of Anny's associates in her film company. In New York, Schmeling remembers, "almost all my friends were Jews."

Foremost was his manager, Joe Jacobs, a little American who mangled the English language, most famously lamenting, "I shoulda stood in bed." Jacobs was often known by his Yiddish name, Yussel, so that in acknowledgment of his power in the fight game he was called Yussel the Muscle. The Nazis were not amused. They became downright furious in 1935 when Jacobs came into the ring in Hamburg after Schmeling's victory in one of his rare bouts in Germany. The crowd, in Schmeling's honor, began to sing the national anthem, raising its arms in the Nazi salute, and Jacobs, somewhat bemused, threw up his arm as well, even as it held a huge cigar. Then the little Jew gave a big stage wink to Schmeling. All this was caught on film. The head of the Reich Ministry of Sports wrote a letter to Schmeling demanding that he get rid of his Jewish manager, but Max Schmeling would not give up Yussel Jacobs.

So long as Schmeling was champion and Hitler was only ascendant, the fighter was safe. Even after Sharkey had beaten him to regain the title in New York back in '32, Schmeling had remained popular because the decision had been an outrageous home-country fraud. Twenty-three of the twenty-five U.S. writers polled at ringside thought Schmeling had won. "We wuz robbed!" Jacobs bellowed. The raw deal made Schmeling a sympathetic figure in the U.S. But the next year, 1933, Max Baer (who wore a Star of David on his trunks) knocked out Schmeling, and his comet began to plummet. He was almost twenty-eight, and he seemed to be washed up. Hitler, by then, was in control.

Not long before, Schmeling had turned to Hitler for help in a sticky little matter involving a currency transaction. The Fuhrer had taken care of things. Now, when the Reich minister of sports demanded again that Schmeling sever relations with Jacobs, the fighter again went directly to Hitler. How quickly things had changed, how naive he was. "In retrospect," Schmeling wrote later, his action was "comical and almost insane." Hitler spent the whole interview flirting with Anny. Schmeling finally forced the issue of Joe Jacobs upon him, but Hitler ignored the subject. When, at last, Schmeling almost wailed, "Loyalty is a German virtue," Hitler grew angry, staring away. Moments later, a young SS officer led the Schmelings off.

His friends at the Roxy Bar on Joachimstaler Strasse in Berlin commiserated with Schmeling. That was his favorite hangout. He and his buddies called it the Missing Persons Bureau because if one of them could not be found at home, then surely he would be at the Roxy. Soon, though, the bar's nickname took on more sinister overtones. The persons, many of whom were Jewish, were not simply missing from home but were missing from Germany — fleeing the regime, even being sent to camps, which were called KZ in savoir faire company. Oh, yes, Schmeling admits, they knew the names.

What is so sadly fascinating about Schmeling is that he never revised the history of his actions during the early years of the Third Reich. He is honest, even as his admissions stain him. Many Germans who looked back on that time made Hitler out to be a bumbling fool. I saw through him, they wanted you to know. Schmeling, however, wrote matter-of-factly in his memoirs that he at first found the Fuhrer "relaxed . . . charming . . . confident." He was seduced. He kept an autographed photograph of Hitler on the wall in his study.

It is so easy for us to think that had we been there then, we would have known, we would have stood up, we would have done something. But, as the old comic vaudeville line went, "Vas you dere, Charlie?" Schmeling and his pals were there, drinking at the Roxy, even as other old friends left Germany or were sent to a KZ (or even committed suicide). Yet they just ordered another schnapps and abided — "impressed," Schmeling wrote, "by the new optimism in Germany as well as by the successes of the new regime." Life was truly somewhat, and they were all frogs in the pot, pretending not to notice that the water around them was slowly approaching a boil. How could they not see? Why did they not act?

Although Schmeling has never spared himself, he does not really explain. "After the war," he wrote in *An Autobiography,* "many, perhaps hoping to fool themselves, claimed to have had no knowledge of what went on. In truth, we all knew. It was no secret that there were camps in Germany; it was openly discussed in the Roxy Bar."

Still, the boxer and others who knew did nothing. Most German Christians were too afraid to act. Schmeling, though, was different. He was like so many athletes, strong and confident, certain he could play with the devil's fire. He was Germany's champion, was he not? "They tried to use me, and I used the Nazis to help others," he said not long ago to his friend Gunnar Meinhardt.

Meinhardt, a former East German weightlifter, is a journalist with the German press agency DPA. He is the only one in his profession whom Schmeling allows to visit, for Meinhardt has become, it seems, the son — the grandson — Schmeling never had. Schmeling loves him. They sit by the window that looks out on the living things of the forest. "I feel I am in harmony with life, with myself," Schmeling has told him.

So, how would you like to be remembered, Max? "I would not like to be remembered as someone who amounted to so much as an athlete but who was good for nothing as a person. I couldn't stand that."

Are you religious? "To me, religion means to give, to do good. I live my life as if there were a God." Do you believe in life after death? "No. There is no other life. We live on solely as someone who is being remembered, someone who is talked about."

He visits Anny's grave and thinks of the old times, good and bad, when they were together, because there will not be any more time for them in the beyond. He simply accepts his great age as "a present from heaven." Who could ever imagine that an old boxer, with seventy professional bouts and many more in the amateurs, whose head was pummeled by Joe Louis, would still be alive, in his ninety-seventh year, alert and sentient and still full of wonder? On the other hand, nothing is absolute; everything is somewhat. "I would never have thought it possible," the very old man tells Meinhardt.

Hitler didn't care that much for sports. When Schmeling refused to accept the Nazi Dagger of Honor, an award that had gone only to the most prominent dignitaries — and that would have made Schmeling an honorary commander in the SA, the storm troopers — the Fuhrer didn't seem disturbed, even though other top Nazis were appalled at Schmeling's audacious rudeness. Hitler did play up the 1936 Berlin Olympics for all they were worth, but as pageantry more than competition. It was Josef Goebbels, the propaganda minister, who was more concerned about the impression sports might make on the larger world. Probably because Goebbels prompted him, Hitler didn't want Schmeling, who by then had had sixty fights and seven losses and looked like a washed-up palooka, to take on the magnificent, young, undefeated — and black — Louis at Yankee Stadium on June 19, 1936.

Then again, nobody else gave Schmeling much of a chance, either; he was fodder for the Brown Bomber, an 8–1 underdog. Nevertheless, while some of Louis's opponents entered the ring scared stiff, Schmeling was not the least bit frightened. A foolish man he might be, but a brave one. That made him a more attractive underdog; so while a few U.S. newspapers called him "the Heil Hitler hero," others tagged him "the terrific Teuton."

Once Schmeling knocked Louis down in the fourth round and took command of the fight, the crowd's latent racism began to surface. Before Schmeling finally knocked out Louis, he could hear ringside cries of "Kill him! Kill him!" Neither was it lost on the German how quickly, in the aftermath, white America displayed its suppressed racial meanness. O. B. Keeler, one of America's most renowned (and beloved) sportswriters, called Louis "the pet Pickaninny."

In the long run, though, Schmeling would pay, because victory made him a Nazi talisman. Hitler greeted Schmeling — along with his wife and mother — when he returned the hero, having crossed the Atlantic in style in the *Hindenburg* zeppelin. This was only weeks before the Olympics. It was the German summer of the century, before the covers came off the guns, when panoply could still blind casual witnesses to hatred. The Games would be a huge success in putting Nazi glamour and organization on display, while German athletes would dominate the medal count. The only fly in the ointment would be the showing of Jesse Owens and other African-American athletes, so Schmeling's knockout victory over another, even more famous black man took on much more meaning as the summer passed.

Ironically, had Schmeling not come to New York the previous December to scout Louis in his fight against Uzcudun Paolino, the U.S. might have boycotted the Berlin Games. Schmeling had agreed to his government's "request" that he meet with Avery Brundage, the American Olympic Committee president, a few days before the committee voted on whether to participate in Berlin. Claiming to speak on behalf of "German athletes," Schmeling assured Brundage that American Jews and blacks would not be discriminated against. Schmeling would come to regret making such a blanket promise, but in any event, because the committee rejected a boycott by only two and a half votes, it is possible that Schmeling's "guarantee" carried the day. Hitler was thrilled by the news: the U.S. would come to his party.

Victories, however, are not always what they seem. Owens would rise above Hitler at the Olympics, a symbol to the world. Likewise, those close to Louis would eventually understand that his defeat at the hands of Schmeling might have been a blessing in disguise. The Brown Bomber had come to think of himself as invincible. He had been slothful in training, cocky going into the ring. Schmeling taught him a lesson. What's more, Schmeling would come to appreciate that his defeat in the return bout saved him from becoming, as he wrote, "forever the 'Aryan Show Horse' of the Third Reich."

By 1938 he was not only a fighter but also a swastika in trunks. Almost no one in the U.S. spared him rebuke. Indeed, in a January 1993 article in the journal *History Today,* authors Robert Weisbord and Norbert Hedderich point out that even in the *Pittsburgh Courier,* an African-American newspaper, Schmeling was paid off in the currency of stereotype so familiar to blacks. "The Nazi-man who would be king" read one caption, and Schmeling was quoted as snarling, "I am going to stop this black domination by regaining the crown." Rumors persisted that his German trainer kept a Nazi uniform in his closet and that Hitler would appoint Schmeling Reich minister of sports should he win.

Meanwhile, Louis, the black champion who couldn't walk into a restaurant and get a meal in much of the country, was transformed into an all-American symbol, guardian of our precious liberty and equality, while Owens raced against horses at state fairs and tried to get a nine-to-five job. Although Schmeling persisted in asserting what he believed — that this should be nothing more than a fight between two men — Louis was moved to rage by all the Nazi propaganda attributed to his opponent. Probably, he never fought so viciously. Probably, too, Schmeling was scared this time. His favorite cornerman, fearful for his life, refused to work the bout, and as Schmeling moved through the crowd toward the ring, he had to cover his head to protect it from the debris that rained down on him. A cordon of New York's finest was needed to shield him from further barrage. The hate was palpable.

Louis's son, Joe Louis Barrow, Jr., says, "The parallels between my father and Max were quite considerable. Max had never really experienced prejudice till he came back over here in '38 and had pickets and felt hatred. Then he realized what so many whites never do — exactly what it is blacks have to go through."

Back home, the Nuremberg laws of 1935 had made it increasingly difficult for Jews. Henri Lewin would go on to become a prominent U.S. hotel executive; in the thirties, he was the adolescent son of David Lewin, who ran the Prince of Wales haberdashery and other carriage-trade businesses. Henri remembers that friends and customers who had known his father for years — "people who had kissed my father" — would ignore him. Anny Ondry had to fold her film company; there were too many Jewish colleagues to replace. The Nazis were especially infuriated that Schmeling would not fire Yussel Jacobs.

Indeed, Schmeling recalls that when he encountered Goebbels one day, the propaganda minister paused only to snarl, "What are you thinking, Herr Schmeling? You just go ahead and do whatever you please. You don't concern yourself with laws. You come to the Fuhrer, you come to me, and still you continue to socialize with Jews."

So when Louis clobbered him in the rematch, rendering him

bloody and unconscious, Schmeling lost his entrée to power. He tossed away whatever chance he had to salvage respect from the Nazis when the German ambassador to the U.S. visited him in the hospital and tried to get him to claim that Louis had fouled him. Schmeling refused, and with that, he was effectively dismissed as a German.

Less than two years later, in 1940, when young men of twenty or so were being drafted, Schmeling, thirty-four, was inducted into the Wehrmacht as a private. The minister of sports had obtained Hitler's blessing to draft the ungrateful boxer. He was assigned to the paratroopers, and in May 1941 he jumped into withering English fire over Crete and was knocked unconscious by the landing. Later he was hospitalized with dysentery in Athens, where a U.S. reporter interviewed him. When he failed to accuse the English army of cruelty in Crete and declared anew that "I have always seen America as my second home," Goebbels was so angry that he ordered Schmeling's name never to be printed again down through all the millennia of the Third Reich.

Of course, had the Nazis known what Schmeling had been up to in November 1938 he would have suffered a far worse fate than being drafted. On Kristallnacht — when Nazi gangs roamed the streets of Berlin and other cities destroying Jewish property, burning synagogues, and assaulting and killing Jews — David Lewin, desperate, told his sons, fifteen-year-old Werner and fourteen-year-old Henri, to go to the Excelsior Hotel, where Schmeling had a suite, find David's old Gentile friend, and tell him of their plight.

There was no house phone, so the two boys waited nervously in the lobby. At last Schmeling appeared, and as soon as the young Lewins explained the situation, Schmeling spirited them up to his room, where he hid them for two days. "He risked everything for us," Henri recalls. "We hid from the housekeepers, waiters, other friends of Max's. He told the front desk he was sick and not to let anyone come up."

The boys cowered, Schmeling sharing with them what food he had, while, outside, the Nazi thugs ran amok. Finally, after two days, as the pillaging and bloodletting abated, Schmeling took Werner and Henri out of his suite, escorting them first to his house in another section of town and then to the Lewin family apartment. Eventually, the boys and their parents escaped to a Jewish enclave in Shanghai, where — frying pan to the fire — they would end up as captives of the Japanese. The family finally made its way to the U.S., though, and both Henri and Werner became successful hoteliers. Today the brothers are nearing eighty.

Henri Lewin has publicly told this tale of Kristallnacht only once, at a Las Vegas dinner in 1989 at which Schmeling was honored. Schmeling cried, but he said he didn't like being "glorified." Even now, even with Schmeling's faxed permission to talk about him, Lewin speaks reluctantly of the awful events surrounding Kristallnacht. "Max was a man of the highest quality," he says. "If they had caught him hiding us, they would have shot him. Let me tell you: if I had been Max Schmeling in Germany in 1938, I wouldn't have done it."

Mike Tyson was at that dinner in Las Vegas, sitting next to Schmeling. Lewin remembers that Iron Mike talked to Schmeling for a long time. Finally, Tyson told him, "I don't like fight people, but I like you."

Schmeling replied, "I like everybody."

After the Louis rematch, Schmeling did not return to the U.S. for sixteen years. By then, he and Anny were back on their feet. Schmeling had, in desperation, returned to the ring for five bouts, in 1947 and '48, when he was in his early forties. That provided him with the nest egg to buy the homestead where he lives in the woods near Hamburg.

When he finally returned to America, in 1954, his first stop was at a Jewish cemetery in New York, where Joe Jacobs was buried. Schmeling then went to Chicago and, unannounced, visited Louis. The two former foes chewed the fat until three in the morning.

Louis was already on hard times, struggling to climb out of a tax hole that grew deeper with each year. Fame fades; interest compounds. Louis, who had saved the honor of Uncle Sam by beating the dirty rotten Nazi to a pulp, had fallen into arrears to IRS, so he would spend the rest of his life broke, troubled, scrambling for dignity and a buck. "America's guest," people would snicker at Louis. Meanwhile, Schmeling, like his defeated nation, prospered. The economy was already becoming global. Coca-Cola is a global taste.

Over the years Schmeling would quietly send Louis money, and when the Brown Bomber died, in 1981, Schmeling asked Henri

Lewin to go to the funeral, with a substantial gift for the widow. That was a sweet closing of the circle, wasn't it? The German Jewish boy whom Schmeling had saved was now a rich American carrying a present to the family of the black man who, by thrashing Schmeling years before, had saved him the injustice of any longer being the Fatherland's pride and joy. "Oh," says Joe Barrow, Jr., "there were always tears in Max's eyes when he talked of my father's death."

So the very old man sits yet by the window. It is best that we cannot visit him, frail and worn, the better only to visualize him there, with the morning papers on his lap, still peering from under those heavy eyebrows at the wildlife that pokes about, peeking back at him. Schmeling may be silent before us, but he is merely tired of talking about the past. He still recalls so much that he did and saw — and what he did not do and chose not to see. For all our goodness and all our shame, most of the somewhat of our lives is constructed of what we failed to do, what we avoided, what might have been.

It is late in the day. The sun must dance through the trees now to play across the very old man sitting by the window. Dinnertime nears. If this is Friday, it will be potato pancakes.

With special reporting by ANITA VERSCHOTH

EUGENE ROBINSON

The Cuban Ali

FROM THE WASHINGTON POST MAGAZINE

HE WENT BACK OUT to sit in the shade with an old friend who had dropped by, Oscar Torres, who used to be one of the doctors for the Cuban national boxing team. As is often the case with men who have known each other for decades, there was more silence between them than conversation. Across the street — a quiet suburban lane of fairly new houses, one of the better addresses in greater Havana — music poured from a neighbor's radio. It was salsa, hot and sweet like Cuban coffee.

The men sipped glasses of fresh coconut milk mixed with splashes of rum from a bottle the doctor had brought, a combination called *saoco.* It was early for rum, but this was a quiet celebration: the day before, in a full-dress ceremony attended by Fidel Castro himself, Stevenson had been honored as one of the top one hundred Cuban athletes of the century. His ovation had been the loudest of all, and the warmest.

Stevenson went inside twice to check the water on the stove. When it was hot, he carried it to the bathroom and poured it into the tub. Now he could take a bath. There's no hot water from the tap at the house of the man who could have been Muhammad Ali, just cold.

Everyone else was ready to go, but Stevenson refused to hurry. He shaved, dressed neatly, combed his salt-and-pepper hair, and took his time pulling on a pair of Italian-style black boots — then abruptly walked out to the car, with an air of impatience.

On the drive to his favorite restaurant, as slowly as he had zipped up those well-worn boots, Stevenson slipped into his public persona.

He became more animated, more voluble; he smiled more frequently, and a light came into his eyes. Now he wanted to talk, especially about Ali — their friendship, and their unconsummated rivalry. He recalled Ali's last visit to Cuba, three years ago: "Someone asked Ali what would have happened if we had fought, and he said it would be a draw. I think that's right. It would have been a draw."

By the time he stepped out of the car he was fully alive. He suffered backslaps from the parking attendants. He signed autographs. He shadowboxed with the bartender and flirted with the waitresses. He posed for pictures. He shook a dozen hands. He remembered everyone's name. It took him fifteen minutes to get from the door to his table, and when he finally sat down he was wearing an enormous, satisfied grin.

Thus did Teofilo Stevenson begin another day on the job.

Officially he is vice president of the Cuban Boxing Federation, but whether he bothers to show up at his office is largely irrelevant. His real work — his role in today's Cuba, his mission, his life — consists of something much more important: being a hero.

No, more than that: being The Hero.

In 1972, at the age of twenty, Teofilo Stevenson went to Munich and won the Olympic gold medal in boxing, heavyweight division. In 1976, he went to Montreal and did it again. In 1980, he went to Moscow and did it again. Three straight Olympic Games, three straight gold medals. But that doesn't begin to tell why he's such a hero.

He was heir to the great traditions of Cuban boxing, stretching back to the dazzling featherweight champion Eligio Sardinas — better known as "Kid Chocolate" — in the 1930s. Stevenson was tall and graceful, and he fought elegantly, keeping opponents at bay with his long jab, wearing them down, and then finishing them off with a right hand like clenched thunder. Only two of his many Olympic bouts even went the full three rounds. But that, too, is just part of the story.

The rest is crisply told in a 1974 headline from *Sports Illustrated:* "He'd Rather Be Red Than Rich."

"Given two, maybe three more years, he probably could become the professional heavyweight champion of the world," the magazine article said. "But he most assuredly will not."

After his Olympic victory in 1972, Stevenson was offered $1 million by American fight promoters to defect, come to the United

States and turn professional. They offered more money throughout the next decade as his victories mounted. Stevenson was handsome, he spoke English, he was a great fighter with a legitimate shot at becoming champion, and he had bankable charisma, the same kind of charisma that Ali had. He even looked like Ali, enough that the two men could be brothers.

That was the fight promoters dreamed of, the money fight: Stevenson vs. Ali.

"Everybody wanted Teofilo," recalls Angelo Dundee, Ali's legendary manager, who at eighty is still hard at work in South Florida, cruising the gyms, looking for the next Mike Tyson, the next Larry Holmes. (There will never be a "next" Ali.)

"I mean, I never went after him because I had the champ, I had Ali. I had the guy who was gonna beat him, see? But everybody else wanted Teofilo, and I mean everybody. They were gonna give him a million dollars. And a million dollars then was money!"

And Stevenson turned it down.

He turned all the offers down, despite having every chance to defect during his frequent trips abroad. He stayed in Cuba, where boxing is all-amateur, where there's no Don King, no Vegas bling-bling, no pay-per-view. He stayed to write a grander legend, and to revel in the love of his compatriots and the praise of his government, especially its Maximum Leader.

In a post-Olympics speech at the Plaza de la Revolucion, where he gathers the multitudes, Fidel Castro praised Stevenson for rejecting the "traffickers of bodies and of souls" who were trying to tempt him with riches. Not for the last time, he spoke of Stevenson as an example for others to follow.

On the wall of his sitting room Stevenson displays a photograph of himself with Castro following one of his early triumphs. Castro wears a boyish look of uncomplicated joy as he raises Stevenson's hand like a referee signaling the winner of a fight. The meaning of the image couldn't be clearer: whenever Stevenson stretched some lug out on the canvas, it was as if Castro himself had KO'ed one of his many enemies.

In 1972, Castro's revolution was just thirteen years old, barely in its adolescence. Teofilo Stevenson became the revolution's first great sports hero — not just because he won, but because he stayed. And because he believed.

Today both the boxer and the revolution have made it into restless middle age. Both have endured blows, bruises, setbacks, and wrong turns. Cuba is a nation that does state-of-the-art biotechnology but struggles to produce basics like paper and soap, a one-party state that provides both universal literacy and universal hard times. Stevenson is a garlanded Hero of the State who has to heat his bath water on the stove.

And who still believes.

The name is pronounced *tay-OH-fee-lo,* with the stress on the second syllable. That sleepy morning, before he heated his bath water and got ready to go out, he was shaking a hangover. The night before, after the ceremony for the top one hundred athletes, he'd done some not-so-quiet celebrating. Now it was almost noon and The Hero was back among the living, but barely.

At forty-nine, he is shockingly unchanged from the Apollonian giant who used to frighten his opponents half into submission before pounding them the rest of the way. The big muscles are diminished but he's kept in shape, and he still carries himself like a king, chin up and shoulders thrown back. He stands six-five but looks taller. His face is unlined; if he dyed his hair, he could pass for thirty-five.

"You must be hungry," he said. "I'll bring you some fish that I prepared myself. It's very good, you'll see. I'm a very good cook." But instead of getting up and going into the kitchen, he yelled the magic word: "Fraymaris!"

Fraymaris, a petite woman with skin the color of winter wheat, is Stevenson's wife. As is the case in most Cuban homes, she is expected to act as an extension of her husband's arms and legs, meaning that she had to drop whatever she was doing and go get the plate of fish that he just as easily could have fetched. The couple have a young son, David, who took my presence as an excuse to misbehave. Fraymaris had to be in three places at once — helping her husband, tending to a guest, and running after a six-year-old who was betting he wouldn't be punished in front of company.

She is Stevenson's fourth wife. He has the fame and status to spend the rest of his life choosing and losing trophy wives, but this time, his friends say hopefully, he seems to have met his match. Fraymaris is trophy-beautiful and also fiercely intelligent — she works as a lawyer, and doesn't hesitate to subject her famous husband to a little cross-examination when necessary.

I had arrived unannounced at ten that Saturday morning. I had no phone number for Stevenson, but a friend of mine who lives in Havana knew he lived in a development called Reparto Nautica several miles west of downtown. It's an upscale neighborhood where most of the homes are well kept and most people have cars. Stevenson's four-bedroom house, occupying most of a tiny lot, is protected by a chain-link fence. A red Mitsubishi sedan sat in the driveway.

Shirtless and in sandals, Stevenson came to the gate, unlocked it, and mumbled pleasantries, then issued three instructions: Come in. Sit. Wait.

The house is far from sumptuous, but comfortable — spotless linoleum floors, casement windows framed by floral curtains, utilitarian furniture. There is even a small swimming pool filling the little back yard, though it contains just a couple of feet of black, brackish water. Stevenson explained that it was far too expensive to fill and maintain the thing.

(Stevenson has a second house as well — a country home, in the little eastern town where he grew up. He keeps a second car out there, a Russian-made Lada. Both houses, and both cars, were gifts from the government. Another retired boxer, a former member of the national team, told me that every Cuban athlete who wins Olympic gold has the same first reaction: "There, that's my house.")

The walls of one sunny little room were covered with memories: The photo of Stevenson with Castro. An autographed photograph of Ali, and a set of Ali's boxing gloves, also signed. An engraved plaque from actor and martial artist Chuck Norris, of all people. Pictures of Stevenson in the ring, including a wall-size collage from one of his biggest fights, the destruction of highly touted American boxer Duane Bobick in the quarterfinals of the 1972 Olympics. Bobick had actually defeated Stevenson once before, and was favored to win the gold medal. The photos on his wall chronicle Stevenson's revenge: the biggest picture shows Bobick, one of boxing's occasional Great White Hopes, hugging the canvas and clearly not about to get up.

Stevenson's fights were amazing to witness, but you had to watch carefully because the endings were sudden.

Typical was his win over the Romanian heavyweight Mircea Simon in the 1976 Olympics. ABC covered the games that year; Howard Cosell called the fight, with George Foreman, the gold medalist eight years earlier, sitting in as color commentator. Cosell began by stating flatly that Stevenson would be the heavyweight champion if he defected and turned professional. Foreman, who was thinner then and had much more hair, agreed.

From the opening bell Stevenson stalks the Romanian, and the Romanian ducks and covers and runs away. Stevenson keeps throwing long jabs with his left, and occasionally one gets through, but the first round ends with few blows having landed. The second round is a repeat of the first — Stevenson advances, Simon retreats, Cosell laments the "disgraceful" lack of action. Foreman decides that although Stevenson clearly is winning, the Romanian is making him look bad. He revises his opinion: Stevenson is too patient, he says, and might not be able to win in the professional ranks after all.

Then, early in the third round, the Romanian starts to fight back. He actually lands a couple of blows. It is clear that his was a survival strategy, and having survived to the last round, he hopes to get lucky. Stevenson is still implacable, but he's getting hit. This could be an upset in the making . . .

It's over.

Only in the slow-motion replay is it clear what happens. Simon gets confident enough to come within range, just for an instant, and Stevenson hits him flush in the jaw with an overhand right. The Romanian goes down faster than the Nasdaq on a bad day, and when he struggles to his feet his legs have turned to rubber. The referee stops the contest.

After the fight, Foreman changes his opinion yet again: Stevenson would have to "pay his dues" as a professional, but "I still say he would be champion of the world."

"Everybody says I always did the damage with my right. But really it was my left. People don't understand that. Pum, pum, pum, with the left. That's what hurt them. Pum, pum, pum. And then the right."

Stevenson was commanding attention at the restaurant table, giving a graphic tutorial on his fighting style. Every time he said "pum" he demonstrated by hitting my shoulder, and it hurt like hell.

On meeting him I had noticed that he has soft hands, as many boxers do. His fingers are relatively short, given his height, but the fist they make is huge, as if he's wearing brass knuckles under the skin. His arm span, almost eighty-four inches from fingertip to fingertip, is freakishly long. "I compared my arm with Ali's, and his only came to there," Stevenson said, pegging Ali's reach with either arm at three inches shy of his own. "Pum."

He has visited his friend Ali in the States, and Ali has been to Cuba twice, most recently in 1998. "I sat with him at this same table," Stevenson said. "He's doing okay. He doesn't like to talk in public, because of the Parkinson's, but he can talk. He's all there. People who don't like boxing always say, 'Look at Ali, he boxed all that time and he's got Parkinson's.' I tell them, 'Hey, look at the pope. He's got Parkinson's, too, and as far as I know, he didn't box.'"

We were at one of the best-known restaurants in Havana, a venerable institution called El Aljibe, where everybody who's anybody eventually shows up. Fraymaris was there, along with little David. Torres, the doctor, had dropped by as well. A Mexican businessman who spied Stevenson across the room sent over a bottle of three-year-old rum, with his compliments, and then came to join the party.

A woman who had been sitting at another table approached with apologies and asked for an autograph — her son would never forgive her if she didn't, she said. Stevenson put her at ease with a smile, then asked her son's name and wrote him a personal message.

Stevenson seemed relaxed and in his element, so I asked the questions I had come to ask: Why didn't you go for it? Why didn't you leave?

"What is a million dollars," he said, "compared to the love of my people?"

It was a pat answer, the one he'd been giving for at least twenty-five years, according to newspaper clippings. I tried a different angle: quite a few Cuban baseball players, such as the Yankees' Orlando "El Duque" Hernandez, have defected over the years, but not many boxers. Why is that?

Stevenson insisted on answering in the English he had learned as a child, rather than in Spanish. "Because they don't have to," he said. "Because in Cuba, everyone goes to school. School is the light, because when you go to school, you can see. They don't have to resort to boxing to earn money. It's not your eyes that you see with, it's your mind."

The vocabulary was rusty, but the thrust of what he had said was clear enough. Time and again he has spoken of his admiration for Cuba's socialist system and his appreciation of the revolution's accomplishments, particularly in wiping out illiteracy, providing an impressive level of medical care, and making sure everyone has a roof over his head, even if sometimes it's a leaky one. One could point out the failings and misdeeds of the Cuban regime, but there was no reason to doubt his sincerity. Still, the answer seemed incomplete.

We spent more than two hours in the restaurant, eating chicken and steak, talking and laughing, drinking rum. Stevenson told war stories. His classical style in the ring, he said, was as much Russian as Cuban, learned from the Soviet trainers sent over by Moscow to further the glory of world socialism. "He had a Russian name," Stevenson said of one of his teachers, "but he was really a Kazakh."

At one point, Stevenson went over to the bar and came back with a huge, custom-rolled cigar, one of the finest you could buy in the country that makes the best cigars in the world. It would have cost $25, even in Cuba — and I knew that Stevenson didn't have $25 on him and couldn't possibly have bought the thing. Watching the interaction from across the room, I was sure that he had somehow muscled, cajoled, or embarrassed the management into giving it to him.

He didn't light it; he just put it in his shirt pocket. I made a note and put a star next to it: this was a different side of Stevenson. Celebrity, I supposed, had its privileges.

A few minutes later, the woman who had obtained the autograph for her son came back over to our table.

"We're leaving now, but I just wanted to thank you for being so generous," she said to Stevenson. "You were so kind, even though I interrupted your meal. This is something that my son will always treasure."

Stevenson offered to pose for a picture, but the woman didn't have a camera.

We finished eating at El Aljibe, and fifteen minutes of hugging and hand-shaking later we were back out on the street. Torres, the doctor, had gone off to pick up his daughter from a soccer game, and Fraymaris had taken David back to the house to do his homework. Stevenson was on the loose, which is how he likes it. He gave directions to the house of Alcides Sagarra, trainer of the national team that won four boxing gold medals in Sydney. Sagarra wasn't home but we spent half an hour there anyway, as Stevenson flirted with the women of the household, roughhoused with teenagers, hugged little girls, and playfully cuffed little boys. Most of the kids were from somewhere in the neighborhood — they had rushed over when word spread that Stevenson was there.

"Now I'm taking you someplace else," Stevenson said, when we made it back out to the car. "I'm taking you to meet a woman who is like an aunt to me."

We drove a few blocks and parked in front of an apartment complex. The usual crowd gathered when Stevenson got out of the car. This time, in addition to the neighbors and passersby who stopped to greet him, people were shouting down from balconies.

Stevenson stopped at one door, positioning himself so that he would be out of the line of sight of whoever answered it. "Go ahead and knock," he whispered. "Ask her if she knows where Teofilo is. Ask if she's seen him around."

The door opened, and there stood a dark, handsome woman with a million-dollar smile. The joke didn't work; she was on to him already. "I'm not sure where Teofilo is, but I know he's around here somewhere," she said. "I was upstairs, on the balcony, and I saw him get out of the car. Teo, where are you?"

Stevenson popped out, and they fell into each other's arms. "This is Aracelis," he said, beaming. "My family." I made a note, with a star: this was another side of Stevenson. Suddenly, he was thirteen years old.

Teofilo Stevenson Lawrens was born March 29, 1952, and grew up in Las Tunas Province in a little town on the north coast called Puerto Padre. His father was an immigrant from St. Vincent; his mother, though born in Cuba, was the daughter of immigrants from St. Kitts. (Hence Stevenson's childhood English.) In those years, Cuba's eastern provinces were full of impoverished guest workers from other Caribbean islands who had come, like Stevenson's parents, for jobs in the cane fields and sugar mills.

According to the story he has told over the years, his potential as a boxer was discovered when a male teacher humiliated him at school one day and he decked the man. Stevenson didn't repeat that story to me. What he said was that his favorite sport, the one he hoped to play at a high level some day, was basketball. Boxing was something he did because he seemed to be good at it.

In 1959, Castro's revolution triumphed and the schools were transformed. Students with special talents were separated out for special training. At age thirteen, Teofilo Stevenson was asked to leave his home and come to Havana to train as a boxer at the national sports complex.

"I lost fourteen of my first twenty fights," he said. "I hated getting hit. What happened was that I decided I hated losing even more."

Stevenson's mother decided not to accompany her son. Instead, she left him in the care of a friend who had moved to Havana several years earlier. "You take care of him," Stevenson's mother had told her. "You're the one who understands him."

That woman was Miss Aracelis, in whose apartment we now sat. She swore that she was seventy-five but seemed much younger; she had no wrinkles, her muscles were firm and toned, and she moved with the quickness and bounce of a woman in her forties. The room where we sat was tiny, typical of Havana apartments, crammed with chairs, a sofa, knickknacks, a little dining table. In a corner sat a small refrigerator; there was no room for it in the closet-size kitchen.

She and Stevenson reminisced about old times, when he had been an unsophisticated country boy plunged into the big city, with all its temptations. He would train during the week, and on weekends he'd come to Miss Aracelis's apartment — it was the closest thing to a home that he knew throughout his teen years, until he won his first Olympic gold medal and Castro gave him a house.

As we sipped more rum, Miss Aracelis laughed out loud at the memory of those weekend visits. "You have to remember that he was a champion at a very young age, a champion in Cuba before he won the Olympics," she said. "He was famous, and the girls loved that. Hah! I swear that one year he came every weekend, and over the course of that year he brought forty-nine different girls here to meet me. Every time he would come, there would be another girl. He'd say, 'Aracelis, I'd like to introduce my girlfriend,' and I'd have to pretend and say, 'Oh, I'm so glad to meet you, I'm so happy for the two of you.' Oh, Teo, you were terrible."

She wagged her finger at Stevenson, and he grinned like a little boy. Teofilo Stevenson, Hero of Cuba, had vanished. In his place sat young Teo, child of the revolution.

On January 1, 1959, when Castro took power, Stevenson was a young black boy from the provinces, at a time when young black boys from the provinces looked forward to lives of backbreaking work and soul-sapping poverty. The revolution promised bounteous fruits — care for the body, development of the mind, relief from material want, pride in self and country, a tomorrow without horizons. I have met very few Cubans who feel the revolution has given them all of these things in full measure, but Teofilo Stevenson is one of them. He got the whole package.

He paid for it, though. He surrendered much of his youth to the revolution, and in his role as hero he never found — at least until now — a stable family life. He drinks more rum than he should, and he knows it. He's working on his fourth marriage.

"That one he has now, Fraymaris, I have to say that she's the only one who ever seemed to know how to handle him," Miss Aracelis told me, clapping Stevenson with a big hug. "Because our man here is not easy. No, he is not easy."

After a while Miss Aracelis started tidying up and checking the time, and it became apparent to me that as happy as she was to see Stevenson, she had something else to do. I suggested it was time for us to go.

"Five more minutes," Stevenson said. "We'll just stay for five more minutes."

Half an hour later, he finally stood to leave.

"No, not home," he said, when we were back in the car. "Turn right here. Now left. We're going one more place."

We ended up at the modest home of Luis Octavio Samada, a retired air force general. Stevenson and Samada are friends — how they met never became clear, and it was difficult to see just what they had in common. Samada is in his seventies, a grand old man who soldiered with Castro's brother Raul during the revolution and then went on to have a long and illustrious military career. After pouring us a bit of rum — rare is the Cuban house where a bottle of rum is not quickly produced for visitors — he drew diagrams on the coffee table of the defensive preparations that thwarted the invasion at the Bay of Pigs. That time, Samada manned a post that saw no action.

We chatted for a while about nothing in particular — sports, beautiful women, the indignities of advanced age. Samada's ninety-nine-year-old mother-in-law sat on a bench in the corner, watching television, rocking slowly back and forth. At one point the electricity went out for a brief while, and Samada's wife had to fetch candles, but the mother-in-law kept staring at the blank screen, kept rocking; she never missed a beat.

As Samada and Stevenson talked about his wives, about his old girlfriends, about the nights he had slept on the Samadas' couch, the nature of the relationship gradually became clearer, even if its genesis remained obscure. This was something very much like father-son. The old general was very proud of the young boxer, and loved him very much.

All of Cuba was very proud of the young boxer, and loved him very much.

Before we left, Stevenson reached into his pocket, took out the cigar he had gotten at El Aljibe, and gave it to Samada.

"Teo is so good to me," Samada said to me. "He knows that I like cigars, and he knows that I can't afford them. Every time he comes to see me, every time, he brings me a cigar."

It was getting late. Time to go.

"Five more minutes," Stevenson said. "Five more minutes."

It was an hour later when I finally had him back at his house and safely in the care of Fraymaris.

"There is really nobody like Teofilo. He is such a good person, very humble, very easygoing. He occupies a special place in Cuba."

The speaker was Alberto Juantorena, the Cuban track star — he was so strong and so swift in the 400-meter and 800-meter runs that they called him El Caballo, The Horse — who now serves as deputy chief of Cuba's entire sports apparatus, and, indirectly, Stevenson's boss. But those words could have come from almost any Cuban official, or for that matter any of Stevenson's friends. Mention Stevenson's name and you get a smile, and kind words, and abundant praise. But often there's a slightly patronizing tone, a hint of indulgence.

Because, in truth, there are things to allow for.

There's the rum. During the course of an average day, Stevenson consumes a lot of it. He's a big man with big appetites and big capacities, and he never seems drunk, never stumbles or slurs. His aim seems to be to pace himself; he alternates sips of rum with sips of water, and somehow manages to achieve a kind of equilibrium. He says he has a technique: "You have to dominate the rum. You don't let the rum dominate you."

His friend Oscar Torres told me several times that Stevenson recently had been given a complete physical, which showed him in excellent health. "Don't forget to note that," he said. "He's really in very good shape. There's nothing wrong with him." But I also heard Torres tell Stevenson flatly: "Teo. Too much rum. Too much."

Then there's his driving. Stevenson is always crashing his cars. Mostly he gets into fender-benders, but in 1987 he was driving his Lada, on a dark spring night, and collided with a motorcyclist who was killed instantly. Stevenson was taken into custody and held for several days. He told authorities that the biker was "driving in the middle of the road without his lights on," and that he never saw him. Eventually he was cleared of any wrongdoing.

He has had off-road mishaps as well (not counting his marriages). In 1977, one of the dangerous alcohol-fueled stoves that are found in so many Cuban homes exploded in his face. Stevenson suffered burns severe enough for some commentators to worry that he would have to give up his boxing career. The injuries turned out not to be so severe, though, and Stevenson went on to win his third Olympic gold medal three years later. Today he bears no apparent scars.

His most recent tangle came in October 1999, at the Miami airport. He was returning from a charity event in Washington organized by Ali. A United Airlines agent named Pedro de Leon demanded to see his ticket, and Stevenson — who, like most loyal supporters of the Castro government, is deeply suspicious of the entire city of Miami — felt he was being hassled and refused to cooperate. Words were exchanged; something of a scuffle ensued. The ticket fell to the floor, Stevenson bent to retrieve it, and when he stood up again de Leon received a head-butt that left him with a cut lip and a chipped tooth. The police were called, but Stevenson was allowed to post bond and board his plane for Havana.

Stevenson said later that de Leon had provoked him.

"He starts to spout insults against the commander-in-chief, against our government, against all of us," Stevenson told the Havana weekly *Trabajadores.* "I tried to ignore him at first, but when he went after Fidel, I had to say to him, 'Don't screw around with me, because I'll kill you right here.'"

Where the two Cuban metropolises, Havana and Miami, are concerned, bygones can never be bygones. Assault charges are still pending against Stevenson, and until some sort of deal is worked out, he risks arrest if he sets foot on U.S. soil.

A few days later, I got to see Stevenson work his hero magic in a much larger room. The Rafael Trejo Gymnasium, a venerated boxing arena tucked down one of the narrow streets of Old Havana, was hosting an afternoon of official competition for young boxers. Stevenson decided to drop by.

The Trejo gym is to Cuban boxing what certain playgrounds in New York City are to basketball — source, sanctuary, shrine. Every day, after school, boys as young as nine come to the Trejo to learn how to box. The instructors are former boxers, sometimes former members of the national team. The gym is run by the state now, like most institutions in Cuba, but it far predates Castro's revolution; the great Kid Chocolate himself taught at the Trejo in the 1940s, after he retired from the professional ring.

The entrance is on Calle Cuba. You walk through a doorway and beneath a set of bleachers, and emerge into an open-air quadrangle in the middle of the block, walled in by more bleachers and the back sides of apartment buildings. At the center of the enclosure is an elevated boxing ring, its precious canvas protected from Havana's sudden rainstorms by a canopy.

There's nothing deluxe about the Trejo. Most of the equipment is old and worn, and the rest is newly donated by foreign tourists who wandered in and became enchanted by the place. Usually, on a given afternoon, about two dozen boys come in to train. Some will be skipping rope, some bashing the tattered heavy bags, some doing calisthenics, some shadowboxing. A pair of boys might be in the ring wearing gloves and headgear, sparring, working, making their moves but putting no force behind their punches. A couple of cigar-chomping old guys from the neighborhood, boxers themselves once, drop by most days to provide running commentary.

Sparring was one thing; a real competition, like the one that Stevenson had come to watch, was something else. These were purposeful encounters, with punches meant to hurt. Theoretical concepts like footwork and hand speed suddenly became quite practical, determining who would be a giver of humiliation and pain, and who a receiver.

Two evenly matched teenaged opponents were in the ring when Stevenson arrived, a clumsy slugger and a punchless dancer. It didn't take long for the distracted crowd to notice the tall, familiar figure who strode toward the ring and then stopped, right in the open where he could hardly be missed.

Trainers, many of them old friends, came over to greet him. Kids pointed at him but didn't quite know whether it was okay to approach. At the next break, the announcer boomed over the PA system that "the great champion" Teofilo Stevenson had arrived.

Then, in a flash, he was out of sight. I found him sitting on a bench beneath the bleachers. He was smoking a cigarette — in his fighting years he would quit a few days before a bout, to let his lungs clear out, and then pick up the habit again afterward. He was hiding, he said, because he didn't want all the kids to see his bad example.

But the kids spotted him, and they quickly had him cornered. They wanted autographs. Most didn't have anything for the champion to write on, so they asked me for sheets of paper from my reporter's notebook. Stevenson sat there for more than half an hour, signing his name for the boys who scrambled down out of the bleachers in seemingly endless numbers.

The interesting thing was the way he changed the event. There was a buzz in the bleachers that hadn't been there before. The trainers ramped up their intensity, yelling louder into their fighters' ears. The boys in the ring stood taller and tried to remember to move the right way, the way a boxer moves, pushing off with the right foot to move left and the left foot to move right. They remembered to jab. The winners didn't look first for Mom and Dad in the stands; they looked for the champ.

Now this was real boxing. Stevenson's being there made it so.

When he left he could light another cigarette — the kids wouldn't see him. Out on Calle Cuba, he (of course) drew another crowd. The street is always busy — just across the way is an old colonial Catholic church popular with devotees of Santeria. Everyone knew who he was, and he was mobbed with handshakes and hugs. Old Havana is a poor neighborhood, and Cubans are not immune to feelings of envy or resentment. Here was a man who everyone knew owned two big houses and two functioning cars, who though not rich was free from want, who would never get hassled on the street by a cop with an attitude or run in circles by a tyrannical bureaucrat, who could travel abroad whenever he wanted — a man who had advantages and opportunities the people of Old Havana could only dream of, and yet no one confronted him with anything but love.

Maybe he could have come to the United States and had all the love and a bank vault full of money, too. He'll never know. And not knowing doesn't seem to bother The Hero one bit.

BOB NORMAN

Backyard Bloodbath

FROM NEW TIMES BROWARD–PALM BEACH

I

THE SICKLY SWEET SMELL of blood fills the dimly lit bathroom where John Ulloa sits dazed on a closed toilet. The silky red fluid gushes from a gash in his forehead, creating a stream that flows over his cheekbone, past his mouth, and drips like a leaky faucet from his chin. It has already dried onto John's short, spiked black hair and his ears. His wife-beater shirt and shorts are soaked in it. The sixteen-year-old boy, who is short, thin, and naturally muscular, struggles to keep his eyes open as his older brother, David, silently limps over with a brown bottle of peroxide. David takes off the cap and, without a word, pours the liquid over the straight, surgical-looking three-inch slit at the top of John's forehead, just below the hairline. As the peroxide does its job, John's legs shake in pain. "I'm dizzy," mutters John, who goes by the name Kid Suicide when he performs. "But I don't think I want to go to the hospital."

After nearly thirty minutes of applying pressure to the cut to slow the bleeding, John walks out to his back yard, where his club, Extreme Fuckin' Wrestling (EFW), continues its show under the bright Saturday-afternoon sun. His friends slam one another on a homemade wooden stage, which is laden with barbed wire and tacks. The boys leap from the roof and crack their faux opponents over the head with real metal chairs and garbage cans. They crash through burning tables and whack their fellow wrestlers with a barbed wire–wrapped baseball bat. They dive from rooftops and ladders to the ground below. The EFW members are not alone:

about forty kids, all of them yearning to see savage beatings, lounge on the grass to watch.

The barbaric show takes place in what seems a wildly incongruous setting: John's solidly middle-class neighborhood in Coral Springs. Surrounding the bloodletting are large, well-kept homes with an average worth of about $150,000, and bordering the rear of the yard is a wide canal that cuts past swimming pools, freshly painted gazebos, and orange trees.

With his head wrapped in a makeshift white bandage that turns redder with every passing minute, John watches the final competition, the "death match." It features his buddies, Giovanni "Psycho" Torres and Jason "The Sensation" Jelonek, and doesn't disappoint the fans. There's plenty of blood, a bed-of-nails stunt, body slams, and a twelve-foot dive, the highest in the club's short history.

But the February 24 show ends in an almost surreal outburst of unscripted violence as the raw, sadistic longings of the crowd and the pumped-up showmanship of the wrestlers collide. Police are called to stop the mayhem. An ambulance arrives and takes John to the hospital as a "trauma alert," which is code for a potentially critical injury. He initially tells the medics his cut was caused by a blow to the head from a folding chair. Later he admits the truth: he cut himself with a razor blade to make sure the crowd and the ever-present EFW video camera got their fill of blood.

EFW is one of hundreds of backyard wrestling clubs that have sprouted up across the country in the last couple years. The participants, who mimic their pro wrestling heroes, say they love the audience reaction and long for stardom. But what distinguishes EFW from the other clubs is that it is truly extreme. Kid Suicide, Psycho, and their compatriots have broken numerous bones and repeatedly been knocked unconscious. Why do they go so far? The answer may lie not in their back yards but inside their homes.

John's obsession with backyard wrestling began, predictably, in front of the television. At about the age of ten, he and David, who is a year older, started watching the World Wrestling Federation. Soon they moved on to Extreme Championship Wrestling, which might be considered the WWF's foul-mouthed, hell-raising, jail-bound cousin. Soon they were idolizing ECW stars such as Mick "Mankind" Foley, Rob Van Dam, and Spike Dudley, all of whom are renowned for spilling buckets of their own blood. The two brothers and Giovanni, who goes by Gio and lives next door to the Ulloa brothers, soon began imitating their heroes and dreaming of staging a show of their own.

At first they practiced simple things like headlocks and fake punches. Then they graduated to various moves, such as body slams, suplexes, and pile drivers. Next it was on to the props of pain. John experimented with razor blades. David practiced taking staples in his head. Gio had thumbtacks stuck into his forehead. They all took shots to the head from metal chairs and learned a trick: if they popped the metal to invert the curve of the seat, it would pop back into place upon impact with a skull to make a louder *thwack.* To perfect their falls, or "bumps," they slammed one another to the ground relentlessly. The secret to avoiding injury, the boys say, is to spread out the impact as much as possible so the arms and shoulders, instead of the backbone and ribs, take most of it. The same theory applies to the high dives. They jump straight out and flip into the air before landing on their backs. Tables are usually positioned below, and crashing through them shortens the free fall and cushions the impact with the ground. John and Gio, the only EFW wrestlers who venture high dives, started from heights just a couple feet up, then graduated to a six-foot ladder, then to a rooftop, and now to the twelve-foot ladder, which is akin to leaping from the backboard of a regulation basketball hoop. It's equal to dives of some of the top pro wrestlers, who rarely leap from heights of more than fifteen feet. John says he doesn't know how high will ever be high enough.

After years of fooling around with such techniques, the EFW held its first show last year, on February 13. Since then they've held about ten more performances, each a little more hard-core than the last. In addition to the founding threesome, EFW has a few other regulars: Jason, a tall and thin seventeen-year-old who prides himself on how much punishment he can take; Edwin Lebron, who at eighteen weighs more than 200 pounds; and Rich Teixeira, a seventeen-year-old who gives EFW some major heft with his 340 pounds. Another half-dozen teens orbit EFW but haven't wrestled much. Several quit after their first show, unable to take the abuse.

As the EFW grew, an amazing thing happened: people began coming. So many, in fact, that the wrestlers began charging admission, earning more than $200 at a show that drew nearly one hundred spectators. John says his performances provide two things he never before had at Marjory Stoneman Douglas High School: attention and respect. "Now I'm living it up at school," he says in his smooth voice. John doesn't just talk about wrestling; he sells it. "They say, 'You're crazy, man.' I mean, I'm small, but people respect me now. They treat you different. Even gangster kids. They like to watch us, and after the show they have, um, gratitude."

David says the teens who come to watch their performances crave blood and destruction. "They aren't really normal," he says of the fans. "But I like how the crowd goes, 'Ooooh' and 'Ahhhh.' That's why we do this. Our fans are ghetto. They're bloodthirsty, our fans. They just want someone to get killed."

EFW always has someone on hand to videotape the proceedings. The wrestlers say they'll cherish the tapes forever — and they hope to sell some of the footage to companies that market the ghoulish stuff. A similar video titled *The Best of Backyard Wrestling,* for instance, is currently being advertised on cable television for $19.95 a pop. The members of EFW have also created a Web site touting their feats.

In addition to making some money from EFW, John dreams of owning a wrestling ring; practicing in a bare back yard is akin to playing basketball on dirt with a volleyball and a peach basket. But a decent ring would cost them about $1,500, far more than they can pay. So last fall, when they forged a loose partnership with a Hollywood-based backyard group called Hardcore Champion Wrestling (HCW), they were ecstatic. HCW is the best organized of Broward County's backyard wrestling clubs (there are at least four of them) and has a ring.

It was, however, a doomed marriage from the start, the backyard equivalent of the Hell's Angels crashing a kiddie party. HCW forbids cursing at its shows, while EFW thrives on profanity. HCW doesn't care for bloodletting, bans self-cutting, and employs just a touch of barbed wire, which is mostly for show. Thumbtacks are a rarity.

"EFW has no wrestling techniques," says sixteen-year-old Nick Mayberry, a wrestler and HCW promoter. "They just hit each other with weapons and go nuts out there. They beat each other senseless and fly off things like they're crazy. Someone always winds up hurt really bad or in the hospital. They think they're gonna get famous, but they're just gonna get killed."

After a few practice sessions and a show last fall, a staple gun terminated the relationship between the two clubs. When Rich shot a thick, half-inch steel staple into David's forehead, HCW banned EFW for life. The stunt was actually a mistake; Rich was supposed to hold the gun away from David's head so it would make only a partial puncture wound and protrude from his head. In the heat of the match he pressed the gun flush against David's forehead. John removed the staple from his brother's cranium. "It took everything I had to pull that thing out," he says, smiling at the memory. Describing the incident, David states the obvious: "It felt like a sharp object entering my skull."

All the EFW veterans have lengthy injury lists and scars all over their bodies that make them unabashedly proud. In addition to the forehead slashing and about 130 shots to the head, David says he's cracked his sternum, tailbone, shoulder blade, and jaw, as well as a few fingers and toes. He's received medical attention for precious few of those injuries. Instead he lived with the pain until, after a few weeks, it subsided. Both his jaw and sternum now make hideous cracking noises if he moves them in a certain way.

"I don't think they healed right," John says. "Pain is no object to me at this point. If you can get past the stinging, I mean, what is pain? It's nothing. You disregard it or whatever."

Jason was knocked unconscious last year when another wrestler slammed him with a folding chair. He's also been hospitalized with a gashed head and recently ripped open his knee when he fell badly on the bed of nails. The other wrestlers sometimes gibe him when he lapses into a stutter or has a memory lapse. Those chair shots to the head, they laugh, don't come without a price.

Gio has potentially the most lasting injury of all. He suffers from bilateral knees — they've taken so much abuse from his falls that they are curved in a way that suggests deformity. He takes medication for the condition and says doctors have told him he will require surgery in a few years.

The bone-crunching pays off, they say, in larger crowds, who push the wrestlers to new extremes. "Everybody just loves violence," David surmises. "I don't know why, but I know they'll always love it. Our fans just want to see us kill each other."

His penchant for blood notwithstanding, John doesn't have a lot of teenage vices. He spends most of his time at home, doesn't like to fight outside the choreographed backyard performances, abstains from cigarettes and drugs, and seldom touches alcohol. Such distractions would only get in the way of his all-consuming dream of becoming a wrestling superstar. Unfortunately school seems to be another such distraction. His academic performance has declined as his interest in wrestling has risen. He has a D average. School isn't so important when stardom beckons.

John's mother has a dream, too: she wishes she could ship him off to military school.

Carolyn Lister is a forty-two-year-old single mom who speaks of John with nervous laughter that hints at helplessness. She says she has tried to keep the kids from breaking their bones and slashing their skin but has been unsuccessful. She's overwhelmed by the testosterone, by the boys' wild energy. "Oh, if I'd only had girls!" she exclaims before letting out her laugh.

Lister, as it turns out, is no stranger to the sometimes violent vagaries of young men. While living in Connecticut some twenty years ago, she married a man she now characterizes as an abusive alcoholic. "I fell in love with the wrong guy. He hit me over the head with a bottle, and that was about all I could take," she says. "I took a flight to Fort Lauderdale to be back with my mother and father."

After divorcing she quickly married a Colombian immigrant named Oscar Ulloa, who had a good job as a maintenance technician and a promising future. Ulloa was stable and calm, she says, and they had two sons in successive Augusts, David in 1983 and John in 1984. David, who has blond hair like his mother, was born without a right leg. Wearing an artificial leg kept him from playing most sports but hasn't slowed him down much in backyard wrestling, where he manages to hold his own.

Nothing, meanwhile, could slow John, who has black hair and the dark complexion of his father. "When Jonathan was born, he had a certain scream and a way about him," his mother recalls. "He had to get the attention from the get-go, that one did. It's not like he doesn't get attention at home — he wants attention from the world. He's a showman, that one."

His motorcycle-riding father is also something of a thrill seeker, and some of John's fondest memories include riding with his dad in a dune buggy. In recent months John and his father have been bonding on a paintball shooting range, where they play war games together. "I love extreme sports, anything that will get the adrenaline pumping," says John. "That's just the way I grew up."

While John was destined to crack his own bones, it was his home that broke first. Three years ago, just as John and David were embarking on adolescence and wrestling was overtaking their imaginations, their parents split up. "He had a midlife crisis and decided to enjoy other things," Lister explains of Ulloa. Her husband (they've yet to divorce) says he left because of a lack of trust. Whatever the reason, both parents agree the split has caused a complete breakdown in parental authority. "I always gave the love and the kisses and fixed boo-boos," Lister says. "My husband always did the disciplining. I always sent them his way. He left at the worst time, when they really needed a fatherly influence, a man."

Asked whether he could stop the wrestling, Oscar Ulloa replies, "It's not my house; I don't live there. I just try to talk to them, to make them understand [the dangers]. At least they are off the streets."

For all her apparent exasperation, Lister sees some value in backyard wrestling; she's even encouraged it by purchasing the boys a trampoline to use as a makeshift ring. "They say in life, you go after what you want," she philosophizes. "When you really want something, you pursue it, and this is something they really, really want. They are so dedicated. It only goes too far when there is an audience to push them. All that bleeding."

Lister says she had no idea the kids were going to have the February 24 show in her back yard and says she just happened to be getting her hair done that day. John has another story. He says his mother knew about the show and left the house because she didn't want to be held responsible if police were called. John, while idolizing his father, clearly holds some deep bitterness toward his mother. "My mom is usually out with her friends, so she's not around much at all," the boy says. "We always make our own dinner. My dad doesn't like it, so he tries to be here. Everybody always says my mom is not really a good mom."

Lister fervently denies her son's claims and counters that she devotes her entire life to her children. Her only parental sin, she says, may be spending too much time in Internet chat rooms in the evenings. "I don't even date anybody," she explains. "I'm lucky if I sit down on the computer and talk to people that way. Since my husband left, my kids are my world."

But that world sometimes seems about to implode. John, she says, is becoming increasingly aggressive. He demands to have his own way, and if he doesn't get it, he storms about the house, banging on walls and occasionally breaking things. "He's never struck me, but it's getting to that age where I'm afraid of him," she says. "I guess it comes with the territory when you have boys."

Hence her dream. "If I had the money, I would send Jonathan's butt to a military school," she says. "That's where he belongs."

John, however, is bent on staying in one place: his own back yard.

On February 24 a racially mixed crowd of about forty teens gathers in John's back yard. Girls in loose-fitting T-shirts over bikini tops lounge on boys' laps as a CD player rips out Nirvana, Kid Rock, and Metallica. A teen named Parker Tindell is there to videotape the show, which he sardonically terms "an adventure in boredom."

EFW's set consists mainly of a large plywood wall, which the wrestlers have set up next to the screened enclosure around the pool. Other than that, there's the stage, the barbed wire, the thumbtacks (they've purchased 1,000 for this show), and their other torturous trappings. A half-dozen tables wait to be smashed, and a can of lighter fluid is on standby. There is no parent here, no authority figure; just kids and their tools of destruction.

To open the show, Kid Suicide is scheduled to wrestle his brother, who goes by Extreme D. David begins the damage when he slams John's head with the garbage can. As the younger boy falls to the ground in mock pain, David staggers around, exhorting the crowd. With the spectators diverted, John deftly pulls out a razor blade and slices his forehead. He knows instantly he's gone too deep, but he isn't about to stop the show.

In the next few minutes, as the blood starts dripping down John's face, David pummels him with the barbed wire–wrapped baseball bat. Then David does the unthinkable: he takes the barbed wire in his hands and presses it against John's forehead, right across the cut. David didn't want to do it, he says later, but it was scripted, and John would "hate" him if he didn't follow the plan. Blood is now spurting out of John's head. But that doesn't keep John and David from climbing the ladder to the top of the screened enclosure over the pool, which is a little more than eight feet high. Two tables are stacked below. John, pretending that he's been thrown, dives onto the tables, breaking them in half. As he lies motionless on the ground and blood pools in the grass beside him, the crowd is loving it. A spectator screams, "Holy shit!" John, who landed well and isn't in much real pain, loves to hear it; he knows he's succeeded in making the crowd believe that he's seriously injured.

David slowly climbs back down, and soon the brothers are body-slamming each other, hard, on the wooden stage, leaving dozens of tacks stuck into their arms and backs. David finally pins John, ending the match. John then staggers over to the video camera. It looks as if a can of red paint has been poured over his head.

"Intense," Parker mutters from behind the camera.

"Film it!" John orders.

"You just spit blood on me," replies Parker, while dutifully videotaping.

Then John stumbles past his family's pool, which is filled with green, murky water. He enters his house and walks across the bare cement floor of his family room, which his mother has been planning to tile for weeks. From there he stumbles into the bathroom, where he can bleed in relative peace. Other than his brother and a few other teens, the house is empty. Lister doesn't see her son until later, at North Broward Medical Center's trauma unit, where doctors stitch his head back together and nurses stick him with IV needles to replenish his fluids. She's told that John lost about a gallon of blood.

But now, as he sits on the toilet with the blood still flowing, John rests. His performance is done.

The show, however, has just begun.

II

Giovanni "Gio" Torres climbs the rungs of a twelve-foot ladder and stands at the top, towering above a small crowd in John Ulloa's back yard. The forty or so spectators call out for Gio to jump; they want to see him dive onto his friend, Jason Jelonek, who lies on a table below. The crowd's objective is clear: to see someone hurt.

Gio, a sixteen-year-old Marjory Stoneman Douglas High School junior who stands five-foot-seven and weighs about 125 pounds, needs courage. He already has thumbtacks stuck into his head, but that's no problem; the tacks sting only for a moment as they enter the skull. The dive, which he calls a "Senton Bomb," could break his neck. The ground is hard, and he has never jumped from such a height. Gio masks his fear with an inscrutable, determined expression as he surveys the scene. In his mind he pictures a huge man with a beer in his hand. Always a beer in his hand. He imagines the man is watching him from behind a darkened screen next door. The image fills Gio with hate, and that emotion inspires him to leave the security of the ladder, dive out, flip in the air, and crash onto the boy on the table.

The man is his stepfather.

Gio, who goes by "Psycho" when he wrestles in the back yard, lands badly. Only his neck and head strike Jason, yet the impact is enough to break the table. Though he intended to fall squarely on his back before springing to the ground, he instead tumbles violently into the dirt. After lying flat for a moment, he knows he is really hurt. But he doesn't stop the show. Instead he calls to the referee, a bespectacled teen named John Summers, and quietly asks, "Did it look good?"

"Yeah," Summers replies.

It feels good to hear that, good enough to dull for at least a moment the terrible pain spreading through his chest.

Gio finished the February 24 wrestling show, but he hasn't breathed easy since. The pain was constant for two weeks. He still doesn't know why it hurts so much. He wonders whether he cracked a rib or bruised a lung, but he'll likely never know because his mom, Maricela Crofts, so hates his backyard stunts that she refuses to take him to the hospital when he gets injured doing them. She wouldn't even ferry him to a drug store for an Ace bandage to wrap around his chest. He had to borrow one from a friend.

"He got hurt, like, once and I told him, 'That's it, if you go over there and you get hurt, don't come crying to me, because you have to learn to deal with it,'" Crofts explains in a thick Puerto Rican accent. "The police have to stop them from doing this before someone really gets hurt."

Crofts wants the cops to stop Gio, because her son refuses to quit. He's as dedicated to backyard wrestling as his buddy and next-door neighbor, John. And like John, Gio saw his family break up years ago. His mother and father divorced when the boy was about ten years old. A year after the split, his mom married William Crofts, who is now fifty-three years old and retired from Lucent Technologies. Gio has grown up in the couple's beautiful, middle-class Coral Springs home, which has a large and expensive boat in the driveway. He's still growing — at just five-feet-seven, he expects to get a little taller. His lips bulge over the braces he wears, and his shoulders and chest have been expanding since he recently began lifting weights. Gio is on the high school wrestling team but is academically ineligible to compete. He desperately wants to be a full-fledged member of the school team and says he has maintained a B average this year (up from a D last year) in pursuit of that goal. But he concedes that his ventures with Extreme Fuckin' Wrestling are largely to blame for his scholastic woes.

Gio loves the backyard grappling; it's the fighting inside his house that disturbs him.

"[My stepfather] would drink, and he would snap at my mom," Gio says. "Other times he just yells at her and threatens her and throws her out of the house."

William Crofts declined to comment for this article, and Gio's mother says only that such things don't happen anymore. The worst incident, Gio says, occurred on the night of December 30, 1996. "I was in my room, and I heard all this yelling and crap, and I walked out there," he explains. "They were out on the patio, and my dad was drinking beer. He threw my mom in the pool. And then he started yelling at her and said, 'Get out of this house!' I've seen him push her, and it pisses me off. But what can I do? I was only five-foot-two then. He's six-foot, 500 pounds."

Gio manages a smile at his exaggeration. His stepfather actually weighs 220 pounds, according to a Coral Springs Police Department arrest report from that night. Gio's mother complained to officers that her husband threw her into the pool, then into the Jacuzzi, then against a wall, and then grabbed her by the hair and shoved her into her daughter's room. William Crofts was arrested for domestic violence and later, his wife acknowledges, was sentenced to probation. (Although the arrest report details the incident, *New Times* could find no record of the case in Broward courts.)

To try to stop Gio from backyard wrestling, his mother and stepfather threaten to exile him to Orlando to live with his father. But the boy says that just makes him angry. And it makes him want to be more hard-core. "I don't like [my stepfather], and that's why I keep doing the backyard stuff," Gio says. "He keeps getting on my nerves. That's why I get the twelve-foot ladder, build a bed of nails, and stick the thumbtacks in my head." He pauses a moment before adding, "That and because I love wrestling more than anything else."

All the EFW members collect wrestling action figures and hang posters of their heroes. Each of them has read *Have a Nice Day,* the autobiography by Mick Foley, one of hard-core wrestling's original stars. But their love of backyard wrestling is no mere hobby; they want to do it for a living and dream of someday attending a professional-wrestling school to begin the climb to stardom.

Only Rich Teixeira, however, comes close to fitting the traditional image of the professional-wrestling behemoth. Gio and John, who from a distance appear almost like twins, are short and thin. Most pros weigh more than both of them put together. But there is one wrestling star who gives them hope, who is cut in their mold, whose very existence helps to keep them going, and his stage name is LSD.

Extreme Championship Wrestling's Li'l Spike Dudley stands five-foot-seven and weighs a mere 140 pounds. Dudley, whose real name is Matt Hyson, says he overcame his diminutive dimensions by taking extreme punishment in the ring (he's renowned for bleeding buckets), by diving from obscene heights (he claims his highest dive is from twenty-five feet), and by training for many years. Now thirty years old, Hyson went to a pro wrestling school in his early twenties and soon began traveling the country on the lowly independent circuit, in which ambitious beginners often perform in poorly attended shows for scant wages. He worked three years before landing his gig at ECW; in this league he has perfected his wrestling persona: a half-witted, burned-out druggie who wears denim suspenders over a tie-dyed shirt. In the past few years, Hyson has realized the EFW members' dreams of good pay and a TV gig. He says he can earn $3,000 a night for pay-per-view performances, and while declining to provide a specific amount, claims his annual pay is six figures.

Though Hyson's success story gives EFW members hope, the pro wrestler is not optimistic about the kids' wrestling success. Young wannabes send backyard videos to the ECW every week, and those usually end up in the trash, Hyson says. "They give the business a terrible name," he says of extreme backyard wrestlers. "There is an art form in doing it safely, and these kids have no regard for that whatsoever. We think they're idiots. When I was a kid, we would wrestle around on cushions, but not anything like these guys. They're going to get hurt."

Despite all his training, Hyson has suffered a slew of injuries. Like John, he often cuts his own forehead with a razor blade to amp up the bleeding. "There are subtleties to how far and deep you go with the blade," he cautions. "I've probably had stitches fifteen to twenty times, and half of them were not self-inflicted."

He also blew his knee out and once required surgery after flying into a rail outside the ring during a high dive. He claims he was the first wrestler to take a staple gun to the head. "There's a little difference, though," he says when told of the boys' adventures. "It wasn't real. There weren't any staples in the gun."

Hyson knows that, as much as he may try to dissuade youngsters from hard-core backyard wrestling, he has helped to inspire it. "My story in the ring is David and Goliath," he says. "I appeal to the children, to the little guy. I'm probably the smallest pro wrestler out there other than the midgets. Any guy who can relate to the underdog can relate to Spike Dudley."

While he knows kids are imitating him, he doesn't feel any responsibility for the dangerous stunts. "It's a show, and if you can't grasp that, then you got bigger problems than pro wrestling," he says. He then mentions Lionel Tate, the fourteen-year-old Fort Lauderdale boy who was recently sentenced to life in prison without parole for killing a six-year-old girl while imitating pro wrestling moves two years ago. Tate's actions can't be blamed on pro wrestling, Hyson asserts: "I never went into a back yard and killed someone mimicking something I saw on TV."

Hyson's disdain for EFW dissipates a bit when he hears that small crowds gather for their shows. "Is that right?" he asks with a note of surprise. "Well, that's tremendous. More power to them."

Hyson is definitely wrong about one thing: the EFW members care deeply about the "art form" of pro wrestling. And they have some genuine wrestling skills (especially John and Gio). The members carefully plan and choreograph their matches, have a championship belt, and predetermine who will win it. But unlike the pros' performances, EFW shows have a raw, unpolished feel and exceedingly long and awkward lulls between moves. And far too often they make mistakes, which usually prove to be gory and sometimes downright frightening.

That brings us back to the February 24 match with Gio, Jason, and Edwin.

The match begins with Jason goading the crowd, which has already been warmed up with John's copious bleeding. Wearing sliced-up denim shorts and a white T-shirt, Jason greets the spectators with an Italian salute — a stiff hand flick under the chin. To make sure they don't miss his point, he shouts: "Fuck you!"

Then comes Gio, who stalks about in the manner of a caged animal. Next Edwin Lebron, whose wrestling name is "Havoc," jumps into the fray, and the bloodletting begins. The beginning of the performance features hard body slams onto a makeshift wooden stage littered with hundreds of thumbtacks. The tacks drive into Jason's back, hands, arms, and legs — a friend later counts 250 holes in his back, which looks as if it has been attacked by a swarm of killer bees.

Jason then slams Gio's head into the tacks. Gio rises to reveal several thumbtacks in his forehead. Blood trickles down his face. Gio is the only member of EFW who takes tacks to his head this way. It's one of his specialties.

Seeking a little blood revenge, Gio grabs some barbed wire, wraps it around Jason's head from behind, and pulls in the manner of a shoeshine. But the metaphorical shoe is Jason's forehead, and the rag is a strand of barbed wire. Jason's head is cut, and Gio's mission is accomplished; there is more blood. Jason counters by grabbing a can of lighter fluid, dousing a table, and lighting it on fire. Then he picks up the smaller boy and slams him through it. The fire goes out.

Then it's time for Gio's twelve-foot dive. Edwin lays Jason, who pretends to be stunned in the classic, cheesy style of pro wrestling, onto the table while Gio climbs the ladder. After a moment of hesitation, Gio, with his stepfather in mind, makes his leap and has a miserable landing. The crowd shouts its approval, and one fan throws an orange at Gio, perhaps in an effort to get him back on his feet.

After a minute on the ground, the boy overcomes the pain. He grabs the orange and throws it at Jason. The crowd laughs. Gio and Edwin then hang Jason upside down from a lower rung of the ladder. Gio leans the bed of nails against Jason's chest, and the crowd loves it.

"Oh shit!" shouts one onlooker.

"Yo, just hit the bitch, yo!" hollers another.

Gio takes a running, diving leap into the back of the bed of nails, compressing them into Jason's stomach. The problem is that Gio doesn't fake it well, and the impact is obviously weak. The lame stunt ends an otherwise memorable EFW match.

The show is officially over, but there's one more bloody fight to go — and this one is unplanned.

Gio isn't the only EFW member who pictures his father at strange times. Rich does, too, but he does it when he's enraged.

Rich Teixeira is a seventeen-year-old, dirty-blond-haired boy who carries his 340 pounds on a six-foot-one frame. His size alone intimidates, a fact that pleases him. "I've been in fights since I was little," he says. "That's just me. I've always been bigger than anyone else, and I have always felt I have that little bit of power. It's a power trip."

But something else drives him to violence, he says: his father. Rich moved to Florida from New England with his mother, Regina Teixeira, last March because, they say, his dad threatened them. They also say Rich's father is thousands of dollars behind on child-support payments. Rich contends he feared his dad until his parents divorced when he was about eleven years old. (Despite extensive efforts *New Times* was unable to reach Rich's father for comment.)

"I know I hate my dad," Rich says. "My mom says he hit me with a closed fist, but I don't remember that. I do remember him beating me with a belt to where I couldn't walk up the stairs. He had a cow whip and used to threaten me with it. A couple of times, he hit me with it. And he had these ninja swords he used to threaten me with, too."

Rich says that, no matter how hard he tries to forget his father, he can't do it. "When I get angry, I start seeing pictures of my father everywhere," Rich says. "I get flashbacks of him beating me as a kid." Before Rich came to Florida, his anger spilled over in high school. He fought another student in the hallway, and the other kid suffered a concussion in the fracas. Rich was convicted of assault, sentenced to probation, and is now undergoing therapy to help him cope with his anger. He says backyard wrestling provides him with an ideal relief valve. "I'm played out on the fighting and violence," he says. "I hate it. All I do now is wrestle."

Rich, who was an honor student in middle school, now ekes out a C average, "just enough to graduate," he says. He attributes his scholastic decline to smoking cigarettes and drinking beer. He says he'll either attend community college or join the army. Like all the EFW kids, Rich has endearing qualities. He's smart, acutely sensitive, and cares deeply about his friends. When something goes wrong during a show — like the time he accidentally staple-gunned David's forehead or when John seriously injured himself with the razor blade — Rich is usually the only crew member who shows emotion. At these times he becomes distraught and seems to cry, but with a boyish machismo, he denies shedding tears. "It's a family," he says of EFW. "That's the way most of us look at it. I needed to get friends down here [in Florida], and these guys are like family to me."

At the end of the February 24 show, however, a member of his real family flashed in his mind: his father. And that was not a good thing.

EFW members have a fitting plan for the end of the performance. In the spirit of blending sex and wrestling that works so well in the professional ranks, they are going to propose the girls in the audience participate in a wet T-shirt contest. But Rich has something else on his mind: that orange. He and his friends work way too hard on the craft of wrestling to be pelted with fruit. So Rich confronts the crowd member who he believes tossed the offending piece of citrus, a skinny, dark-complexioned fifteen-year-old named Frankie. Soon, the two of them square off in the middle of the back yard.

"Fuck you!" Rich yells.

"Like I fucked your mama last night," Frankie shoots back.

Rich gets in Frankie's face.

"Wop!" Rich yells.

"What the fuck are you?" says Frankie, backing off a bit.

"I'm 340 pounds of person who will beat the shit out of you!" Rich replies, his head shaking in rage and his massive belly bumping Frankie backward. Rich then exhorts Frankie to hit him, to provide Rich with an excuse to beat him into the ground.

Some in the crowd seem to believe this is all still part of the show. They laugh and watch in anticipation, perhaps of a body slam onto a bed of thumbtacks. Rich, too, is still caught up in the excitement. He's demonstrative and wild, much like his pro wrestling idols. Later he admits he was still pumped up from the show and wasn't really prepared for what followed: Frankie, dancing around and appearing understandably nervous, looks away for a moment before shooting a stinging right to Rich's jaw.

Rich, stunned from the blow, stumbles backward. Frankie runs. But the smaller boy winds up cornered between a pool enclosure and a plywood wall. (Almost two months later, Rich will still be a bit hazy about the events that ensued. All he will remember seeing are images of his father.) What the crowd sees is Rich storming up to Frankie, wrapping his huge hands around the boy's neck, and lifting him off the ground. Frankie doesn't breathe. His tongue is forced from his mouth, his feet shake helplessly a foot above the ground, and his eyes roll back into his head.

After a few seconds, Rich lets Frankie fall to the ground like a rag doll. A friend of Frankie's then throws two vicious punches to the same spot over Rich's left eye. Rich falls like a redwood tree straight back into a large bush. The bush doesn't stand a chance; it is broken into pieces.

Frankie gets to his feet and runs onto the street. Rich, as if rising from a dream, stands up and follows him. Blood flows from above Rich's eye. Out on the driveway and street, the two shout taunts at each other.

"I'll lay you out, you fat bitch!" Frankie repeats over and over.

Then three police cars pull up and Frankie escapes down the street. The mere presence of the cops acts as a sedative; the threat of violence recedes. The spectators disperse, and medics arrive. Coral Springs police officer Brian Tarbox finds John; the self-inflicted razor blade wound has reopened, and blood drips down his chin.

Tarbox says there's little he can do to stop the kids from wrestling, so he focuses on John's parents' liability. "Do you know if somebody gets hurt doing this 'rassling thing, their parents are going to own your parents?" Tarbox asks John.

The boy just nods.

"How old are you?"

"Sixteen," John answers.

"Plenty old enough to know this is stupid."

On their radios the police call in medics to treat John and Rich. "This is the stupidest thing I've ever seen," Tarbox mutters. Gio stands quietly in John's front doorway. "I can hardly breathe," he says to one bystander. "I think I may have to go to the hospital."

Officer Rex Kirkpatrick of the Coral Springs gang unit arrives in a bulletproof vest. He announces to EFW members milling about outside: "This is over. You do realize that, don't you? You can't do this ever again."

The boys nod.

Medics soon determine that John needs emergency medical care. In addition to the cut, he also has a hematoma on his forehead, likely from a chair shot. The EMTs wrap a collar around his neck, lay him on a backboard, and load him into the ambulance. Rich's mother arrives and tells the police about her son's problems: the threats, the lack of child support, the probation, and the anger.

Finally John's mom, Carolyn Lister, comes home. In a blue spring dress over a bathing suit, she appears to have been at the beach. (She said later that she was getting her hair done.)

"You need to get control of your kids," Tarbox admonishes her.

Lister tells the officers she has tried to no avail. John has taken over the house, she complains.

"Has he hit you?" Tarbox asks.

"No, but he's thrown and broken things," she says.

Before heading to the hospital to see her son, Lister complains the authorities simply don't understand. For her, backyard wrestling isn't a troubling trend, it's an inevitability. So she calls for official regulation. "I just wish the city would get a place where they could do this under some kind of supervision," she says. "They could use fake blood."

In the end Tarbox decides not to arrest anyone. He says he hates what he sees, but since it's all consensual and takes place on private property, he's powerless. With no victim there's no crime, and he believes charging Lister with child neglect is unwarranted.

Though the bloodbaths continue, the Coral Springs Police Department has managed to slow them down. They've been called to John's back yard, mostly following neighbors' complaints, a half-dozen times in the past couple years. Indeed EFW doesn't charge admission anymore because cops threatened to arrest the wrestlers for running an unlicensed business.

The February 24 show went further and got uglier than planned. The wrestlers didn't want the police to come. John didn't want to lose a gallon of blood (though he was determined to lose a cup or two). Gio didn't want to injure his chest. Rich didn't want to get in a fight or gash his eye. He's still a bit hazy about the fight and says he was in a sort of trance when he was holding Frankie by his neck. "All of a sudden, I thought, 'What am I doing?'" Rich recalls of the moment before he let go.

Of the three injured, just John went to the hospital — and only because the medics gave him no choice. Gio's mom refused to take him there. Rich's mother took him to the emergency room, but after waiting a couple hours, they left in frustration. Rich ultimately opted for butterfly bandages, and now both he and John boast thick scars, lifelong mementos from the show.

Of all the wrestlers, only Rich resorted to violence in the chaos following the show. The others called for order. It's not about hurting anyone, they say. People get hurt only when they screw up. It's about the craft of professional wrestling in its rawest form.

But they won't be practicing that craft before crowds in John's back yard, Lister promises. She says the February 24 debacle led her to ban shows on her property. EFW members say that won't stop them. Just moments after the police left John's house, Jason was already plotting the group's next move. "We won't be able to do it here," he said with resignation, "but we have a great place out in a field where we can have our next show."

It's scheduled for April 21.

JULIET MACUR

"Please Let Me Die"

FROM THE DALLAS MORNING NEWS

I

SHE HAD BEEN THERE for seven days, holed up in her dorm room, wrapped inside a cocoon of bedcovers.

The phone was off the hook. The shades were drawn. She could hardly move.

But she cried.

Casi Florida, one of the best high school distance runners Texas has ever seen, felt delirious and hopeless.

Her athletic ability. Her college scholarship. Her Olympic dream for Sydney in 2000. All that she had worked for, all that defined her, was disappearing.

Just as her body was disappearing.

Casi was five-foot-six and only 93 pounds, a stick figure.

She despised every inch of that bony body, every strand of Breck Girl blond hair that for weeks had been falling out in clumps. She hadn't taken a shower in days because she didn't want to see her reflection in the bathroom mirror.

Her limbs felt like chopsticks, her ribs like piano keys. Her skin was pale, a ghostly contrast to the black circles beneath her eyes.

On the inside, things were worse. The lightest touch of her skin sent sharp pains through her veins. When she brushed her hair, the pressure on her scalp caused her to lose control of her bowels.

Her body was saying goodbye to the world. And she wanted to go. She prayed for God to take her.

"Please let me die," she whispered into the blankets. "I can't live like this anymore."

It was September 1996, one year after Casi had left her hometown of Joshua, twenty miles south of Fort Worth, to attend Abilene Christian University on a track scholarship. She was a nineteen-year-old sophomore who could run far and fast.

In high school, she won four state championships in distance events. Her first year at ACU, she won the junior national cross country championship and the NCAA Division II indoor title in the 5,000-meter run. Two summers in a row, she competed against the world's best runners as part of the U.S. junior national track team.

Casi was a high-profile athlete at ACU, but during that week of despair, she thought nobody would notice she hadn't been around campus.

Maybe her Aunt Donna back in Joshua had tried to call but got a busy signal. She knew her mother wouldn't have called; she never did. She rarely saw her roommate. And her track friends and coaches surely would write off her absence as just another Casi thing.

That whole week, she hadn't been to class or track practice. She was too weak — and, in her mind, too fat — to go anywhere. She was mortified that days and days had passed since her last long run.

She also knew something was wrong with her body, very wrong. So she stayed put in her room, mostly in the shadows, curled up in her misery.

Without fanfare or goodbyes, Casi Florida vanished from ACU and the world of elite track, just as her body was vanishing inch by inch, pound by pound.

She didn't know she had anorexia nervosa, a deadly psychological disorder that causes people to starve themselves. Though she had become skeletal, she saw herself as fat and disgusting and lazy.

"I can't believe this is happening," she thought. "It's my nightmare."

Casi (pronounced *kay-cee*) showed up at ACU for "Welcome Week" with those turquoise blue eyes, that friendly smile, and a high-pitched laugh that made everyone want to laugh, too. People gravitated toward her.

At first, good times did, too.

Playing a giant game of Twister in the gym was so fun, with all those arms and legs and bodies intertwined. In her dorm room, she decorated with glee, tacking up pictures of Aunt Donna and high school coach Jack Wilson.

Her world was changing, and she could hardly contain her joy.

"Nice to finally meet you," Casi said as her track teammate and freshman roommate, D'Anne Bragg, arrived at their dorm room. "Isn't this going to be great?"

D'Anne, a discus thrower from Childress, couldn't help but notice Casi's stair-stepper machine sitting in the middle of the small space.

"Do you work out a lot?" D'Anne asked.

"Yeah, I usually run about 100 miles a week, then I do the stair-stepper and other stuff," said Casi, then a lithe, muscled 108 pounds. "Do you work out a lot?"

D'Anne just laughed.

"Well, not as much as you do," she said. "I can guarantee that."

Later, D'Anne realized that Casi worked out almost incessantly. In the morning. During the day. In the afternoons during practice. At night. Between classes. Before dawn.

Still, they became fast friends, both small-town girls who came to Abilene with big dreams. They smiled a lot. Talked a lot. Laughed a lot. And dreamed a lot.

Mostly, Casi dreamed about escaping her hometown.

She considered Joshua boring and dreary. No movie theater. No bowling alley. No roller-skating rink. No fun. Nearly 4,000 people with nothing to do but get into everyone else's business.

Casi had seen her mother, unmarried and only fifteen when Casi was born, stagnate inside the city limits, struggling to care for her crew of five children and stepchildren. Casi's father skipped to Seattle shortly after her birth and never kept in touch. Her stepfather, Bill Shipley, came into the picture when Casi was three.

Growing up, Casi lived in a chalky white trailer home with her mother, stepfather, and three brothers. A fourth would come later. It was a packed house and a tense house.

Mr. Shipley had a bad temper and a thunderous yell, and for as long as she can remember, Casi considered him an angry, abusive, threatening man. (Mr. Shipley did not respond to repeated interview requests for this story.)

So Casi always looked for reasons to get out of her house. And when she was eight, she stumbled upon her ticket out of town.

She discovered running.

One afternoon, she stood in her yard and spied a summer track camp for kids across the street at Joshua High School. She crossed over and tugged on the coach's shirt.

"Can I be a long jumper?" Casi asked.

"Sure you can," said Jack Wilson, Joshua High's track and cross country coach. He was in his mid-forties, wore glasses, and dressed neatly. To Casi, he looked gentle and patient, like the kind of father she had yearned for.

After a few enthusiastic leaps into the long-jump pit, Casi approached Mr. Wilson again. "When can I come back to practice?" she asked.

"Whenever you want," he replied. "We're here every day."

So was Casi.

Year after year, she looked forward to those summer practices when she would long-jump and tag along with the big kids as they circled the track. It was a much better option than staying home.

Her stepfather was always upset, threatening to harm his wife or Casi when things didn't go right. And to him, they never went right.

Casi and her mother believed Mr. Shipley blamed Casi for everything. Dirty dishes? It was Casi's fault for not cleaning them. He didn't sleep well? Casi's fault. He was fighting with his wife? Casi's fault.

To get away from that stress, Casi moved in with Aunt Donna when she was fourteen. But her family problems didn't go away, so sports became her sanctuary.

In high school, she played volleyball and basketball before running track in the spring. She first ran sprints and hurdles, though Mr. Wilson considered her more of a long-distance runner. He even signed her up for cross country, but she never came to practice.

"Forget cross country," Casi thought. "Two miles! That's so far! Too much pain!"

Midway through her sophomore track season, Casi pulled a hamstring while hurdling. At Mr. Wilson's suggestion, she ran longer distances as part of her recuperation. The first time she ran the two-mile race, she broke the school record.

Mr. Wilson was right. She was a natural long-distance runner.

Her junior season, she won the Class 4A state championship in the mile and was second in the two-mile.

She liked the success, especially because it made Mr. Wilson smile. How she wanted to run fast for him. How she wanted him to love her like a daughter. So she vowed to run faster and, to her, that meant getting lighter.

During the summer before her senior year, Casi ran full-throttle. She was on the main roads of Joshua all the time, like clockwork. Everyone noticed.

"Oh, it's lunchtime. There's Casi running down the street."

"Yep, time for supper. There's that Casi again."

When she ran, she was in a world of her own. She was not her stepfather's scapegoat, not her mother's burden.

Running, she was at peace — and it gave her a reason to live. She would say she never felt her feet hit the pavement.

She never felt herself gasp for air. She just pushed and pushed, then pushed some more.

Her mind was clear. She was in control.

In a high school parent newsletter, a cover feature on Casi read: "To release tension and to lose weight, Casi began to participate in athletics. To prove to her family that she could 'amount to something in life,' she began to compete."

And when she won, she felt a rush of pride. She was important! Talented! Not the worst person on earth!

Her senior year, Casi felt that way often. She ran the mile in 4 minutes, 55 seconds, the fastest time in the state.

She also won the "triple crown" — the state cross country meet and one- and two-mile events. Her Class 4A state record of 10:41.60 in the two-mile still stands.

But within an instant of each victory and each state record, she felt worthless again — because her complicated, miserable home life still ate away at her.

She tried to hide her problems, but Mr. Wilson could see what she was going through. When he coached football just across the street from Casi's house, he saw how Mr. Shipley would yell and yell at his kids.

He heard the tirades. He saw how Casi was suffering and considered taking her into his house because he thought she deserved better.

In fact, when things got particularly bad, Casi did stay at Mr. Wilson's home.

"You can stay with us whenever you need to," Mr. Wilson had told her. "You're safe with us."

Casi's future looked safe, too. It seemed so promising.

College coaches across the nation knew her name, her best times, her grade-point average (3.6) and SAT score (750). More than forty recruiting letters streamed in, enough to fill three shoeboxes.

Arkansas. Rice. Vanderbilt. Baylor. Some of the nation's best NCAA Division I track programs wanted her. But in those moments of what was supposed to be Casi Florida's greatest glory, her life began to tumble.

By then, the obsession about her weight became her defining characteristic. She went from 127 pounds in the eighth grade to 108 by her senior year. That's what everyone knew about her: "Casi's always on a diet. . . . She looks like a cancer patient."

She would spend hours shopping in the supermarket, picking up jars and cans, analyzing the calorie and fat contents.

Everything was too fattening. She would leave with only a bag of grapes.

Mr. Wilson knew about her obsession. Often, his wife even packed Casi a lunch, and he would make her eat a bite of meat during lunch, or else practice was off.

College coaches found out about her eating habits, too. During her recruiting trip to Arkansas, coach Lance Harter saw signs of anorexia.

For dinner, Casi had ordered only a plain baked potato and a salad with no dressing from a large menu.

"Isn't there something you like?" Mr. Harter asked. "Is something wrong? Do you feel sick?"

"No, no, no," Casi replied. "This is just what I normally eat."

Mr. Harter asked his team members to see what else Casi ate during the trip. "Nothing," they said. Afterward, Mr. Harter talked to the coach at Rice, another school that Casi had visited. She hadn't eaten much on that trip, either. Word of her eating disorder was spreading, from coach to coach. Soon, many schools that had been interested in her stopped calling her.

Casi was hurt by the rumors but undeterred. She set her sights on Vanderbilt University, in Nashville, Tennessee. It was far from Texas and it was the home of country music; what more could she ask for? But Vanderbilt denied her admission at the last minute, saying her test scores weren't high enough. She was devastated.

By that time, most other track programs had given out their scholarships. So Mr. Wilson contacted ACU, which he had attended for a semester. The coaches there snapped her up.

Despite her eating disorder, Casi had received a college scholarship after all. And in her dorm room that week in September, she realized she was blowing that opportunity. In fact, her whole world was slipping away.

In the darkness of her bed, she remembered her stepfather's mean words, which through the years had shriveled her soul: "You're going to be a nobody. You're no good."

Now she knew: he was right.

A few times that week, out of guilt, Casi had dragged herself out of bed to run down the hallway to exercise. She could barely walk. She looked pitiful, and she noticed people's stares.

"They all think I'm crazy," Casi thought. "They always did."

Back in her room, she covered her head with a blanket. She tried to think good thoughts but just couldn't.

Instead, she reached beneath her mattress and pulled out her secret stash of laxatives.

Though she had eaten only grapes for weeks, she swallowed yet another pill even as she thought, "I threw all of it away. I ruined my life." Her stomach grumbled.

Then Casi slept for twenty-four hours straight.

She woke trembling with fear. What was happening? Was she dying? She placed her phone back on the hook and waited for her aunt to call. The phone rang several hours later.

"Aunt Donna?" Casi said, nearly hyperventilating while crying hysterically. "I need help. I can't stop sleeping."

"Don't worry, honey," said Donna, unaware of how Casi had spent the last several days. "You're probably just tired. You'll feel better in a couple days. If you don't, I'll come and see you."

Her aunt's voice had soothed her, but Casi was still frightened. She tried to give herself pep talks. That didn't work. Then she knew what she had to do to feel better, the same thing that she had done since she was eight.

Run.

She needed to run, but not just down the hall. She needed a real run. The four-mile loop around campus, the one that she had run time after time after time, was calling her.

"I need to work out," she thought as she looked at her body and saw nothing but flab. "I need to snap out of this."

So Casi groaned, wiped her tears, and rose slowly from her bed. Dizzy, aching, exhausted, she slipped out of her robe and into her usual baggy sweatpants and sweatshirt.

She laced her track team sneakers and carefully pinned up what was left of her hair.

A week earlier, sick of her shoulder-length hair falling out in chunks, she had taken dull scissors and sawed it off. But she had left the hair long in the front so it would seem — to her, at least — that nothing had changed.

But plenty had changed. She could feel it.

Her chest felt tight. It hurt when she breathed. Her joints ached. She felt faint. But she heard those words echoing inside her head.

Run. Run. Run.

So she opened the door, said a prayer and was gone.

Fifteen minutes later, alone on a city street, she collapsed.

In a voice only she could hear, she said, "I'm having a heart attack."

II

Casi Florida hardly had the strength to open her dorm room door, much less run four miles that September day five years ago.

But she ran.

She ran down Abilene's main drag, past Rick & Carolyn's Burgers and Fries, past J&J's Bait and Tackle.

She had run the same route many times, never stopping, because she had long before promised herself she would never break off a run before completing it. She wouldn't slow down to catch her breath, let alone pause to stretch a tightening muscle.

To stop would be to give in to weakness.

No way would she do that.

Until now.

Less than a mile from her dorm at Abilene Christian University, she felt a sharp pain in her chest. She gasped for breath. She doubled over.

Then Casi Florida, the national champion long-distance runner, collapsed.

"Oh, my gosh. This is it," she said as fear shot through her body. "I'm having a heart attack."

She was certain she would die right there on the street, alone. When she didn't, and she thanked God she didn't, she gathered enough strength to rise and walk back toward campus. There, as if it were sweet heaven itself, Gray Stadium beckoned her to the track where she had always felt safe.

She spotted Jon Murray, her cross country and distance coach, who had often seen signals of her distress and tried to help. "My chest . . . my heart," she said to him. "Please help me."

She had come to ACU from Joshua High School weighing 108 pounds with 9.3 percent body fat — thin, but typical for an elite runner. (The average woman has about 20 percent to 28 percent body fat.) Not once, her coaches say, did they think Casi had anorexia, an eating disorder that causes people to see themselves as fat though they may be wafer-thin.

So Mr. Murray and head coach Wes Kittley didn't worry when Casi began to lose weight — because her running times kept improving.

Then, the summer before her sophomore year, she ran poorly and looked pale and gaunt during the Junior World Championships in Australia. By then, her eating habits and irrational exercise regimens were well known. She ran from class to class, always in a sweat suit, always carrying a plastic bag of grapes. On campus, she was known as "grape girl."

It all convinced Mr. Murray that Casi needed help.

He asked her to undergo eating-disorder counseling that fall, but he was too late. She wound up in bed, in the dark, where she made the dangerous decision to go on a run.

That afternoon, she stood before him at sunset, her eyes red and swollen, her manner frantic as she pleaded for help.

This time he spoke directly. "We're going to send you away so you can get help," Mr. Murray said. It would be a week-long program at Shades of Hope Treatment Center in nearby Buffalo Gap. "You're going to die if you don't do this."

In the past, Casi had denied having an eating disorder. She

thought her strict diet and constant exercise were typical for elite runners.

In her mind, anorexia was for other girls, ones they made movies about. She would even watch made-for-TV movies about people such as singer Karen Carpenter and think, "Those poor, poor girls. I feel so sorry for them."

Slowly and painfully, she learned that she was just like them.

Casi went for a physical before checking into the treatment center. When a nurse hooked her up to a heart monitor, an IV, then took blood samples, Casi lost it.

"I'm fat! Look at me," Casi yelled, grabbing her thighs. "Don't try to feed me!"

The test results were shocking.

"You're on the verge of a heart attack," the doctor said. "Your heart, your liver, your kidneys — they're about to give out. Basically, your body is eating itself."

Even then, Casi didn't believe it. She thought, "They're just jealous. They're just trying to get me to do what they want me to do."

Shades of Hope is a cluster of quaint yellow buildings tucked away from the main road. Every room is painted pink. In that pastel world in which everyone seemed to smile constantly, Casi responded with a perpetual frown.

During check-in, the questions came rapid-fire. "What do you eat? . . . Do you throw up? . . . Do you get your 'monthly visitor'?"

She answered softly, embarrassed that her coach would hear. She ate grapes, her "natural laxatives." She didn't throw up because she didn't eat. And her menstrual period? Although she was nineteen, she had never had it.

After moving in, Casi was counseled individually and in groups. She ate six times a day, disgusted by the toast, eggs, peanut butter, rice cakes, and Ensure.

She was ordered to sit still. No runs. No walks. No climbing stairs. She was not even allowed to cross her legs.

There wasn't much to do.

No newspapers. No telephone calls. No TV. Patients couldn't use the bathroom in private, lest they vomit.

"Not too long ago, I was dreaming about going to the Olympics," she thought. "Now I can't even do a sit-up without getting in trouble. This is so stupid. I don't belong here."

After a week, she was told she had to stay until she got better.

Casi soon returned to tricks of making food disappear without eating it, tricks she had perfected in high school. She slipped food from her plate into her shirt cuffs. She stuck rice cakes with peanut butter to the roof of her mouth. Later, she tossed the food into the garbage.

Patients at Shades of Hope weren't fooled. They played those games too. So during weekly "Family Day" sessions, they tattled: "I saw Casi putting food into her sleeves. . . . I saw Casi running up and down the stairs of the dorm. She was also doing leg lifts."

Casi hated those nights, because Mr. Murray and her Aunt Donna heard the accusations and knew she wasn't ready to go home. She also felt like a burden because they visited her so often.

"He's only here because I'm his runner," she thought. "Aunt Donna feels like she has to take care of me because I'm family."

For forty-two days, Casi felt unloved, and she denied all. Even as she gained healthy weight — a pound one week, two the next — she told herself, "I need to lose weight to get back to running."

Finally, she said, she heard the voice of God.

Maybe her therapy finally had sunk in. Maybe she had become sick of killing herself. But the voice came in a dream: "You have a problem. You need help."

Rather than run from the pain again, rather than hide from it, Casi finally turned to face it. She started to recognize the sources of the hurt inside her: the anorexia, her emotionally torn mother, her angry stepfather, her low self-esteem.

She believed her eating disorder had started because her home life was so chaotic. She dieted and ran because she could control those things.

She even figured out when her illness started. The summer before high school, as she bounced on a trampoline at home and saw her reflection in a mirror, she noticed "fat" jiggling. She was five-six and 127 pounds.

The month before school began, she lost twenty-two pounds by limiting each meal to one piece of fruit. Everyone raved about her new looks, even boys who had long ignored her.

Little did they know that as she lost weight, she also lost herself.

She heard her stepfather's words: "fat . . . slut . . . bastard . . . lazy." She saw her mother hurt, humiliated, and made ineffectual at Bill Shipley's hands. She knew about Mr. Shipley's past convictions for DWI and public intoxication, and that scared her.

Desperate for solace, Casi once tried to contact her birth father; his wife answered, saying he wanted no part of her.

Through therapy, Casi accepted three critical pieces of information: 1. She was not at fault. 2. She didn't have to be perfect — or seem perfect — at all times. 3. She had the strength to face her demons.

Face them she did, during a "Family Day" group therapy session when her aunt and mother came for a role-playing exercise. Casi screamed at her mother: "I wish you had adopted me out a long time ago. Why didn't you stop Bill from hurting me? Why didn't you protect me?"

Debby Florida, Casi's mother, had secured a restraining order against Mr. Shipley in 1993, claiming there was "clear and present danger" for her and her children. The order said he had grabbed her arms so hard he left marks, then threatened to knock her head through the wall. It also said that he repeatedly had threatened to punch her.

Nearly two years later, they were divorced.

Hearing her daughter's pain, Debby Florida stood in front of the patients and their families. And wept.

She told Casi, sobbing, "I didn't know what to do. That man abused me for fifteen years. He controlled me. I'm sorry. I'm so, so sorry."

After three months of treatment, Casi Florida left Shades of Hope, three days before Christmas 1996.

She had gained seventeen pounds and was back at 110, her weight just before starting college. Her $15,000 bill at Shades of Hope was paid by ACU and private donations.

Back at school, Casi opened up about her eating disorder, even speaking to the Fellowship of Christian Athletes.

She didn't run her sophomore spring but was allowed to return to cross country the next fall — on several conditions.

Mr. Murray, her distance coach, wrote an actual contract for her: Go to counseling. No extra workouts. Eat three meals a day.

But at the national cross country meet, where she had placed second as a freshman, she finished sixty-ninth.

So Casi relapsed.

She would eat because she knew people were watching; then she would use a toothbrush to gag herself into throwing up, a technique she learned from another patient at Shades of Hope. One day she even broke a blood vessel in her right eye because of the vomiting.

She believed, again, that everyone considered her fat. In her head, she could hear them saying, "She was so tiny and so good. Now look at her. She must be pigging out."

Mr. Murray knew Casi had broken their agreement. At a loss as to how to save her from herself, he decided that he had only one choice.

In April of her junior year, he told her that she was no longer welcome on the team.

"I'm sorry, Casi," he said. "You're banned from the track, banned from the weight room. You're not even welcome to come down and watch. You know what it takes to get better, but you're just not willing to do it. Until you change, you're kicked off the team."

By summer's end, she had packed up and left Abilene. And descended into darkness once more.

Casi had no money, no college degree, no scholarship, no place to go. She drove to Joshua and got a job at the local gas station. When not crashing with friends, she lived in the back of her mother's pickup truck in the station's parking lot. At night, she cried until her face puffed up like a balloon.

"I'm a nobody, just like my stepfather always said," she thought. "He always said I'd work at a gas station."

Casi soon got a job at a weight-loss center, where, ironically, she was a nutrition counselor. The job fell through after two months, and she followed it with two jobs in Fort Worth.

In the meantime, University of Texas at Arlington track coach John Sauerhage had offered her a scholarship. She signed and planned to attend that fall, but she fell out of shape and never showed up at UTA. She was bulimic then, too, meaning she ate but threw up meals.

Casi eventually moved into Fort Worth's downtown YWCA. The

naive, sheltered small-town girl lived alongside junkies, alcoholics, and runaways, paying minimal rent for a marginal room. She was terrified and embarrassed, so she purposely lost touch with friends and family.

Each night, Casi Florida sat quietly in her room while voices, stomping feet, and slamming doors boomed in the hallway. She prayed for God to give her control over her life. She prayed that somebody somewhere would truly love her someday, not just because she was a good runner, not because it was a family obligation.

Then one day she walked out of a restaurant after lunch. Across the street, sparkling in the sun, she saw an answer.

She saw the U.S. Army recruiting station.

III

She wanted out.

Out of her life, her body, and her situation.

Enough of being a failed athlete, college dropout, and imperfect woman.

So in Fort Worth that day, Casi Florida didn't pay attention to the posters or pitches in the U.S. Army recruiting station: See the world. Serve your country. Learn new skills.

To her, the words and pictures meant nothing. She just wanted to escape her life and become somebody else.

Joining the Army would make it happen.

No one there needed to know she had been one of the nation's best distance runners. No one needed to know she had nearly starved herself to death, or that anorexia and bulimia had ravaged her body and soul.

So, four days before Christmas 1998, two years after leaving an eating disorder treatment center and five months after dropping out of Abilene Christian University, Casi joined the Army for a four-year stint — enough time to reinvent herself.

She quickly learned it would be a painful process.

Her first stop was Fort Leonard Wood in south central Missouri. A voice over the intercom broke the night's silence at 4:30 A.M.: "Get up!"

Morning formation at 5:00 A.M. Yelling. Push-ups. Twenty-mile marches under thirty-pound packs. Gas chamber exercises that felt like swallowing shards of glass.

All that, just in basic training.

Early on, Casi regretted enlisting. "Why did I leave school? What I would give to be back at ACU right now." But she forged ahead and eventually even boasted about her experiences.

She told her Aunt Donna over the phone about finishing second on the obstacle course and becoming an M-16 "sharpshooter." To ACU track coach Jon Murray, she wrote, "I was on a bayonet assault course on my twenty-first birthday!"

Casi pretended to love the challenge but often questioned her decision. Was joining a mistake?

She wasn't sure. But she didn't go AWOL, and life drastically improved three months later.

It was the day that she met a soldier named Rodney Chatman and wondered, "Was this the reason God let me sign up for this?"

The classroom was silent before the officer began the interrogation.

"Who led drills this morning?" he bellowed to the sixty soldiers in front of him.

Casi Florida leapt to her feet. "Sergeant Argumito!" she shouted with conviction.

"Wrong!" the officer replied. "Sit back down!"

Casi's face turned bright red as she slid into her seat. "I never should've done that," she thought.

Across the room, Rodney Chatman thought otherwise. One look at Casi, and he was smitten.

Rodney grew up in St. Petersburg, Florida, where he had attended Eckerd College on a basketball scholarship. He joined the Army while working toward his master's degree in urban planning at the University of Florida. He thought something was missing from his life and needed a place to "find himself."

Little did he know, he would travel the path of rediscovery holding someone's hand.

Soon after they met, Rodney and Casi were virtually inseparable. They coyly waited for each other in the chow line. They shined boots together. They became soul mates and never cared that she was white and he was black.

Rodney saw an honesty and kindness in Casi that he hadn't seen in anyone else. Casi thought Rodney understood her and never judged her. He was the person she had been waiting for.

He didn't know she once was a great runner. He wasn't bound to her by family ties. He simply liked her.

She couldn't believe it.

"I scare men away," she told him one night. "I used to be real skinny. I had an eating disorder. I have scars on my liver. My heart might not be strong. My body may take a toll later in life. And my family . . ."

"Everybody has problems," Rodney said.

Then he wiped away her tears.

Five months later, on September 9, 1999, Casi and Rodney were married in a civil ceremony in Killeen, Texas, where Rodney was stationed at Fort Hood. They didn't invite anyone.

In fact, Casi kept the wedding a secret for several weeks. She didn't know how her family, friends, and past coaches like Joshua High School's Jack Wilson would react to her interracial marriage.

The people closest to her didn't mind.

"Rodney gives her love and affection that she's never had before," her Aunt Donna said. "He helps her see things in a different perspective, in a way I couldn't do or Coach Wilson couldn't do, or her mom couldn't do."

"They both act like each other hung the moon," said Debby Florida, Casi's mother. "She's happy. He's happy. That's what matters."

Though Rodney was all Casi had hoped and prayed for, he couldn't magically cure her eating disorder. The Army couldn't, either.

Sometimes, she vomited more than five times a day during those first seven months of marriage when she and Rodney lived apart. Stationed in North Carolina then, Casi didn't tell Rodney her secret until she transferred to Fort Hood.

Stomach acid from her vomit had worn away the enamel of her teeth. She needed several cavities filled.

"You know when I go into the bathroom, lock the door, and turn on the water?" she screamed one afternoon. "I'm not always taking a bath! I'm throwing up! You can divorce me because I'm crazy. I'm not good enough for you."

He hugged her.

The next day, he left a note on the front door that said, "I love you more than you'll ever know."

"Who is that person?"

In the couple's living room, Casi turns the pages of her scrapbook and shakes her head. It's a weekend in June. More than three years have passed since she last ran competitively.

"Who is that person?" she says. "Those shorts won't even fit over one of my legs now. What on earth was going through my mind?"

Casi is twenty-four and 135 pounds, thin and muscular, no longer curveless. Just last year, she became confident enough to wear shorts, sleeveless shirts, and even a bikini.

Her cheeks are rosy. Her eyes sparkle.

She is happy.

Casi and Rodney, the Chatmans, will get discharged from the Army on November 4, 2002. Until then and perhaps for years after, Casi will thank God for giving her the strength to control her eating disorders.

But, she admits, her illness still lurks.

Sometimes, she worries about Army weigh-ins and pressures at work in the finance office. Sometimes, she panics because she has the body of a woman, not a pre-pubescent girl. Sometimes, she regrets that she's no longer a world-class runner.

And sometimes, but not often, she exercises too much or throws up her food.

"The disease is so bad, you'll battle it the rest of your life," says Casi, who hasn't gone to therapy since leaving ACU. "You just can't let it get the best of you every day. I have to be prepared because that monster will always come back."

Rodney is there to help fight it. He'll see the beginnings of a relapse, like her staring into a mirror and worrying, and he'll soothe her.

"I'll just tell her how beautiful and smart she is," says Rodney, twenty-seven. "It's just hard for her to believe it."

They recognize that full recovery from her eating disorders is a long process — because food stares her in the face every day. Her compulsive exercising is difficult to control, too. In the Army, working out is a necessity. Casi does it to the hilt.

She rises at 4:00 A.M. to work out, then frequently returns to the gym at lunch. Sometimes she'll play basketball with Rodney after work, or even go running again.

She is one of the most physically fit people at Fort Hood, according to a physical test that includes a two-mile run, sit-ups, and push-ups. Her score, adjusted according to age and sex, is one of the best among 42,000 soldiers.

Her commanders rave about her abilities, but only a few people on base know she had Olympic aspirations. She, on the other hand, thinks about it often.

"I still think I can run professionally," Casi says. "But I have to be healthy for my husband. Then again, I'll dream about the Olympics until I'm eighty. By that time, I won't be able to run anymore, and my dream will be over."

By that time, she also should be out of Texas. She and Rodney plan to move to Florida, where he'll finish his master's degree and she her bachelor's. She wants to become a kindergarten teacher.

Someday, too, she wants a house — without mirrors or bathroom scales. And someday, she wants to have children. If she can.

Doctors told her that complications from her eating disorders may have left her infertile. Her anorexia and bulimia also may have irreversibly damaged her heart, kidney, and liver. And after not having her menstrual period (or estrogen) until she was nearly twenty, she may have osteoporosis, or brittle bones, due to lack of calcium.

For now, though, Casi doesn't want to think about any of that. She doesn't want to know the long-term effects of her illnesses, avoiding doctors as much as she can. For now, she and Rodney just want to enjoy life.

They like to take vacations and went to Key West last winter. At home, Rodney likes to watch the History Channel. Casi relaxes by listening to Reba McEntire while searching the Internet for phone numbers of past friends and coaches.

She's trying to contact people who haven't heard from her since she left ACU and disappeared without a trace.

Casi Florida — the new, the old, the reinvented and redefined — is trying to tell everyone that she's back.

"My other life was so confusing and crazy," she says, removing the lid from a large plastic trunk in her living room. "It's all a blur now because I'm such a different person."

She carefully pulls out objects covered in tissue and newspapers. She unwraps them, revealing one trophy after another, then plaques, ribbons, and medals. They're vestiges from another life, awards from races ranging from the Fort Worth Turkey Trot 10K to the NCAA championship.

When the trunk is empty, her prizes cover the living room and dining room floors.

"In our future house, we're going to get shelves to show off these trophies," Rodney says, looking at the sprawling pile of memories.

"I know. I accomplished a lot," Casi says with a laugh. "Whoa! We're going to need a separate room for these things!"

WILLIAM NACK

A Name on the Wall

FROM SPORTS ILLUSTRATED

> The feeling had gone out of everything. It was like we were zombies. You didn't care anymore. July was terrible. The [North Vietnamese] whacked Ripcord, that hill we were on, with mortars and rocket fire. Day after day, night after night. I was getting shell-shocked. I didn't care if I got out. At night you could hear the [enemy] yelling from the jungles all around, "GI die tonight! GI die tonight!" This was our deathbed. We thought we were going to be overrun.
>
> — Spc. 4th Class Daniel Thompson, wireman at Firebase Ripcord, Vietnam, July 1970

THERE WERE ALWAYS LULLS between the salvos of incoming mortars, moments of perishable relief. The last salvo had just ended, and the dust was still settling over Firebase Ripcord. In one command bunker, down where the reek of combat hung like whorehouse curtains, Lt. Bob Kalsu and Pfc. Nick Fotias sat basting in the jungle heat. In that last salvo the North Vietnamese Army (NVA), as usual, had thrown in a round of tear gas, and the stinging gas and the smoke of burning cordite had curled into the bunkers, making them all but unbearable to breathe in. It was so sweltering inside that many soldiers suffered the gas rather than gasp in their hot, stinking rubber masks. So, seeking relief, Kalsu and Fotias swam for the light, heading out the door of the bunker, the threat of mortars be damned. "Call us foolish or brave, we'd come out to get a breath of fresh air," Fotias recalls.

It was Tuesday afternoon, July 21, 1970, a day Kalsu had been eagerly awaiting. Back home in Oklahoma City, his wife, Jan, was due to have their second child that very day. (They already had a twenty-month-old daughter, Jill Anne.) The Oklahoma City gentry viewed the Kalsus as perfectly matched links on the cuff of the town. Jan was the pretty brunette with the quick laugh, the daughter of a successful surgeon. Bob was the handsome, gregarious athletic hero with the piano-keys grin, the grandson of Czech immigrants for whom America had been the promised land and Bob the promise fulfilled. As a college senior, in the fall of 1967, the six-foot-three, 220-pound Kalsu had been an All-America tackle for Oklahoma, a team of overachievers that went 10–1, beating Tennessee in the Orange Bowl. The next season, after bulking up to 250 pounds, Kalsu had worked his way into the starting offensive line of the Buffalo Bills, and at season's end he had been named the Bills' rookie of the year.

While in Vietnam, Kalsu rarely talked about his gridiron adventures. Word had gotten around the firebase that he had played for the Bills, but he would shrug off any mention of it. "Yeah, I play football," he would say. What he talked about — incessantly — was his young family back home. Jan knew her husband was somewhere "on a mountaintop" in Vietnam, but she had no idea what he had been through. In his letters he let on very little. On July 19, the day after a U.S. Army Chinook helicopter, crippled by antiaircraft fire, crashed on top of the ammunition dump for Ripcord's battery of 105-mm howitzers, setting off a series of explosions that literally sheared off one tier of the hill, the bunkered-down lieutenant wrote his wife. He began by using his pet name for her.

> Dearest Janny Belle —
>
> How're things with my beautiful, sexy, lovable wife. I love & miss you so very much and can't wait till I'm back home in your arms and we're back in our own apartment living a normal life. The time can't pass fast enough for me until I'm back home with all my loved ones and especially you Jan and Jilly and Baby K. I love and need you so very much.
>
> The wind has quit blowing so hard up here. It calmed down so much it's hard to believe it. Enemy activity remains active in our area. Hopefully it will cease in the near future.
>
> I'm just fine as can be. Feeling real good just waiting to hear the word again that I'm a papa. It shouldn't be much longer until I get word of our arrival. . . .
>
> I love you, xxx-ooo.
>
> Bob

Kalsu was, in fact, involved in the gnarliest battle going on at the time in Vietnam: an increasingly desperate drama being played out on the top of a steep, balding shank of rock and dirt that rose 3,041 feet above sea level and 656 above the jungle floor. From the crest of this two-tiered oblong promontory, on a space no bigger than two football fields, two artillery batteries — the doomed 105s and the six 155-mm howitzers of Battery A, Kalsu's battery — had been giving fire support to infantrymen of the 101st Airborne Division, two battalions of which were scouring the jungles for North Vietnamese while pounding the ganglia of paths and supply routes that branched from the Ho Chi Minh Trail in Laos, twelve miles to the west, spiderwebbing south and east around Ripcord through Thuathien Province and toward the coastal lowlands around Hue.

Atop that rock, Kalsu was caught in a maelstrom that grew stronger as July slouched toward August. On July 17, four days before his baby was due, Kalsu was made the acting commander of Battery A after the captain in charge was choppered out to have a piece of shrapnel removed from a bone in his neck. Kalsu and his men continued their firing missions as the NVA attacks intensified. With a range of thirteen miles, Battery A's 155s were putting heavy metal on enemy supply lines as far off as the A Shau Valley, a key NVA logistical base ten miles to the southwest, helping create such havoc that the enemy grew determined to drive the three hundred or so Americans off Ripcord. As many as five thousand NVA soldiers, ten to twelve battalions, had massed in the jungles surrounding Ripcord, and by July 21 they were lobbing more than six hundred rounds a day on the firebase, sending the deadliest salvos whenever U.S. helicopters whirled in with ammo and soldiers raced for the helipad to carry the shells on their shoulders up the hill.

Kalsu humped those ninety-seven-pound explosive rounds along with his men, an officer exposing himself to fire when he could have stayed in the bunker. "A fearless guy, smart, brave, and respected by his troops," recalls retired colonel Philip Michaud, who at the time was a captain commanding the ill-fated battery of 105s. "Rounds were coming in, and he was out there. I told him a few times, 'It's good to run around and show what leadership is about, but when rounds are blowing up in your area, you ought to hunker down behind a gun wheel. Or a bunker.' The guy thought he was invincible."

The grunts loved him for it, and they would have followed him anywhere. David Johnson always did. Kalsu and Johnson, by most superficial measures, could not have been more different. Kalsu was white and the only child of middle-class parents — city-bred, college-educated, married, a father, devoutly Catholic. Johnson was black and the seventh of eleven children raised on a poor farm outside of Humnoke, Arkansas. He was single and childless, a supplicant at the Church of God and Christ. What the two men shared was a gentleness and childlike humanity that reached far beyond race. So James Robert Kalsu, twenty-five, and Spc. 4th Class David Earl Johnson, twenty-four, became inseparable. "They just clicked," recalls former sergeant Alfred Martin. "You saw one, you saw the other."

That lull in incoming fire on July 21 nearly brought the two friends together again. Johnson was standing outside Kalsu's bunker on the pock-marked hill. Cpl. Mike Renner, a gunner, was standing by his 155 with a sergeant who was dressing him down because the jack on the gun had broken, leaving the crew unable to raise it to a different azimuth. At that moment Kalsu and Fotias rose out of the bunker. They stood at the door for a moment, Fotias with his back to it, and Kalsu started reading to him from a piece of paper in his hand. "[It was] a letter he had received from his wife," Fotias says. "I remember the joy on his face as he read the letter to me. He said, 'My wife's having our baby today.'"

Some rounds you heard falling, some you didn't. Fotias did not hear this one. Jim Harris, the battalion surgeon, was across the firebase when he heard the splitting crack and turned his head toward it. The 82-mm mortar landed five feet from the bunker door. "I can still feel the heat of the blast coming past me and the concussion knocking me over," says Renner. "It flipped me backward, my helmet flew off, and the back of my head hit the ground."

Johnson fell sprawling on the ground. Fotias, at the mouth of the bunker, saw the sun go out. "I remember this tremendous noise," he says, "and darkness. And being blown off my feet and flying through the door of the bunker and landing at the bottom of the steps, six feet down, and this tremendous weight crushing me. I couldn't see. I couldn't hear. I had dirt in my eyes, and my eyes were tearing. I rubbed them, and then I could see again. I pushed off this weight that was on top of me, and I realized it was Bob."

Kalsu was really a boy trapped inside a large man's body — a player of pranks whose high-pitched cackle would fill a room. He laughed so heartily that he drooled, the spittle coursing from the corners of his mouth down around his dimpled chin and on down his chiseled neck. Once, on hearing the punch line of an off-color joke, he slammed a fist so hard on an adjoining barstool that the stool broke into pieces. He had the appetite of a Komodo dragon, but he loved kids even more than food. Some valve must have been missing in his psyche: his ego, unlike that of most jocks, was not inflatable. He always favored the underdog (he arranged the selection of one girl as high school homecoming queen because no one paid her much mind), and he turned down a high school sports award on grounds that he'd already received too many. "It'll mean more to somebody else," he told his mother, Leah.

Kalsu was born in Oklahoma City on April 13, 1945, and he came of age in the suburb of Del City at a time when coach Bud Wilkinson was leading Oklahoma through its gilded age. From 1953 into '57 the Sooners won forty-seven consecutive games, still a record for a Division I school, and finished three straight seasons ('54 to '56) undefeated. Twice during that run, in '55 and '56, they were national champions. Like every other eighteen-year-old gridiron star in the state, Kalsu aspired to play in Norman. Even as Wilkinson's program faltered in the early 1960s — the Sooners were 16–14–1 in the first three years of the decade — the coach's aura was so strong that there was only one place for a local kid to go. When Wilkinson recruited Kalsu out of Del City High in '63, Kalsu signed on.

He was not the first in his family to make the big time in Oklahoma college sports. Bob's uncle, Charles Kalsu, played basketball at Oklahoma State for Henry Iba, whose legend in college hoops was writ as large as Wilkinson's was in football. The six-foot-six Charles was a second-team All-America in 1939 and played pro ball with the old Philips 66 Oilers. Charles's brother Frank Kalsu, three inches shorter and two years younger, yearned to follow him to Oklahoma State. "Frank and Charles were extremely competitive," recalls their younger brother, Milt. "Frank went to Stillwater thinking he could play. He lasted half a semester and came home." Frank married Leah Aguillard, of French Canadian ancestry, became a sheet-metal worker at Tinker Air Force Base in Midwest City, Oklahoma, and settled in Del City.

Frank saw in his son, Bob, an open-field run at fulfilling the dreams that he had left behind in Stillwater. "That's what made him drive his son to be a college athlete," Milt says. "He'd wanted to play basketball for Iba." Frank put the teenage Bob on a rigorous conditioning program long before such regimens were common. Milt still remembers Bob chuffing through four-mile cross-country runs among the tumbleweed and jackrabbits while Frank trailed behind him in the family car.

Early on, the boy began to live for the playing of games, for competition, and he approached everything as if it were a last stand. "He played every kind of ball imaginable," says Leah. "He was even on a bowling team. He loved to play cards — canasta, hearts. We'd play Chinese checkers head-to-head. We played jacks when he was seven or eight. He played jacks until he was in high school. He'd never quit when he lost. He'd say, 'Mom, let's play another.'"

Bob liked football well enough — the butting of heads, the grinding contact, the fierceness of play in the trenches — but the game he loved most was golf. He was a four or five handicap. On Sundays, Bob would go to 7:00 A.M. Mass at St. Paul's Church so he and Uncle Milt could make an 8:30 tee time. They sometimes got in fifty-four holes in a day, and they spent hours behind Bob's house hitting balls, always competing. "We'd see who could get [the ball] closest to a telephone pole," Milt recalls.

Kalsu never played a down for Wilkinson, who resigned after his freshman season. However, over the next four years, including a redshirt season in 1964, Kalsu matured into one of the best offensive linemen ever to play for the Sooners. He also developed his talent for leading men, which was as natural as the stomping, pounding gait that would earn for him the nickname Buffalo Bob. Steve Campbell, three years behind him at Del City High, remembers summers when Kalsu, preparing for the next Oklahoma season, would call evening practices for high school players and run them as if he were a boot-camp sergeant. He simply put out the word that he would be working out at the high school and that all Del City players should be there.

Kalsu would appear in a jersey cut off at the sleeves, in shorts and baggy socks and cleats, and begin sending the young men through agility and running drills, racing up and down the field with the players and finally dividing them up for a game of touch football. "We were ready and willing followers," Campbell says. "He had a very commanding air about him."

Fact is, in his comportment on and off the field, Kalsu rarely put a cleat down wrong. "He did everything the way you're supposed to," says former Sooners defensive end Joe Riley, who was recruited with Kalsu. "He didn't cut classes. He never gave anybody a minute's trouble. He became the player he was because he believed everything the coaches told him. He didn't complain. We'd all be complaining through two-a-days, and he'd just walk around with a little smirk on his face. He was a little too goody-goody for some of us, but we respected him. And once you got to know him, you liked him."

By his third year of eligibility, 1966, Kalsu was starting on a squad that was showing signs of a pulse. The year before, in Gomer Jones's second season as coach, the Sooners had gone 3–7, and Gomer was a goner. In '66, under new coach Jim Mackenzie, Oklahoma went 6–4. When Mackenzie died of a heart attack in the spring of '67, Chuck Fairbanks took over, and his rise to the practice-field tower presaged the sudden ascension of the team, which would have one of the wildest years in Sooners history.

Like their 2000 counterparts, the '67 Sooners had not been expected to win their conference, much less make a run at the national title. For guards Eddie Lancaster and Byron Bigby, the tone of the season was set on the first play of the first game, against Washington State in Norman on September 23, when they double-teamed a defensive lineman and rolled him seven yards down the field, springing tailback Steve Owens for a twelve-yard gain. Next thing Lancaster knew, Kalsu was standing over him and Bigby and yelling, "Good god, awright! Look at this! Look at what you did!"

Bigby turned to Lancaster and said, in some amazement, "You know, we can do this." The Sooners won 21–0. They kept on winning, too, and nearly pulled off the whole shebang, losing only to Texas, 9–7. Kalsu was smack in the middle of it all. Elected team captain, he took the job to be more than that of a figurehead. He took it to mean that he should lead, which he did in the best way, by example.

Steve Zabel, an Oklahoma tight end at the time, recalls the day Buck Nystrom, the offensive line coach, got peeved at the taxi-squad players who were going against his linemen in the "board drill," in which two players lined up at opposite ends of an eight-foot-long plank and ran into each other like mountain goats, the winner being the one left standing on the board. Disgusted by what he saw as a lack of intensity, the 215-pound Nystrom — "the meanest coach I was ever around," says Zabel — got on the board and turned his cap backward. Without pads or a helmet, he took on all his linemen, one by one. Finally Kalsu got on the board.

Kalsu, at 220 pounds, had become the biggest hammer on the Sooners' offensive line. He took off down the board. "He hit Buck so hard that he lifted him off the board and planted him on the ground with his helmet on Buck's chest," says Zabel. "Everybody was running around yelling, 'Kalsu killed him! Kalsu killed Buck!'"

That night Zabel and center Ken Mendenhall were walking into a Baskin-Robbins when Nystrom came out, holding an ice cream cone in one hand and his two-year-old son, Kyle, in the other. He was wearing the same T-shirt he'd worn at practice, and his arms were discolored. "Zabel! Mendenhall!" Nystrom blurted. "Wasn't that the greatest practice you ever saw?" He handed his cone to Zabel, the boy to Mendenhall, and raised the front of his shirt, revealing the black-and-blue imprint of a helmet. "Look at this!" he said gleefully. "Boy, ol' Bob Kalsu liked to kill me!"

On the field that year Kalsu was everywhere, urging the troops on, picking them up off piles. Every time Owens, the tailback, looked up from the ground, there was Kalsu. Owens would win the Heisman Trophy in 1969, but in '67 he was an unbridled galloper who often ran up the backs of Kalsu's legs. One day the exasperated captain took Owens aside. "Listen, Steve, I'm on your side," he said. "Find the hole!"

Owens was in ROTC, and he remembers Kalsu, a cadet colonel, marching his battalion around the parade grounds like so many toy soldiers. "He was all over us all the time," says Owens. "He took that job seriously, too."

Before Kansas State played Oklahoma, Wildcats coach Vince Gibson, who had been studying film of the Sooners, approached Fairbanks on the field. "Kalsu is the best blocking lineman I've ever seen," Gibson said. In fact, after the Sooners' coaches studied all their game film of 1967, Fairbanks said that "our average gain on all plays going over Kalsu, including short yardage and goal line plays, is 6.2 net yards rushing. . . . This is what we coaches grade as . . . near perfection."

Kalsu "wasn't better than other players because of his ability,"

Fairbanks recalls. "He was better because he was smarter and technically better. He was a little more mature in his evaluation of what was happening on the field. There were no problems coaching him. You didn't have to try to motivate him. He came to practice every day with a smile on his face."

At season's end Kalsu appeared to have it all. An appearance in the Orange Bowl. All-America honors. A solid chance at a pro football career. And his marriage, after the Orange Bowl, to Jan Darrow. She and Bob had had their first date on October 15, 1966, and she knew that very night she'd found her mate. "A really cute guy who made me laugh," she says. "I came home, threw myself on my sister Michelle's bed, and said, 'I just met the man I'm going to marry.'"

Jan was the third of nine kids — five girls and four boys — and by the summer of 1967 Kalsu had been embraced as the tenth sibling in the Darrows' seven-bedroom house on Country Club Drive. "I always wanted brothers and sisters, and now I got 'em," he told Ione Darrow, the mother of the brood. Kalsu may have been a fearsome lineman, but what the Darrows discovered was a large, lovable kid who liked to scare trick-or-treaters by jumping from behind trees and who failed grandly in his experiments as a pastry chef. Diane Darrow, four years older than Jan, walked into the kitchen one day and saw Bob with his huge hands in a mixing bowl, squashing the batter. She asked him what on earth he was doing. He said he was making an angel food cake for Ione's birthday. Diane wondered why he wasn't using a wooden spoon. "The box says mix by hand," he said.

Around the Darrows' dinner table, everyone would stop to watch the spectacle of Kalsu's eating. Whole salads disappeared at two or three stabs of a fork. Glasses of orange juice vanished in a single swallow. Kalsu could devour a drumstick with a few spins of the bone, stripping it clean. He also played games endlessly with his new siblings, cheerfully cheating at all of them.

Bob and Jan were married on January 27, 1968, and when they returned from their honeymoon in Galveston, Texas, during spring break, the Darrow family sang the news: "Buffalo Bob, won't you come out tonight?" He had been drafted in the eighth round by the Bills of the American Football League. The NFL's Dallas Cowboys and the AFL's Denver Broncos had also shown interest, but both had backed away, leery of Kalsu's military commitment. Having completed ROTC, he would be commissioned a second lieutenant after graduation in May. He was not immediately called to active duty, however. By the time he reported to the Bills that summer, Jan was six months pregnant.

Within a few weeks with the Bills, Kalsu had worked his way into the lineup, taking the place of the injured Joe O'Donnell at right guard and starting nine games that season. No one watched Kalsu more closely than Billy Shaw, Buffalo's left guard and a future Hall of Famer. Shaw was twenty-nine in '68, nearing the end of his career, and he saw Kalsu as a threat to his job.

"Bob had a lot of talent," says Shaw. "He had real good feet, and he was strong, good on sweeps. In those days we had only one backup, and he was Joe's and my backup. Our forte was foot speed, and Bob was right there with us. He really fit in with how we played, with a lot of running, a lot of sweeps, a lot of traps."

Shaw and O'Donnell were mirror images of each other — both six-foot-two and about 252 pounds — and when Kalsu joined them, the three looked like triplets. At the Bills' urging, the six-foot-three Kalsu had gained weight by lifting weights and devouring potatoes and chicken ("His neck got so big that even his ties didn't fit him anymore," says Jan), and he was listed at 250 pounds on the Bills' roster. "The thing I noticed is that he was so mature for a young player," says Shaw. "He wasn't your normal rookie. He wasn't in awe."

Bob Lustig, the Bills' general manager at the time, says Kalsu "had a good future in pro football." Lustig recalls something else: "He not only had the talent, but he also had the smarts. He didn't make the same mistake twice."

Kalsu also brought to Buffalo the same love of horseplay and mischief that had marked his days in Oklahoma. He and one of his rookie roommates, John Frantz, a center from Cal, filled a trash can with water and carried it into the head at training camp. They thought their other roommate, rookie tackle Mike McBath, was sitting on the toilet in one of the stalls. They lifted the can and dumped the water into the stall. They heard a thunderous bellow that sounded nothing like McBath. It was six-year veteran Jim Dunaway, Buffalo's six-foot-four, 281-pound defensive tackle, who rose from the dumper like Godzilla and screamed, "Whoever did that is dead!"

Kalsu and Frantz bolted in a panic and hid in the closet of their room until Hurricane Dunaway had blown over, and they laughed every time they saw the big tackle after that. "Bob was always stirring the pot," says Frantz. "As good an athlete as he was, he was an even better person."

Frantz and McBath used to hit the night spots, chasing girls, but no amount of coaxing could get Kalsu to go along. "Some of the married guys chased around, but Bob, never," says Frantz. "He loved his wife and his kid. He was totally at ease with himself, confident in who he was. We'd go out, and he'd laugh at us: 'You guys can do what you want. I've got what I want.'"

Only seven active pro athletes would serve in Vietnam: six football players and a bowler. Most other draftable pro athletes elected to serve in the reserves. Kalsu's family and friends urged him to go that route. "I'm no better than anybody else," he told them all. It was early 1969. The Vietnam War was still raging a year after the Tet Offensive, and there was no hope of its ending soon. Frantz pleaded with Kalsu to seek the Bills' help in finding a slot in the reserves. "John, I gave 'em my word," Kalsu said, referring to his promise, on joining ROTC, to serve on active duty. "I'm gonna do it."

"Bob, it's hell over there," Frantz said. "You've got a wife, a child."

Kalsu shook his head. "I'm committed," he said.

That September, after nearly eight months at Fort Sill in Lawton, Oklahoma, Kalsu went home one day looking shaken. His uniform was soaked with sweat. "I have orders to go to Vietnam," he told Jan.

They spent his last weeks in the country at her parents' house, with Jan in growing turmoil over the prospect of losing him. They were in the laundry room washing clothes when she spoke her worst fear. "What if you die over there?" she asked. "What am I to do?"

"I want you to go on with your life," he said. "I want you to marry again."

She broke down. "I don't want to marry again," she said. "I couldn't."

"Jan, I promise you, it'll be all right."

They had been married in the St. James Catholic Church in Oklahoma City, and a few weeks before he left, they went there together. Jan knelt before the altar. "If you need him more than I do," she prayed silently, "please give me a son to carry on his name."

Bob was gone before Thanksgiving. In one of her first letters to him, Jan gave Bob the good news: she was pregnant again.

If his letters didn't reveal what he was facing in Vietnam, Jan got a sense of it in May 1970 when, seven months pregnant and with Jill in tow, she met him in Hawaii for a week of R and R. Bob slept much of the time, and he was napping one day in their room when fireworks were set off by the pool. "He tore out of that bed frantic, looking for cover," Jan says, "terror and fear on his face. I got a glimpse of what he was living through."

At the end of the week they said goodbye at the airport. "Bob, please be careful," she said.

"You be careful," he said. "You're carrying our baby."

Jan returned to Oklahoma, Bob to Vietnam — and soon to Firebase Ripcord. For the last three weeks he was on that rock, it was under increasing siege, and his men saw him as one of them, a grunt with a silver bar working the trenches of Ripcord and never complaining. "He had a presence about him," says former corporal Renner. "He could have holed up in his bunker, giving orders on the radio. He was out there in the open with everybody else. He was always checking the men out, finding out how we were, seeing if we were doing what needed to be done. I got wounded on Ripcord, and he came down into the bunker. My hands were bandaged, and he asked me, 'You want to catch a chopper out of here?'" Renner saw that Kalsu had been hit in the shoulder. "I saw the bandage on him and saw he was staying. I said, 'No, I'm gonna stay.'"

The men of Battery A, trapped on that mountaintop, bonded like cave dwellers in some prehistoric war of the worlds. "Our language and behavior were pitiful," says Renner. "We behaved like junkyard dogs. If you wanted to fight or tear somebody else up, that's what you did. It was the tension. But I never heard Lieutenant Kalsu cuss. Not once. He was such a nice guy."

As was the other gentle soul of the outfit, David Earl Johnson. "A kind, lovable person," recalls his sister, Audrey Wrightsell. Growing up in their little Arkansas community, David played most sports. His junior high coach Leo Collins says that David was good at just about everything and best at basketball and track. "One of the best athletes you could ever wish for in a small school," says Collins. "He was so easy to manage, a coach's dream."

Like Kalsu, Johnson did not take the easy way out of the war. He was paying his way through Philander Smith College in Little Rock, majoring in business administration, when he decided not to apply for another student deferment. "I'm tired of this," he told Audrey. "I'm gonna serve my time."

So it was that Johnson landed on Ripcord with Kalsu, in the middle of the most unpopular war in U.S. history. In May 1970, during a protest against the war at Kent State in Ohio, National Guardsmen had fired on student protesters, killing four. Criticism of the war had become so strong that as the NVA massed to attack Ripcord, the U.S. command in Vietnam decided not to meet force with more force, which would have put even more body bags on the evening news. So Ripcord was left twisting in the boonies.

The men made the most of their fate. Kalsu tried to make a game of the darkest moments. He and Big John, as Johnson was known, "were always laughing and joking," says former sergeant Martin. "For [them], everything was a challenge." When the sling-loads of ammunition would arrive by chopper, Kalsu would call out, "Let's get that ammo off the pads!" He and Johnson would take three of those 97-pound shells apiece and hump them up the hill together. The contest was to see who could carry the most. "Johnson was the biggest man we'd seen until Kalsu came along," says Martin.

They died together at five o'clock that summer afternoon. Fotias rolled Kalsu off him and saw the flowing wound behind the lieutenant's left ear. Kalsu was pulled out of the bunker, not far from where Johnson lay dead, and Doc Harris came running over. He looked down at Kalsu and knew that he was gone.

Renner, dazed from the concussion, saw that Kalsu was dead and picked up Beals, wounded in the blast, and started to carry him to the aid station. "Lieutenant Kalsu has been killed," Renner said. "I don't know what the hell we're gonna do now."

In a hospital where he had been flown after taking shrapnel, Martin got word that Kalsu and Big John were dead. "I sat there and cried," he says.

That evening, the battalion commander on Ripcord, Lt. Col. Andre Lucas, learned of Kalsu's death. Lucas would die two days later, as the firebase was being evacuated, and for his part in defending it, he would win the Congressional Medal of Honor. As battle-hardened as he was, he seemed stunned by the news about Kalsu. "The tone went out of the muscles on his face, and his jaw dropped," Harris says.

On July 21, 1970, James Robert Kalsu thus became the only American professional athlete to die in combat in Vietnam.

At 12:45 A.M. on July 23, at St. Anthony Hospital in Oklahoma City, Jan Kalsu gave birth to an eight-pound, 15½-ounce boy, Robert Todd Kalsu. When Leah Kalsu visited her that morning, Jan fairly shouted, "Bob is going to jump off that mountain when he finds he has a boy!"

That afternoon, as the clan gathered in the Darrow house to head for a celebration at the hospital, there was a knock at the front door. Sandy Szilagyi, one of Jan's sisters, opened it, thinking the visitor might be a florist. She saw a uniformed Army lieutenant. "Is Mrs. James Robert Kalsu home?" he asked.

Sandy knew right then. "She's at St. Anthony Hospital," she said. "She's just given birth to a baby."

The young lieutenant went pale. Turning, he walked away. Sandy called Philip Maguire, the doctor who had delivered the baby, and told him who was coming. At the hospital, the lieutenant stepped into Maguire's office and sat down. He was shaking. "Do you think she'll be able to handle this?" he asked. "I don't know what to do. I'm not sure I can do this."

Maguire led the officer to Jan's room, slipped into a chair and put his arm around her. "Jan, there's a man from the Army here to see you," he said.

"Bob's been killed, hasn't he?" she said.

The officer came in and stood at the foot of the bed. He could barely speak. "It is my duty . . ." he began. When he finished, he turned and left in tears.

Jan asked to leave the hospital immediately with her baby. She did one thing before she left. She asked for a new birth certificate. She renamed the boy James Robert Kalsu, Jr.

The funeral, a week later at Czech National Cemetery, brought people from all around the country, and the gravesite service was more anguished than anything Byron Bigby, Kalsu's old Sooners teammate, had ever seen. "I looked around," he says, "and there was not a dry eye. We walked out of there biting our lips."

Barry Switzer, who had been a young assistant under Fairbanks during the '67 season, was walking to his car when he turned and looked back. What he saw haunts him still. "Bob's daddy got his wife and Jan back to the car," Switzer says. "After everyone was gone from the gravesite, he went back and lay down on the casket."

Three decades have passed since Kalsu died. Jan has sought ways to deal with the void, but times were often difficult. She struggled financially, frequently living from one government check to another, determined to remain at home while raising her kids.

She did not have a serious relationship with a man until the mid-eighties, when she began seeing Bob McLauchlin, an Oklahoma businessman. In 1986 they visited the Vietnam Veterans Memorial in Washington, D.C. They found Kalsu's name on the wall, and McLauchlin shared Jan's bereavement. They married in 1988. Last fall McLauchlin took Jill and Bob Jr. to a reunion of Ripcord survivors in Shreveport, Louisiana. Her children persuaded Jan not to go. They didn't want to see her cry as she had for so many years.

Jill and Bob Jr. have suffered a keen ambivalence for years. From all they have heard about their father from Jan and the Darrow clan, they have grown to love and admire him without having known him. They are proud of all he accomplished and the honorable way he conducted his life, but they are angry at him, too. They grew up fatherless, after all, having to comfort a lonely, grieving mother whose pain and struggles continually touched them.

The children turned out well. Jill, outgoing and warm, is a housewife in Oklahoma City, the mother of three with a fourth on the way. Bob, soft-spoken and reflective, is an aviation lawyer in Oklahoma City and the father of two. Asked what he would say to his father, Bob says, "I would embrace him and tell him I love him. It would not be derogatory, and it would not be mean, but I would ask him, 'Did you fully contemplate the consequences of your decision? I feel like I lost out, and I wish you had not made the decision to go.'" Bob Jr. considers what he's said for a moment, then goes on: "I'm equally proud he made the decision. That's the kind of man I want to be, to have the integrity that he had." That, of course, is the rub. Bob Kalsu made that decision precisely because he was the kind of man he was.

All who knew him remember him in different ways. The clan, as a family man. The football players, as a tough jock. Then there are those who knew Kalsu on that terrible hill. They have the most painful and poignant memories of him. Fotias has trouble talking about Kalsu, his voice soft and filled with sorrow. So does Renner. He walked over to Kalsu's body lying outside the bunker and peered into his motionless face. He would see that face for years. Now, however, "I can't see the face anymore," Renner says. "I can see his silhouette. I can't see a lot of their faces, only their silhouettes."

Renner is having trouble getting out the words. They come in a whisper. "I've thought of him every Memorial Day," he says. "In my heart, I pay homage to him. And Johnson. They are all very important." He closes his eyes and bows his head and quietly weeps.

MARK KRAM, JR.

Joe's Gift

FROM THE PHILADELPHIA DAILY NEWS

THE HOLLAND BOYS and their cousin, Lancer Perkins, had gone to Chennault Park early that June day for a picnic sponsored by a local TV station. The three ate free hot dogs at a tent that had been set up, stood in line to enter the amusement area, and then, one by one, sped down the big water slide until a custodian hurried them along so others could play. With the temperature well above ninety by noon and inching upward, the boys searched the park for another place to cool down, only to come upon a pond that was swarming with bathers. The boys walked along the edge of it, then one spotted a secluded spot beyond a grove of trees.

"Look!" shouted Perkins, eleven. "Nobody is over there! Come on!" Off he ran, and the two others followed, Harry Holland, Jr., eleven, and his brother, LeMarkits Holland, ten.

LeMarkits remembers Joe Delaney was sitting under a nearby tree chatting with a woman as the boys approached the edge of the pond. Just weeks from reporting for his third NFL season as a running back for the Kansas City Chiefs, Delaney had come to Monroe from his home in Haughton, about ninety miles away to help promote the events at the park that day. From his position under the tree, he had an unobstructed view of the boys, who locked hands and waded slowly into the shallows. Step by step they splashed on until suddenly, in the blink of a startled eye, they fell together over an unseen ledge on the bottom of the pond and found themselves clawing at the air bubbles that surrounded them. Delaney sprang to his feet.

LeMarkits bobbed up to the top, then slid under again. Water overwhelmed him, forcing itself into his breathing cavities and down into his lungs. But just as the cold depths of the pond prepared to carry him away and claim him, a hand drew upon him and clamped on to his arm. With otherworldly force, the hand swept him into the light of day, where LeMarkits gulped for air. The hand propelled him into the shallows, but before it did, LeMarkits caught a glimpse of it that would remain embedded in his psyche for years to come. The pinkie on that hand had a small scar on it. LeMarkits crawled to the bank.

He remembers the woman with whom Delaney had been sitting shouting hysterically, "Help! Somebody help!"

LeMarkits gagged, then doubled over and vomited.

People from other parts of the park began running to the scene.

LeMarkits looked back at the pond, which now shimmered placidly in the sun. They were gone, Harry and Lancer and the brave soul who saved him, Joe Delaney. And LeMarkits just stood there and began to sob.

Close to eighteen years have passed since that day at Chennault Park — June 29, 1983 — and yet LeMarkits Holland cannot escape the horror of what happened to Joe Delaney and the others. In the bad dreams that have plagued him through the years, he always could see himself standing there on the bank as police divers drag up Harry and Lancer, eyes closed and splayed beneath a team of paramedics. Then up came Joe, his body tangled up in weeds. LeMarkits used to wake up in a cold sweat and shout, "No! No! Come back!" but the dreams he has had lately have been less graphic than just oddly spooky. All he sees now is that big hand with the scar on the pinkie.

"Crazy," LeMarkits Holland says with a sigh. "Even in dreams that are about something else, suddenly that hand just seems to come out of nowhere. And that happens over and over again."

All of our lives have a certain trajectory, the arc of which is drawn by circumstances that can be beyond our control. In the case of Joe Delaney, whose arc was only beginning to soar, the circumstances that conspired to bring him down from his trajectory came upon him unforeseen, suddenly, and altered the lives of an array of people. Bobbing in his steep wake are his beloved widow, Carolyn, who summoned a courage to endure that she could not know she had;

their three daughters, only two of whom barely remember him but are shepherded by his spirit; and, alas, LeMarkits. Overlooked in the hysteria that surrounded the incident was that one of the three boys — LeMarkits, then unidentified in published accounts — did not just swim to safety on the bank of the pond as reports indicated. Carolyn Delaney confirms that young LeMarkits also would have died if Joe had not saved him.

Today, LeMarkits Holland has found himself in search of yet another rescuing hand. At twenty-seven, Holland sits behind bars on a drug conviction here at the Ouachita Parish Correctional Center, or as it is known locally, "The Pea Farm," the grounds of which are used by inmates to grow produce. Wearing a red jump suit and sandals, Holland is ushered by a guard into a bare interview room at the prison and joined on this December day by his attorney, Robert C. Johnson. In jail since police picked him up in September, Holland pleaded guilty to distribution of cocaine and conspiracy to distribute cocaine and was sentenced on each count to five years, to run concurrently. Only too aware that he is squandering the second chance that Joe Delaney so courageously provided him, Holland says: "He would not be too happy to see me sitting in here."

No one surely had more to live for when he died so tragically than Joe Delaney. Well apart from the fact that he had a big career ahead of him with the Chiefs — with whom he had won AFC offensive rookie of the year honors in 1981 — Delaney could look forward to years of bliss with Carolyn and their three daughters: Tamika, seven, Crystal, four, and Joanna, four months. While Delaney was coming off a subpar year in 1982, in part due to an eye operation he'd had during the off-season to fix a detached retina, the Chiefs were prepared to sign him to a lucrative contract just before he died. In fact, the Delaneys were supposed to leave for Kansas City two days later and set up housekeeping there before the start of training camp. When Carolyn Delaney looks back on what happened instead, she is overcome with a sadness that remains just beyond words. Softly, she says, "Things were just going so well for us."

The years have not been easy for Carolyn and her children. With the only love she could ever imagine gone, Carolyn dedicated herself to the upbringing of her three daughters, taking on jobs as a day-care teacher and then as a driver for one of the local casinos.

While she is still only forty-three and youthful in appearance, she has not even gone out on a date since Joe died, concerned it somehow would interrupt the sacred bond she still has with her deceased husband. Carolyn has done a good job with the three girls, two of whom are off on their own and the youngest of whom is a star academically in high school. Joe would be proud of how Carolyn has held the household together, despite the fact that her income has been small and back taxes recently have forced her to sell the home she and Joe built years ago.

Carolyn Delaney was upset to hear what has become of LeMarkits Holland. While it had been years since she had been in contact with him or his mother, Nora Stubblefield, she had hoped that he had gone on and done well for himself, that the spirit of Joe would live on in him. But this is the wrong ending somehow. To hear that Holland is in jail on a drug conviction only enhances the deep sorrow Carolyn has endured in varying degrees since that June day nearly eighteen years ago. With pity in her eyes as she sits at her dining room table in Haughton a couple of months ago, she says that what happened to Holland leaves her feeling angry. She adds that Joe would "feel real bad about it," but is equally certain her husband would have kept in close contact with Holland. She says, "Joe would not have allowed that child to give up on himself."

But that appears to be just what LeMarkits Holland did so long ago. Inwardly, he became walled in by shadows, deeply troubled by the death of his older brother Harry and the others. He wondered why he had been the one who had been spared and not Harry, whom he remembers today as a "good kid who never got into trouble." While his mother conceded that she should have received counseling, she says she was overcome with grief over the loss of Harry and spiraled into alcoholism. LeMarkits stayed alone in his room for days on end. When schoolteachers corrected him, he became consumed by an unspoken rage, beneath which stood a hidden reservoir of tears over Harry, Lancer, and Joe. With eyes lowered and hands folded on the table before him at The Pea Farm, LeMarkits says, "Sometime I feel like it should have been me who died."

He sighs and adds, "Everything changed that day."

The Wednesday that Joe Delaney died began strangely. In the early morning hours, as he prepared to leave for Monroe, it was as if he had some deep premonition that he would not be back. Carolyn remembers that he kept running back into the house to kiss his daughters goodbye, and asked if the two oldest, Tamika and Crystal, could join him on his trip. Carolyn told him no, that they would only get in his way. But he just seemed to oddly linger. When he asked her what she had planned for the day, she told him she had some shopping to do and would begin packing for Kansas City. They were scheduled to leave that Friday.

"Joe," she finally said. "You better get on now."

Then he kissed her, got into his baby blue Cougar, and drove off.

"I remember that day as if it were yesterday," says Carolyn. "He just did not want to leave us."

Joe and Carolyn had grown up down the street from each other in Haughton. Joe was one of eight children and had a twin sister, Joann. Carolyn remembers that Joe had it hard as a child, that he "only had two pair of pants to his name." They began dating at Haughton High School, where Joe won all-state honors as a wide receiver and defensive back and distinguished himself as a sprinter. Carolyn attended Northwestern State University in Natchitoches with Joe, but dropped out after a year, when she and Joe wed and their eldest daughter, Tamika, was born. Converted to a running back by head coach A. L. Williams, the five-foot-ten, 185-pound Delaney became the only State player to rush for 3,000 career yards. The couple had their second daughter, Crystal, when Joe was in his senior year, toward the end of which the Chiefs selected him in the second round of the 1981 NFL draft. Carolyn says, "We were just so in love."

Delaney showed immense promise with the Chiefs; you wonder today just how far he could have gone with his talent. That rookie year, he gained 1,121 yards on 234 carries (4.8 average) in fifteen games, set four club rushing records, and was bestowed with honors: AFC offensive rookie of the year; Pro Bowl starter; team MVP. Carolyn remembers that he used to toss his weekly check on top of the TV — $11,000. Slowed by the eye operation that delayed his participation in training camp and held to just 380 yards on 95 carries in eight games during strike-shortened 1982, he had every reason to expect that the year ahead would bring better days as he drove into Chennault Park that day in June 1983. There, he signed autographs, chatted with some old friends, and by two o'clock had found a shady spot beneath a tree by the pond.

LeMarkits Holland remembers him sitting there as he approached the pond but was unaware of who he was; he had not even heard of Delaney at that point. Holland had been dropped off at the park with his brother, sister LaMisa, and Lancer by his dad, Harry Sr., who had gone off to buy beer and ice. In the care of aunts and uncles who also were at the park that day, the three boys had no way of knowing that the pond was a dangerous place. Only later would LeMarkits discover that a hole had been dug by the builders of the water slide and that it had been filled in with water. Consequently, the pond fell precipitously to a depth of twenty feet at the edge of the shallows, so it was as if a trapdoor had fallen from beneath the three boys. Though Delaney did not swim well, he bolted for the pond as if he had a football under his arm and dived in. Out came LeMarkits. Delaney dived back in again and vanished below the surface.

"Someone ran to get help, but I just stood there," Holland says. "An ambulance came, then the police, and then a diver went in to get them. They got Harry, then Lancer, and then Joe Delaney. They stretched them out there on the grass and worked on them, but Harry and Joe were dead. I was so scared."

Carolyn was relaxing in a rocking chair on the porch with Joanna on her lap when the phone rang inside the house. She held the baby in one hand and picked up the receiver with the other. Coolly, the caller told her that her husband had been in an accident and that she should come immediately to St. Francis Medical Center in Monroe. When Carolyn pressed her for details ("What kind of accident? Is Joe okay?"), the caller replied, "All we can say is that you should come to Monroe. We have your husband here." Upset, Carolyn hurried down the street and found her cousin, Billy Johnson, who offered to drive her to Monroe. On their way out of Haughton, Carolyn stopped off to see her mother-in-law, who was sitting on her porch. "Miss Eunice, they just called from Monroe and said Joe was in an accident," Carolyn said. "Do you want to come along with us?" But Eunice just said quietly, as if she knew something was terribly wrong: "No. You go."

Uneasy silence filled the car as Johnson headed east on Interstate 20 and stood on the accelerator; Carolyn just looked out her window at the passing swampland and wondered what possibly could have happened. She later would discover that by then it was "all over the news," but the radio was off in the vehicle. Uncertain exactly where St. Francis Medical Center was located, Johnson stopped at a convenience store in Monroe to ask for directions, only to learn what had happened from the clerk behind the counter. Shaken, he came out and told Carolyn, "We are not too far away." He paused, then said again and again as they drove on: "Everything is going to be all right." They found the hospital and hurried into the emergency room.

Standing in the corridor there was a police officer, whom Carolyn approached to identify herself. Carolyn told him, "They said my husband is here." The police officer held up a piece of jewelry, a gold chain with her class ring attached to it. He said, "Does this belong to your husband?" When she told him it did, and told him she was sure, she was directed to a small room and told that a doctor would be in to see her shortly. Carolyn said anxiously, "Where is Joe? What happened to him?" She was told again that the doctor would be in shortly, but an hour passed and he still had not showed up. Carolyn walked out in the hallway at that point and was intercepted by a nurse. Says Carolyn: "I will never forget the look on her face."

Gravely, the nurse said, "Mrs. Delaney, your husband drowned around 2:30 this afternoon."

Carolyn looked at her with widening eyes and said, "No! Joe was coming to an event here. He was not supposed to be anywhere near water!"

The nurse replied sorrowfully, "All I know is they said he drowned in Chennault Park and was already dead when he got here."

Suddenly, Carolyn was sucked down into a whirlpool of unspeakable grief. Given a sedative by the doctors, she awoke to find herself in a hospital bed that evening. One of the nurses told her: "You have to identify the body." But Carolyn could not bring herself to do it; she would never see Joe in death. Cousin Billy identified the body that evening at the hospital. Carolyn was sedated again and only later told by doctors what had happened: Joe had died trying to save three boys from drowning in a pond. One of them — Harry Holland — was pronounced dead at the scene. The other — Lancer Perkins — died early Thursday at the hospital.

Gold crosses were placed in the hands of the two boys at their funeral on July 3. Nora Stubblefield was overcome with anguish. How could it be, how could it possibly be, that son Harry was gone? The day is still so unreal to her: the boys in their coffins, the flowers everywhere, the pews overflowing with people. With tears running down his cheeks, LeMarkits stared in at the body of his dead brother, but he sat in the car when the service ended and did not go to the gravesite in the churchyard. LeMarkits says, "I could not stand to look at them sticking Harry in no hole."

Joe Delaney was buried the following day, July 4, in Haughton. Three thousand mourners filed into the gymnasium at Haughton High School, including a contingent of twenty club officials and teammates from the Chiefs. Owner Lamar Hunt said, "Joe was a good man, a real good man." Coach John Mackovic, who had replaced Marv Levy during that offseason, and others eulogized Joe as a hero, and a telegram showed up from President Reagan, who assured that Delaney has "surely earned his place in heaven for having sacrificed his life for those three boys." Carolyn held Joanna in her arms as she stood with her two other young daughters at Hawkins Cemetery, where Joe Delaney lies under a headstone paraphrasing a quote from John 15:13. "Greater love hath no man than to lay down his life for another."

Going to jail has given LeMarkits Holland time to think. With no prior criminal record to speak of other than some disorderly conduct charges stemming from some street fights, Holland says he was "just in the wrong place at the wrong time" when the cops grabbed him, and he has no intention of ever going back behind bars. He plans to better himself, get a job and perhaps his graduate equivalency degree, and take care of his three sons, ages nine, seven, and two, who are in the custody of family and friends. He wants them to remember the three people who died that day in the pond.

"They would not even be here if Joe Delaney had not jumped in and saved me," says Holland, who has an upper tooth capped in gold. "And I would not be in jail today if I had just stopped to think how lucky I was that he got to me. When the boys get older, you better believe they will know who Joe Delaney was. And Harry and Lancer."

He pauses and with a sigh adds, "Lord help me get through this."

But LeMarkits Holland has been in captivity far longer than since September. What happened that tragic day at Chennault Park has held him in an iron grip, just as it has held his parents, Carolyn Delaney, and her three daughters. In the case of Holland, then just in the fifth grade, it was especially horrifying to lose Harry, to whom he looked up with pride. Harry was always an easygoing child, just like his dad that way, and LeMarkits followed him everywhere. They fished together, played ball together, and occupied a bedroom together. Harry was always well behaved, did his chores without being asked twice, but LeMarkits could be a problem for his mother, Nora, who remembers: "He got his share of whuppings." Quietly, LeMarkits says: "I always think about Harry."

Change came over LeMarkits in the wake of the deaths. A wall just seemed to go up between him and everyone else in the world. Oddly, he says he began to systematically erase Harry from the premises: he sold his bicycle, gave away his books, beanbag chair, and other belongings, and set fire to his clothes. The boys had twin beds, but LeMarkits told his mom to get rid of them, that he would burn them, too, unless she did. When LeMarkits would shout out in his sleep, Nora would come into his bedroom and wake him up, only to find him curled up in a ball on his single bed and dripping with sweat. Only rarely would LeMarkits bring up the subject of what happened at the pond, during which he would say sadly: "If only Harry was still here." But whenever that would happen, Nora would just reply with a weary sigh: "Please, Marty. Not today, okay?" And once again that wall would go up.

Nora Stubblefield was in a long free fall herself. On the day Harry drowned, she was supposed to have had the day off at the nursing home where she worked. She had planned to go to Chennault Park that day, but her supervisor summoned her in with the promise that she could leave early. When Nora finally got to the park that afternoon, she saw an ambulance heading the other way and thought, "Oh God, somebody came down with heat stroke." She discovered otherwise when daughter LaMisa came running up to her and, with eyes wide with panic, told her: "Mama! Mama! Your son is drowning!" Nora hurried along with her, certain that she had been referring to Marty. Harry hated the water; he even hated taking baths. Says Nora, "Marty would swim in the cesspool behind the house."

But it was Harry who was lying on the bank when she got to the pond; LeMarkits was standing off to the side with tears in his eyes. Hysterically, Nora cried, "Who pushed him in? I'll kill him!" She then passed out. When she came to later in the hospital, she looked up at her surroundings and screamed: "My baby!" A doctor gave her a sedative and she slipped into a deep sleep.

All that followed is a long blur to Nora, who says she began chasing away the sadness that enveloped her with booze and cigarettes. When she and her remaining children attended the funeral for Joe Delaney in Haughton, it only added to her ordeal to overhear scowling bystanders say: "Look at that country hick from Monroe." Rumors had spread that she had been with Delaney at Chennault Park, that the two of them had been having an affair, but Nora told Carolyn back at her house that she had never even heard of her husband. Steeped in an alcoholic haze and soon out of a job ("I just stopped caring," she says), Nora began assigning blame to herself for what happened. She blamed her supervisor for calling her into work on her off day, which would have been her first in twelve days. She blamed her former husband, Harry, who dropped the boys off at the park and went to pick up picnic supplies. Why had he not been there?

Harry understands why she blamed him. "I used to sit down and cry about it," says Holland, a custodial supervisor at the University of Louisiana at Monroe. "I could have stayed there until their mama got there. But they had their aunts and uncles around and I thought they would be fine. And when I left they were at the water slide, not that itty-bitty pond."

Grief over young Harry blinded both parents to the deepening problems LeMarkits faced. Along with his inability to open up to anyone, his teachers told Nora that he just seemed to be in "outer space" in class, not hearing a single word that had been said. Corrected by a superior, he would suddenly lash out, which along with his propensity for fisticuffs earned him suspensions from schools. When a teacher recommended to her that he undergo psychological counseling, Nora replied: "What he is gonna *get* is a whupping." When LeMarkits was once again suspended in the tenth grade, Nora was by that point a contractor and began using LeMarkits as a helper on the job. LeMarkits did not go back to school. Well before his twenty-first birthday, he was running with what Nora calls a bad crowd and was on an express for either jail or an early grave.

Nora has come to blame herself. "I should have been stronger," says Nora, who has conquered her alcoholism and says she has placed herself in the hands of God. "I used to blame Harry Sr. and everyone else, but I should have been there for him more than I was. I realize that now. But losing Harry was just so hard to swallow. I could not get over the fact that I had just seen him at 6:00 A.M. and when I saw him again, he was lying there by that pond and did not have a single breath still in him."

What Nora has become increasingly thankful for is that Joe Delaney saved even one of her sons that day. Had both of them died, she is certain she would have been swept under. She calls Delaney "heroic," says that he would have to be to do what he did for a stranger. Now she says she has to do her part, which is to help LeMarkits "get his life back together." Currently the driver of an eighteen-wheeler, Nora says she and LeMarkits have talked over the idea of leaving Monroe once he gets out. He is eligible for parole next month. She and her new husband plan to build a house in Texas, where LaMisa is a staff sergeant in the Army. Nora says it was a blessing that LeMarkits was arrested, that he can soon begin over and carry on the spirit of the person who saved him. Says LeMarkits, "If I ever come back to jail, it will be for working too hard."

LeMarkits has not been back to Chennault Park since the drowning, nor does he have any desire to go there again. The part of the pond where the three drownings occurred was drained and filled in, part of a court judgment that Carolyn, Nora and Harry Sr. won against the city of Monroe. Chennault Park still has a big pond nearby that on a hot summer day can seem inviting to young boys. Surrounded by evergreens inhabited by chirping fowl, the pond on cold winter days is a study in solitude: a turtle suns itself in a bare spot in the weeds, a convoy of ducks paddles by. There is no indication that a courageous man once died near here, only a sign that someone placed here the day after the deaths occurred that said: "No Swimming."

Another strange thing happened a day before Joe Delaney passed; Carolyn says it was another premonition. Out that day to take Joanna for a checkup, she had come home to find Joe sitting at the dining room table with the Bible open and a pad of paper. He was drawing a picture. She walked over with the baby in her arms and looked over his shoulder, curious to see what he was working on. Oddly, on the paper before him was a depiction of hands folded in prayer. She asked him, "Why did you draw that, Joe?"

Joe looked up at her and replied, "Somehow it just came to me. And I want you to have it, just so you know that God does hear prayers."

Carolyn wonders how their life together would have been, the impact his daily presence would have had on their daughters. Would they better off somehow? Or are they stronger today because they had to be? No one can ever know that; the trajectory of their lives was irrevocably altered back at Chennault Park. Going in the pond for those boys exacted an immeasurable price, but she knows Joe would do it again, even if he knew that the child he saved would end up behind bars. Carolyn still holds out hope that LeMarkits will find himself. He is still so young. But whatever becomes of him in the years to come, she can carry within her the knowledge that this is true: the deeds of her husband will live on for as long as courage is a virtue.

Carolyn cannot bear to even hang pictures of Joe anywhere in her house, a three-bedroom rancher somewhat smaller than the home she and Joe once had. Up above the fireplace are framed photographs of her daughters, the older ones in cap and gown, but it would be too hard for her to display shots of Joe. They would remind her once again of the years that were stolen from them. Somewhere in the house there are boxes with old pictures of Joe, along with his scrapbooks, trophies, and other odds and ends. Joanna has told her that she would like to have them one day when she has a house of her own. She wants to decorate a room with them, if only to conjure up a connection to a man who died before she even knew him. Joanna's sisters remember him.

Tamika, twenty-five, says Joe used to play the guitar and take her fishing. "But I know what people have told him: that he considered others before himself," said Tamika, whose legacy of tragedy was passed down to her daughter, six, and son, two, when her fiancé was gunned down in California in a drive-by shooting. "Now I have two children who will never know their father." Tamika works with the mentally ill.

Crystal, twenty-one, says she remembers how her father used to take her to the corner store for candy. "It was hard for us growing up without a father," said Crystal, a fine high school athlete who was placed in counseling by Carolyn at a young age. "But Mom was always there for us." Crystal attends community college.

Joanna, seventeen, agrees. "She is such a strong person. But she has never gotten over Daddy." Joanna will attend LSU in the fall and study nursing.

One day her daughters would like to see Carolyn find someone to share her life with. But whenever they say, "Mama, when are you going to go out on a date?" Carolyn laughs and replies, "Where am I ever going to find another man like your dad? He was my soul mate." Secretly, she fears that if she found someone else that Joe would stop visiting her, which always has been an event to which she has looked forward. Someone once told her that she was only dreaming, that by not seeing Joe in death she did not allow herself any closure. While early on she would not accept the fact that Joe was dead, certain that it was someone else in the pond and that Joe would come back, the passing years have convinced her that he is gone, but only in the flesh. Certain that she was awake one day before she sold their old house — or was she? — she says that Joe sat down on the edge of her bed.

"Carolyn," he said. "I have always been there for you and I always will."

She asked him what she should do.

Gently, he placed a caressing hand on her cheek and said, "But the time has come to move on."

KARL TARO GREENFELD

Blind to Failure

FROM TIME

WHEN HE SAW Erik Weihenmayer arrive that afternoon, Pasquale Scaturro began to have misgivings about the expedition he was leading. Here they were on the first floor of Mount Everest, and Erik — the reason for the whole trip — was stumbling into Camp 1 bloody, sick, and dehydrated. "He was literally green," says fellow climber and teammate Michael O'Donnell. "He looked like George Foreman had beat the crap out of him for two hours." The beating had actually been administered by Erik's climbing partner, Luis Benitez. Erik had slipped into a crevasse, and as Benitez reached down to catch him, his climbing pole raked Erik across the nose and chin. Wounds heal slowly at that altitude because of the thin air.

As Erik passed out in his tent, the rest of the team gathered in a worried huddle. "I was thinking maybe this is not a good idea," says Scaturro. "Two years of planning, a documentary movie, and this blind guy barely makes it to Camp 1?"

This blind guy. Erik Weihenmayer, thirty-three, wasn't just another yuppie trekker who'd lost a few rounds to the mountain. Blind since he was thirteen, the victim of a rare hereditary disease of the retina, he began attacking mountains in his early twenties.

But he had been having the same doubts as the rest of the team. On that arduous climb to camp through the Khumbu Icefall, Erik wondered for the first time if his attempt to become the first sightless person to summit Mount Everest was a colossal mistake, an act of Daedalian hubris for which he would be punished. There are so many ways to die on that mountain, spanning the spectacular (fall through an ice shelf into a crevasse, get waylaid by an avalanche, develop cerebral edema from lack of oxygen and have your brain literally swell out of your skull) and the banal (become disoriented because of oxygen deprivation and decide you'll take a little nap, right here, in the snow, which becomes a forever nap).

Erik, as he stumbled through the icefall, was so far out of his comfort zone that he began to speculate on which of those fates might await him. For a moment he flashed on all those clichés about what blind people are supposed to do — become piano tuners or pencil salesmen — and thought maybe they were stereotypes for good reason. Blind people certainly shouldn't be out here, wandering through an ever changing ice field, measuring the distance over a 1,000-foot-deep crevasse with climbing poles and then leaping, literally, over and into the unknown.

The blind thrive on patterns: stairs are all the same height, city blocks roughly the same length, curbs approximately the same depth. They learn to identify the patterns in their environment much more than the sighted population do, and to rely on them to plot their way through the world.

But in the Khumbu Icefall, the trail through the Himalayan glacier is patternless, a diabolically cruel obstacle course for a blind person. It changes every year as the river of ice shifts, but it's always made up of treacherously crumbly stretches of ice, ladders roped together over wide crevasses, slightly narrower crevasses that must be jumped, huge seracs, avalanches, and — most frustrating for a blind person, who naturally seeks to identify patterns in his terrain — a totally random icescape.

In the icefall there is no system, no repetition, no rhyme or reason to the lay of the frozen land. On the other hand, "it is so specific in terms of where you can step," Erik recalls. "Sometimes you're walking along and then boom, a crevasse is right there, and three more steps and another one, and then a snow bridge. And vertical up, then a ladder and then a jumbly section." It took Erik thirteen hours to make it from Base Camp through the icefall to Camp 1, at 20,000 feet. Scaturro had allotted seven.

A typical assault on Everest requires each climber to do as many as ten traverses through the icefall, both for acclimatization purposes and to help carry the immense amount of equipment required for an ascent. After Erik's accident, the rest of the National

Federation of the Blind (NFB) team discussed letting him stay up in Camp 1, equipped with videotapes and food, while the rest of the team and the Sherpas did his carries for him. No way, said Erik. No way was he going to do this climb without being a fully integrated and useful member of the team. "I wasn't going to be carried to the top and spiked like a football," he says. The next day he forced himself to head back down through the icefall. He would eventually make ten passes through the Khumbu, cutting his time to five hours.

Sometimes, when Erik is giving a motivational speech for one of his corporate clients, such as Glaxo Wellcome or AT&T, a fat, balding, middle-aged middle manager will approach him and say, "Even I wouldn't do that stuff." Erik calls it the Even I Syndrome. And he has to resist an impulse to say, "You're fat, out of shape, and you smoke. Why would you even think of doing any of this stuff? Just because you can see?" Erik is not impatient or smug, but he tires of people assuming that sight will trump all other attributes and senses combined.

By all accounts, Erik is gifted with strong lungs, a refined sense of balance, a disproportionately powerful upper body, rubbery legs, and flexible ankles. His conditioning is exemplary and his heart rate low. He is stockier than most mountaineers, who tend toward lanky, long muscles. But he possesses an abundance of the one indispensable characteristic of a great mountaineer: mental toughness, the ability to withstand tremendous amounts of cold, discomfort, physical pain, boredom, bad food, insomnia, and tedious conversation when you're snowed into a pup tent for a week on a three-foot-wide ice shelf at 20,000 feet. (That happened to Erik on Alaska's Denali.) On Everest, toughness is perhaps the most important trait a climber can have. "Erik is mentally one of the strongest guys you will ever meet," says fellow climber Chris Morris.

Everybody gets sick on Everest. It's called the Khumbu Krud, brought on by a combination of high altitude, dirty food, fetid water, intestinal parasites, and an utterly alien ecosystem. On Erik's team, at any given moment, half the climbers were running fevers, the others were nauseated, and they all suffered from one form or another of dysentery, an awkward ailment when there's a driving snowstorm and it's thirty below outside the tent. You relieve yourself however you can, in the vestibule of your tent or in a plastic bag. "It can be a little bit gross," says Erik. "But if you go outside and take your pants down, you'll have two inches of snowpack blow into your pants in about ten seconds."

Scaling Everest requires the enthusiasm and boosterism of a physical-education teacher combined with the survival instinct of a Green Beret. You have to want that summit. And if you whine and bitch along the way, your teammates might discard you before you get there. Erik, beneath his beard and quiet demeanor, was both booster and killer. "He was the heart and soul of our team," says Eric Alexander. "The guy's spirit won't let you quit."

Erik walks through these Kathmandu streets with remarkable ease, his red-tipped cane searching out ahead of him, measuring distance, pitch, and angle. You give him little hints as he goes — "There's a doorway. Okay, now a right — no, left, sorry" — and he follows, his stride confident but easily arrested when he bumps into an old lady selling shawls, and then into the wheel of a scooter. The physical confidence that he projects has to do with having an athlete's awareness of how his body moves through space. Plenty of sighted people walk through life with less poise and grace than Erik, unsure of their steps, second-guessing every move. And certainly most of the blind don't maneuver with Erik's aplomb. As he takes a seat in a crowded restaurant, ordering pizza, spaghetti, ice cream, beer — you work up an appetite climbing Everest — he smiles and nods as other diners ask, "Hey, aren't you the blind guy . . . ?"

With his Germanic, sculpted features and light brown hair, Erik looks a bit like a shaggy, youthful Kirk Douglas. He is a celebrity now: strangers ask for his autograph, reporters call constantly, restaurants give him free meals. But is his celebrity the circus-freak variety — of a type with the Dogboy and the two-headed snake?

At its worst, Erik fears, it is. Casual observers don't understand what an achievement his Everest climb was, or they assume that if a blind guy can do it, anyone can. And indeed, improved gear has made Everest, at least in some people's minds, a bit smaller. In the climbing season there's a conga line to the top, or so it seems, and the trail is a junkyard of discarded oxygen tanks and other debris. But Everest eats the unready and the unlucky. Almost 90 percent of Everest climbers fail to reach the summit. Many — at least 165 since 1953 — never come home at all, their bodies lying uncollected where they fell. Four died in May. "People think because I'm blind, I don't have as much to be afraid of, like if I can't see a 2,000-foot drop-off I won't be scared," Erik says. "That's insane. Look, death is death, if I can see or not."

Everest expeditions break down into two types: those like Erik's, which are sponsored and united by a common goal, and those like the one described by Jon Krakauer in *Into Thin Air,* in which gangs of climbers pay $65,000 each for the opportunity to stand on top of the world. But as conditions become more arduous, these commercial teams start squabbling, blaming weaker members for slowing them down and sometimes even refusing to help teammates in distress.

Many pros wouldn't go near Erik's team, fearing they might have to haul the blind guy down. "Everyone was saying Erik was gonna have an epic," says Charley Mace, a member of the film crew. ("Epic" is Everest slang for disaster.) Another climber planned to stay close, boasting that he would "get the first picture of the dead blind guy."

For Erik, who knew almost as soon as he could speak that he would lose his vision in his early teens, excelling as an athlete was the result of accepting his disability rather than denying it. Growing up with two brothers in Hong Kong and then Weston, Connecticut, he was always an athletic kid, a tough gamer who developed a bump-and-grind one-on-one basketball game that allowed him to work his way close to the hoop. He was, his father Ed says, "a pretty normal kid. While bike riding, he might have run into a few more parked cars than other kids, but we didn't dwell on his going blind."

His blindness was a medical inevitability, like a court date with a hanging judge. "I saw blindness like this disease," he explains. "Like AIDS or something that was going to consume me." Think about that — being a kid, ten, eleven years old, and knowing that at some point in the near future your world is going to go dark. Certainly it builds character — that mental toughness his fellow climbers marvel at — but in a child, the natural psychological defense would be denial.

When he lost his vision, Erik at first refused to use a cane or learn Braille, insisting he could somehow muddle on as normal. "I was so afraid I would seem like a freak," he recalls. But after a few embarrassing stumbles — he couldn't even find the school rest rooms anymore — he admitted he needed help. For Erik, the key was acceptance — not to fight his disability but to learn to work within it; not to transcend it but to understand fully what he was capable of achieving within it; not to pretend he had sight but to build systems that allowed him to excel without it. "It's tragic — I know blind people who like to pass themselves off as being able to see," Erik says. "What's the point of that?"

He would never play basketball or catch a football again. But then he discovered wrestling. "I realized I could take sighted people and slam them into the mat," he says. Grappling was a sport where feel and touch mattered more than sight: if he could sense where his opponent had his weight or how to shift his own body to gain better leverage, he could excel using his natural upper-body strength. As a high school senior he went all the way to the National Junior Freestyle Wrestling Championship in Iowa.

Wrestling gave him the confidence to reenter the teenage social fray. He began dating when he was seventeen; his first girlfriend was a sighted woman three years older than he. Erik jokes that he is not shy about using his blindness to pick up women. "They really go for the guide dog," he explains. "You go into a bar, put the guide dog out there, and the girls just come up to you." He and his friends devised a secret handshake to let Erik know if the girl he was talking to was attractive. "Just because you're blind doesn't make you any more selfless or deep or anything. You're just like most guys, but you look for different things," Erik says. "Smooth skin, nice body, muscles — that stuff becomes more important." And the voice becomes paramount. "My wife has the most beautiful voice in the world," Erik says. Married in 1997, he and his wife Ellie have a one-year-old daughter, Emma.

Erik first went hiking with his father when he was thirteen, trying to tap his way into the wild with a white cane and quickly becoming frustrated stubbing his toes on rocks and roots and bumping into branches and trunks. But when he tried rock climbing, at sixteen while at a camp for the disabled in New Hampshire, he was hooked. Like wrestling, it was a sport in which being blind didn't have to work against him. He took to it quickly, and through climbing gradually found his way to formal mountaineering.

Watching Erik scramble up a rock face is a little like watching a spider make its way up a wall. His hands are like antennae, gathering information as they flick outward, surveying the rock for cracks, grooves, bowls, nubbins, knobs, edges, and ledges, converting all of it into a road map etched into his mind. "It's like instead of wrestling with a person, I am moving and working with a rock," he explains. "It's a beautiful process of solving a puzzle." He is an accomplished rock climber, rated 5.10 (5.14 being the highest), and has led teams up sections of Yosemite's notorious El Capitan. On ice, where one wrong strike with an ice ax can bring down an avalanche, Erik has learned to listen to the ice as he pings it gently with his ax. If it clinks, he avoids it. If it makes a thunk like a spoon hitting butter, he knows it's solid ice.

Despite being an accomplished mountaineer — summiting Denali, Kilimanjaro in Africa, and Aconcagua in Argentina, among other peaks, and, in the words of his friends, "running up 14ers" (14,000-foot peaks) — Erik viewed Everest as insurmountable until he ran into Scaturro at a sportswear trade show in Salt Lake City, Utah. Scaturro, who had already summited Everest, had heard of the blind climber, and when they met the two struck an easy rapport. A geophysicist who often put together energy-company expeditions to remote areas in search of petroleum, Scaturro began wondering if he could put together a team that could help Erik get to the summit of Everest.

"Dude," Scaturro asked, "have you ever climbed Everest?"

"No."

"Dude, you wanna?"

Climbing with Erik isn't that different from climbing with a sighted mountaineer. You wear a bell on your pack, and he follows the sound, scuttling along using his custom-made climbing poles to feel his way along the trail. His climbing partners shout out helpful descriptions: "Death fall two feet to your right!" "Emergency helicopter-evacuation pad to your left!" He is fast, often running up the back of less experienced climbers. His partners all have scars from being jabbed by Erik's climbing poles when they slowed down.

For the Everest climb, Scaturro and Erik assembled a team that combined veteran Everest climbers and trusted friends of Erik's. Scaturro wrote up a Braille proposal for the Everest attempt and submitted it to Marc Maurer, president of the National Federation of the Blind. Maurer immediately pledged $250,000 to sponsor the climb. (Aventis Pharmaceuticals agreed to sponsor a documentary on the climb to promote Allegra, its allergy medication; Erik suffers from seasonal allergies.) For Erik, who already had numerous gear and clothing sponsors, this was the greatest challenge of his life. If he failed, he would be letting down not just himself but all the blind, confirming that certain activities remained the preserve of the sighted.

He argued to anyone who would listen that he was an experienced mountaineer and that if he failed, it would be because of his heart or lungs or brain rather than his eyes. He wasn't afraid of physical danger — he had made dozens of skydives and scaled some of the most dangerous cliff faces in the world — but he was frightened of how the world would perceive him. "But I knew that if I went and failed, that would feel better than if I didn't go at all," Erik says. "It could be like [the wrestling] Junior Nationals all over again. I went out to Iowa, and I got killed. But I needed to go to understand what my limits were."

Oxygen deprivation does strange things to the human body. Heart rates go haywire, brain function decreases, blood thickens, intestines shut down. Bad ideas inexplicably pop into your head, especially above 25,000 feet, where, as Krakauer famously wrote in *Into Thin Air*, climbers have the "mind of a reptile."

At that altitude, Erik could rely on no one but himself. His teammates would have to guide him, to keep ringing the bell and making sure Erik stayed on the trail, but they would be primarily concerned about their own survival in some of the worst conditions on earth. Ironically, Erik had some advantages as they closed in on the peak. For one thing, at that altitude all the climbers wore goggles and oxygen masks, restricting their vision so severely that they could not see their own feet — a condition Erik was used to. Also, the final push for the summit began in the early evening, so most of the climb was in pitch darkness; the only illumination was from miner's lamps.

When Erik and the team began the final ascent from Camp 4 — the camp he describes as Dante's Inferno with ice and wind — they had been on the mountain for two months, climbing up and down and then up from Base Camp to Camps 1, 2, and 3, getting used to the altitude and socking away enough equipment — especially oxygen canisters — to make a summit push. They had tried for the summit once but had turned back because of weather. At 29,000 feet, the Everest peak is in the jet stream, which means that winds can exceed one hundred miles per hour and that what looks from sea level like a cottony wisp of cloud is actually a killer storm at the summit. Bad weather played a fatal role in the 1996 climbing season documented in *Into Thin Air.*

On May 24, with only seven days left in the climbing season, most of the NFB expedition members knew this was their last shot at the peak. That's why when Erik and Chris Morris reached the Balcony, the beginning of the Southeast Ridge, at 27,500 feet, after a hard slog up the South Face, they were terribly disappointed when the sky lit up with lightning, driving snow, and fierce winds. "We thought we were done," Erik says. "We would have been spanked if we made a push in those conditions." A few teammates gambled and went for it, and Jeff Evans and Brad Bull heroically pulled out fixed guidelines that had been frozen in the ice. By the time Base Camp radioed that the storm was passing, Erik and the entire team were coated in two inches of snow. Inspired by the possibility of a break in the weather, the team pushed on up the exposed Southeast Ridge, an additional 1,200 vertical feet to the South Summit. At that point the climbers looked like astronauts walking on some kind of Arctic moon. They moved slowly because of fatigue from their huge, puffy down suits, backpacks with oxygen canisters and regulators, and goggles.

With a 10,000-foot vertical fall into Tibet on one side and a 7,000-foot fall into Nepal on the other, the South Summit, at 28,750 feet, is where many climbers finally turn back. The 656-foot-long knife-edge ridge leading to the Hillary Step consists of ice, snow, and fragmented shale, and the only way to cross it is to take baby steps and anchor your way with an ice ax. "You can feel the rock chip off," says Erik. "And you can hear it falling down into the void."

The weather was finally clearing as they reached the Hillary Step, the 39-foot rock face that is the last major obstacle before the true summit. Erik clambered up the cliff, belly-flopping over the top. "I celebrated with the dry heaves," he jokes. And then it was forty-five minutes of walking up a sharply angled snow slope to the summit.

"Look around, dude," Evans told the blind man when they were standing on top of the world. "Just take a second and look around."

It could be called the most successful Everest expedition ever, and not just because of Erik's participation. A record nineteen climbers from the NFB team summited, including the oldest man ever to climb Everest — sixty-four-year-old Sherman Bull — and the second father-and-son team ever to do so — Bull and his son Brad.

What Erik achieved is hard for a sighted person to comprehend. What do we compare it with? How do we relate to it? Do we put on a blindfold and go hiking? That's silly, Erik maintains, because when a sighted person loses his vision, he is terrified and disoriented. And Erik is clearly neither of those things. Perhaps the point is really that there is no way to put what Erik has done in perspective because no one has ever done anything like it. It is a unique achievement, one that in the truest sense pushes the limits of what man is capable of. Maurer of the NFB compares Erik to Helen Keller. "Erik can be a contemporary symbol for blindness," he explains. "Helen Keller lived one hundred years ago. She should not be our most potent symbol for blindness today."

Erik, sitting in the Kathmandu international airport, waiting for the flight out of Nepal that will eventually return him to Golden, Colorado, is surrounded by his teammates and the expedition's seventy-five pieces of luggage. Success has made the group jubilant. This airport lounge has become the mountaineering equivalent of a winning Super Bowl locker room. As they sit amid their luggage, holding Carlsberg beers, they frequently raise a toast. "Shez! Shez!" shouts a climber. That's Nepali for Drink! Drink! "No epics," a climber chimes in, citing what really matters: no one died.

In between posing for photos and signing other passengers' boarding passes, Erik talks about how eager he is to get back home. He says summiting Everest was great, probably the greatest experience of his life. But then he thinks about a moment a few months ago, before Everest, when he was walking down the street in Colorado with daughter Emma in a front pack. They were on their way to buy some banana bread for his wife, and Emma was pulling on his hand, her little fingers curled around his index finger. That was a summit, too, he says. There are summits everywhere. You just have to know where to look.

MICHAEL LEAHY

Transition Game

FROM THE WASHINGTON POST

HE IS INTO STOICISM SUDDENLY, and this is unlike him. Like a general who finds himself in deep snows with inexperienced troops, he has seemed at moments like a man trying to make peace with his fate, as if able to see a cold winter ahead. "Whatever happens, happens," he said the morning of his official return to basketball this week. It is one of his regular lines now.

It does not sound like Michael Jordan. It alternately sounds grim, casual, forced, defiant, resigned — the sum of his mercurial moods. His left knee hurts, hurts bad. Not at this instant perhaps, not every day, but many days now, the aches not from a tear or sprain, but simply a function of age and wear. It's a slow breakdown that only rest can undo, with the result that he must sometimes sit out practices, which in turn has slowed his conditioning and at times dulled his shot. What a migraine is to any worker, tendinitis is to the athlete: when it hits he's essentially useless — until it passes.

Already a pattern has developed, cycles of bad days and better days for him. Tuesday night, Halloween eve, was the dreariest yet. In resting the knee, Jordan missed three consecutive practices before the Washington Wizards' regular season opener at Madison Square Garden and the cost was obvious — a dreadful shooting night, balls thrown away. He knew people were "going to rip me," as he later put it. "Jordan's Return a Sad Sequel," screamed a headline in one New York paper.

Forty-eight hours later, he seemed reborn — for a half, at least, against a pack of young, mediocre defenders. The Wizards won, so it mattered less Thursday night in Atlanta that he missed fourteen of his last twenty-two shots, or that he wore down in a fourth quarter that saw him futilely throw up three straight off-balance shots that did not touch so much as the rim. By then, Jordan had already dunked in the game's first quarter, albeit at low altitude, lifting 20,000 into delirium. He had eleven points in the game's first six minutes, on his way to thirty-one.

In the end, he played forty minutes, the most of anyone on the floor, and at least eight minutes more than his coach, Doug Collins, had set as a general limit for a man three months from his thirty-ninth birthday. "Michael didn't want to come out," Collins said afterward. "But at thirty-eight, he cannot win the game . . . by himself."

Tonight Jordan takes another step on a journey that began in secrecy in Chicago gyms last winter, then was made official in September by a terse press release whose impact was eclipsed by the sight of a smoldering Pentagon and the tomb that was once the World Trade Center. He plays his first regular season game at MCI Center, in a city still shaken and shaky, a place that could use a distracting extravaganza.

But for Jordan, it is just game three of a grueling eighty-two-game campaign, the length of which has even intimates wondering whether the questionable knees and the rest of his body will hold up.

"There is no way Michael can probably play heavy minutes night after night and not risk a breakdown," John Bach, a Wizards assistant coach, said one day during training camp. "The knees, the back, the Achilles' — you don't know what it might be, but it could be anything at thirty-eight. He's the greatest competitor there could be, but we need to protect him against those . . . urges. Already you can see he's needing to nurse some pains."

The aches have been a sensitive topic since the start of training camp in Jordan's hometown of Wilmington, North Carolina. Collins encouraged the belief that the pain in his knee was merely a normal, temporary effect of the team's rigorous preseason workout regimen; that, certainly, it wasn't anything serious.

The coach would laugh dismissively and convincingly when someone pressed him about the possibility of tendinitis. It took Tim Grover, who as Jordan's personal trainer was more responsible than any other person for having transformed Jordan from skinny wunderkind to strapping power hulk, to acknowledge the problem one evening while in a restaurant picking up food for the Jordan coterie. "We've worked through every challenge except the tendinitis; we know we have to deal with it," he said.

Still, a consensus emerged among observers who could not believe he was suffering even as Jordan gingerly walked around with an ice pack on the knee: he was just coasting, building his wind for fifty-point games, denying the obvious on nights when the gulf between what he was and is became easy to discern. Jordan and his heralded comeback have become a Rorschach test: people see in him what they wish to see, what they have been conditioned by the years to expect and need.

Bach has this story. He shared it with Jordan the first time Jordan retired, when he escaped to try his hand at baseball. He shook Jordan's hand and said how happy he was that Michael would be getting out of the sport on top; that he could still painfully remember an old Joe Louis being pounded between the ropes by Rocky Marciano, and Joe DiMaggio limping after fly balls, and a corpulent Babe Ruth flailing briefly for a barnstorming semipro team called the Bushwick Reds in a game Bach had watched as a child.

"Not going to happen to you, Michael," he remembers saying, and then let Jordan know the psychic cost of comebacks he'd seen; how desire at some point dwarfed a player's skills; how he thought the aging returnees, like Louis, found it impossible just to deal with the expectations surrounding their return; that the pressure alone upon them appeared to have been crippling. It was both a sports story and a homily, a small warning; for Bach, a selfless coach, loved the player. Jordan nodded at the tales, thanked Bach for all his guidance, wished him luck.

And now Jordan was back again, fifty minutes from stepping out on a court in a Detroit suburb for his first game in three years, surrounded by hysteria, the noise of which is seeping through the walls of the Wizards' locker room. His summer scrimmages had prepared him for nothing like this. He has not felt this kind of pressure in three years. He will not again look as nervous as he did this night, his reïntroduction to NBA competition.

Jordan sat on a stool while a dozen strangers stared at him. An NBA locker room is, by rules, a sanctioned peep show before a game, open for forty-five minutes to anyone with the right pass. If and when in their presence he steps into the Wizards traveling blue and black trunks and jersey, it will be construed as the instant of his passage from the Chicago Bulls, the moment of no return.

But Jordan is not going to give it to them. He wanted this transition to happen in private so he gazed clear through them with a stare he perfected two decades ago. He sat there on the stool in his black satin T-shirt and sunglasses whose light-sensitive lavender lenses are turning charcoal, his eyes dark and occluded. Then his bass voice punctured the silence, gently admonishing a TV cameraman: "Man, no pictures." A stocky security guy reinforced the point. "Hey, get that camera away — he doesn't want any filming."

Finally, Jordan fingered the trunks and jersey. "It's not the Bulls," he murmured of his new uniform, faintly wistful sounding, and then, as if hearing his own voice, quickly added, "But it's not bad."

He rubbed the trunks' fabric some more, looking for a different tone, and then he found it, something more upbeat into which he injects a small snort — part-laugh, part curt assessment. "It's an improvement," he said, meaning the design of the uniform over some old Wizards creation. He rubbed the fabric against a silver bracelet on his wrist. "Not bad — okay."

A couple of journalists entered the room, men who've written flattering things about him since he was young in Chicago. The relationship between the NBA and reporters is generally a symbiotic one. But around Jordan, power flows only one way. Reporters are sharecroppers: they till him only at his pleasure, and in this moment, preoccupied by what awaited him outside, he had nothing to say. The two men leave. Another writer, who had predicted his comeback amid much disdain, sidled up, patted his arm, and said, "I didn't get any apology letters."

"Don't expect any either," Jordan said, unwilling to give this man a morsel tonight either. "You ought to know that."

"Ready?" Grover asked over his shoulder.

"No pictures," the security guard warned again.

Jordan got up from the little stool and took a seat a few feet away on a training table. A Wizards trainer rolled up his trousers and applied a translucent film of conductive jell to the knee; its smell, like Ben-Gay, filled the entire locker room. Jordan, sniffing, leaned his head back. No one talked. Grover's gaze did not leave Jordan's face, as if he was measuring his boss's reactions behind the charcoal shades.

It was a reminder, if anyone needed another, of how everything hinges for the moment on a knee that is nothing more or less than aching. "Hmmmm, hmmmm," Jordan said, and an ultrasound treatment began to increase the knee's blood flow, the trainer wielding a black cylindrical instrument, rubbing the knees with a silver-dollar-sized patch at the tip, making a circular motion, like a man with an electric sander.

The trainer rolled down the cuff and Jordan stood up, breaking the quiet. "Gettin' the feelin', feelin' it now, feelin' it," he said, mock serious, hearing the laughs he wants, letting the sharecroppers till him a little. He took off his sunglasses and smirked, rolling big brown eyes at this scene — the hyper rumpled strangers, the cameras, the hysteria. It's been three years, he observed sideways to a friend, but not much has changed. "Nothing," he added, making this sound like confirmation of what he has intended all along.

"Feelin' it," he called, laughing, and then was gone, to put his uniform on alone apparently in a side room, alone being the milieu he wants, alone meaning only he will know what it looked and felt like when the transformation is complete. The least known secret about Michael Jordan, a close friend had said a week earlier, is that no one takes from him anything he doesn't want taken. His voice echoed from behind a wall. "Feelin' it," he said to no one.

Against the Pistons, he wasn't bad, he wasn't great; somewhere in between, like a mortal, like a thirty-eight-year-old man a full step slower. It will be a microcosm of his preseason and his regular season opener in New York. But no sooner did the game begin than it was interrupted so the giant TV screen at midcourt could show President Bush providing an update of the military campaign in Afghanistan.

The crowd was rapt in a way it seldom gets for politicians, heads craning, while Jordan alternated looking straight ahead at the court and down at the floor. Jordan, who gave away his $1 million salary this year to the relief effort for families of victims, studied the back of his hand. It was not a sign of disrespect but merely one more indication of something decidedly apolitical and task-oriented about him: he is a man, now as in his beginning, almost solely about games.

To this point it had been left to some of his teammates and rivals to step before microphones in arenas and express sympathy for the victims of September 11, as well as appreciation for rescue workers, and a few words about country.

The one time Jordan did talk, before Washington-area firefighters, cops, and their families at a preseason intersquad scrimmage at MCI, he uttered not a word about the tragedy; only saying that he much regretted he would not be playing because his foot bothered him and he had a long season ahead. He didn't want to say that much. He agreed only after an imploring Collins and a Wizards executive, Susan O'Malley, told him that the news of his absence from the scrimmage ought to come from him personally.

It was enough for him once to simply be a relentlessly hardworking, graceful, charismatic, law-abiding demigod, especially in times when the most pressing matters on Americans' minds were O. J. Simpson's trials and the saga of Bill Clinton and Monica Lewinsky. He was the welcomed athlete who did not kick cameramen in the groin or get arrested. It was a low bar to jump over.

But, since September 11, he has appeared somewhat diminished as a transcendent athletic symbol — the sporting metaphor of the moment having become for the moment the team that played across town from Jordan's on Tuesday night, the Yankees, who in their comeback victories have been portrayed as resilient as New York resolved to be. Jordan's political remoteness, a quality that once spoke wholly of Jordan's commitment to sports and winning, now seemed to some to border on a middle-aged man's self-absorption. The world to which Michael Jordan has returned is a very different place.

But so is he changed. In moments when he sounds most passionate now, the man whose late father once said he had a "competition problem" talks not of winning championships but of how he simply loves a game, that getting to the playoffs is a good goal, that he wants to be a teacher, especially to the younger Wizards.

He can be hard on them, as he was, famously so, on so many of his Chicago Bulls teammates. Now and then, he has been combustible, exploding one day during a scrimmage when the NBA's top draft pick, nineteen-year-old Kwame Brown, fresh out of high school, complained that he was brushed and fouled on a drive to the hoop. "You don't get a call on a goddamn touch foul," Jordan seethes, proceeding to question Brown's toughness and manhood. "Get your goddamn ass back on the floor and play, rook' . . . I don't want to hear that ——— out of you again."

Having come to camp overweight and sometimes headstrong, Brown triggered Jordan's ire frequently. One day, the two were playing a casual one-on-one game. Thinking he has a leaning, jabbing Jordan off-balance at one point, Brown dared to say, "You reach, I'll teach."

"You reach," Jordan snapped, "and I'll knock you on your goddamn ass." He was not through, railing at Brown, destroying him through the rest of the game, insisting at the end that Brown stay and call him "Daddy" in front of their teammates — "breaking him down," one person said later, "probably to build him up. But there was a lot of breaking down."

Jordan always has trained special attention on teammates whom he thought needed molding and haranguing. He is always testing somebody, in ways big and small. One evening two nights after the game with Detroit, Tyrone Nesby — brought to the Wizards by Jordan last year but a major disappointment because of temper tantrums that led to his being removed from the team bench during a game — sat down near him in the locker room, looking to hang out.

Jordan was surrounded by an Imelda Marcos–like pile of shoe boxes, all Nikes with his likeness on the instep. Nesby pointed at a pair with mustard-colored trimming that Jordan wore in Detroit. "Those the mustard, Mike?" Nesby asked. "I like 'em."

"You like 'em."

"Yeah."

"You sayin' you're gonna get some of these mustards, T-Nez?"

Something in Jordan's tone already had Nesby off-balance. "Y'all were talkin' about the shoes. Just sayin' I like 'em, like the mustards."

"The mustards are for a starter."

"What, I'm just sayin'."

"You gotta get sixth man shoes."

Nesby tried coming back with his own line, but against Jordan, nobody wins these games either.

The past and present ruler donned his headphones to listen to a CD and turned his attention toward a TV set, where a tape was running of a recent Miami game. Among all the Wizards, only Jordan studied the screen. Across the room, Tyronn Lue and Courtney Alexander discussed the merits of rival hip-hop artists. "I want you to respect him," Lue was saying to Alexander about some rapper.

"That's whack," somebody shouted. Young men guffawed, and

then were gone. Only Jordan remained. He stared at the TV, gently bobbing his head to whatever was on those headphones. He likes popping in Marvin Gaye and Jill Scott before games; half-jokes that if he listened to his teammates rap he might be so amped he would throw up air balls and crazy passes. He's suddenly the older generation. "Old school," as Lue teases.

And then Brown walked by, and he clasped the kid's arm, motioned for him to bend, whispered something in his ear, rubbed his head. He is nothing so much as avuncular these days, quicker to forgive, looking to advise, prone to praising when he can find reason. He regularly awards T-Nez with complimentary fist knocks after big plays, and hugs Alexander during a timeout, after the talented second-year player has shown signs of breaking through a preseason slump.

That leaves only someone in need of talking to him, and so far Collins has comfortably assumed the role, twelve years after having lost his job as coach of the Jordan-led Bulls. "He's so coachable," said Collins. "No one works harder than Michael Jordan. . . . He just wants to get better."

But better at what? To what end? What, if anything, is left for him in a game? Is there still time for a grounded comet to inspire or has America moved on, looking for someone new? In Madison Square Garden the other evening, the crowds cheered Jordan but roared at the mention of heroic firefighters. Jordan waved, looking content just to be there, happiest in his life when he's found a game on a huge stage. That might have to be enough. That might be all there is.

MIKE LUPICA

Recalling Brother's Bravest Hour

FROM THE NEW YORK DAILY NEWS

IT IS A FOOTBALL SUNDAY. The Giants' game, their first home game since September 11, is on the television. So this is a day for the brother to remember football things. All days are hard, he says. You just hope tomorrow will hurt a little less, he says. At least the football things make Chris Suhr smile. He is a kid on the Sundays he remembers. His brother Danny is so very much alive.

"I can hear his voice right now," Chris Suhr said yesterday. "I hear him wondering why the linebacker wasn't over in the flat where he was supposed to be. Why one of those SOBs wasn't covering the tight end closer. That sort of thing. Crying because one of the Giants would miss an assignment and the other team would score."

Chris Suhr is twenty-one months a fireman, no longer considered a rookie, in the department's regular rotation now. His brother Danny was with Engine Company 216, out of Williamsburg, Brooklyn. Danny Suhr was one of the first firemen killed on the morning of September 11, on his way with the rest of his company into tower two when someone who had fallen from tower two, or jumped, landed on top of him. Then Father Mychal Judge, the Fire Department chaplain, was killed after giving Danny Suhr the last rites of the Catholic Church.

We have talked all the time since that day about how firemen and police officers and all the emergency workers are the real heroes of the city. Danny Suhr was always his kid brother's hero, long before he tried to lead everybody into tower two, back when he was No. 90

of James Madison High and No. 90 of the semipro Brooklyn Mariners, and captain of the Fire Department football team until he finally decided he was too old a couple of years ago, a couple of years before he became one of the firemen of the city who died much too young.

"He had that football mentality," Chris Suhr said. "Here I come. Rush the building the way you would the quarterback. He was always ready to go. You couldn't block him and you couldn't stop him. A little over six feet, maybe 250, maybe more. A square box of a guy."

Chris remembers the big game between the Fire Department team and the one from the NYPD back in 1993, remembers the Fire Department being down three touchdowns but then his brother, No. 90, forcing a fumble and making a big interception and bringing them all the way back for a 22–21 win.

"I think it might have been the last time the Fire Department beat them," Chris Suhr said.

These were good football memories for him, good ones, on a football Sunday much too quiet in the apartment. Chris Suhr said, "He loved the Giants, but he loved football more." This fall Danny Suhr, once All-City for Madison, had agreed to be a volunteer assistant coach at South Shore High for his old Madison teammate, Tom Salvato. The two Suhr brothers even played together in a touch-football league over on Randall's Island.

The Fire Department games were in the spring, Baker Field at Columbia sometimes, sometimes at St. John's. The Brooklyn Mariners played in the fall, on Saturdays usually. Danny Suhr played inside linebacker, some tight end. Sometimes he would be so sore the next day that he would get on the couch at the family's home on East Nineteenth in Brooklyn, between Avenue R and Avenue S, St. Edmund's Parish, and stay there all afternoon watching pro football, the Giants and Jets both. Yelling about the coverage. Sometimes calling plays before they even happened.

"He was always the most advanced football guy in the room," his brother said yesterday. "He was great, my brother."

They all came in a hurry on Engine 216, on streets Danny Suhr knew around the World Trade Center because he used to go pick up his wife Nancy when she worked downtown. Nancy: the girl he'd fallen in love with when he was in the eighth grade and she was in the seventh, with whom he opened N&D Pizza, for Nancy and Danny, on Avenue U and Twenty-ninth. When he had gotten the call in Williamsburg he had left her a message, telling her he was on his way to the World Trade Center, and that he loved her; that he would see her later.

The engine pulled up near tower two and then No. 90 of Madison High and all his other teams, the square box of a guy, the linebacker who always wanted to be first to the quarterback or the ball, was running to get ahead of the other guys, wanting to be first in, probably thinking this was the fire of all their lives, until a part of the sky fell on him and killed him.

"He was everything on a football field except real fast," Pudgie Walsh, Danny Suhr's old coach with the Brooklyn Mariners and with the FDNY team, said yesterday. "He had to pick that day to be fast."

Danny Suhr was fast from the back step of Engine 216 on the eleventh of September. There were people inside who needed him.

"If my brother had somehow known that one of them in the company might have to die, over there trying to save people's lives, he would have said, 'I gotta go,'" Chris Suhr said. "He would have done what he did, called Nancy, and then he would have gone, never really believing this thing could stop him, either."

Chris Suhr has been working out of Rockaway, expects to be back soon with Engine Company 280 in Brooklyn. He was on vacation the morning of September 11 when he heard what had happened downtown. He got down there as soon as he could and when he did, he started to hear rumors about what had happened, not finding out for sure that his brother was gone until late in the afternoon.

"He wanted to save lives," Chris Suhr said. "And he did. The guys in his company are alive today because they were trying to give him CPR in the ambulance."

Chris Suhr said that before September 11, he and his brother made sure to attend line-of-duty funerals for firemen together. He said that as sad as those occasions were, they were also occasions of pride for both of them, and a chance to spend a few hours together, at a time in both their lives when that had become more difficult, even if they both still thought they had all the time in the world. They would both be in their dress uniforms, two big young guys from Brooklyn, the Suhr brothers, Chris a miniature version of Danny, side by side, honoring the family business, and maybe each other.

"Now I had to put on that uniform for him," Chris Suhr said. "And I have to keep putting it on for funerals, knowing he's not coming.

"You would have liked him," the brother said. "Everybody did." He went back to watching the football game, the only other voices in the room belonging to the announcers.

MIKE BIANCHI

Nightmare Is Real for Mourners

FROM THE ORLANDO SENTINEL

WHAT MUST THEY HAVE been thinking as they filed into the memorial service Thursday and saw the sad faces with faraway eyes and heard the wistful music and smelled the fatal fragrance of funeral flowers?

Would this all be for them someday too soon?

Dale Earnhardt died in a race car a couple of months before his fiftieth birthday. And there sat Jeff Gordon, twenty-nine, somber-faced in a church pew. Was he contemplating his own mortality? Would he make it to thirty? Adam Petty died last year in a race car. He never made it to twenty.

And what was Dale Jarrett thinking as Earnhardt's widow, Teresa, made her way to the front of the church? She turned toward where the other drivers sat, blew a kiss, and tearfully whispered the words, "Thank you." One wrong swerve, one twitched nerve, one treacherous curve, and couldn't that just as easily be Jarrett's wife, Kelley, standing on trembling legs in front of a roomful of forlorn friends?

And what was Michael Waltrip thinking as he watched twelve-year-old Taylor Earnhardt trying to hold back tears, trying to be brave, trying to figure out why God took her daddy away? Was Waltrip wondering if he would be there to give away his own little girls — Caitlin Marie and Margaret Carol — at their weddings?

These are the morose reflections racers contemplate when they attend the funeral of a friend. Which is why they rarely do. There were a handful of Winston Cup drivers at Earnhardt's memorial ceremony Thursday, but there were many more who weren't there.

Earnhardt would have understood the mass truancy. He, too, refused to go to funerals. You have to understand racers. They are trained not to think about dying. That's why they avoid funerals as if they were clogged carburetors. It hurts them to see the survivors suffer; reminds them too much of their own families.

Why do you think it is drivers always carry their young kids to the car with them just before the beginning of every race? Why do you think the last thing they do before they hit the ignition switch is hug their children and kiss their wives? Because, deep down, they know. They know every time they get into a race car that they might have to be cut out of it.

And now, they really know. Because if the indestructible Earnhardt can be put into an early grave, they all can. If Earnhardt must walk through the valley of the shadow of death, nobody is immune. To achieve anything in racing, you must navigate that nebulous line between danger and disaster. It's like English racer Jackie Stewart once said, "In my line of work, the fastest are too often listed among the deadest."

Earnhardt's death finally began to set in Thursday for many fans who have been holding impromptu vigils since the fatal crash of their hero Sunday in the Daytona 500. In the aftermath of a tragedy, the optimists always say, "At least the sun's going to come up in the morning." Appropriately, it didn't Thursday in North Carolina.

The dank, dreary day seemed an appropriate climax to a sunless, joyless week. Raindrops mixed with teardrops. Shivering fans stood outside the invitation-only ceremony and cried out whatever tears they had left.

"I think this weather is God's way of saying the world is a cold and lonely place without Dale Earnhardt," says Terry Wright, who made the trek from Trenton, New Jersey.

Inside the church, the ceremony is ending, and fellow drivers file out one by one by one.

They are ashen-faced, as if they've just seen a ghost.

Or worse:

Maybe they've just seen themselves.

GENE WOJCIECHOWSKI

Last Call

FROM ESPN.COM

I'VE COVERED SUPER BOWLS, Final Fours, Wimbledon, the U.S. Open, NBA Finals, pennant drives, the four Majors, the Monaco Grand Prix, NHL playoffs, and the Summer Games. I've played hoops with and against Michael Jordan, lost a Nassau bet at Pebble Beach to the owner of America's worst golf swing, Charles Barkley, had Reggie Jackson and Ryne Sandberg threaten to pummel me, had Bobby Bowden fall asleep on my shoulder while riding in the back of a Florida Highway Patrol car. I've sat at the knee of John Wooden and Gene Mauch, sat on the couch as Bill Walton immersed himself in Deadhead tunes, sat in disbelief as Tiger Woods hit balata so far I'd need two Lasik surgeries to track the ball.

I've seen some stuff.

But nothing — not Larry Bird Night at the old Boston Garden, not Christian Laettner's shot to beat Kentucky, not watching the Final Four–bound Utah Utes dancing fully clothed in a shower — beats a November afternoon I spent with Al McGuire in 1991.

McGuire died last Friday in the wee hours, which figures, since he was always big on last calls. The funeral Mass is tonight at Gesu Church in Milwaukee and the place will be packed like a Marquette-DePaul game. Father Robert A. Wild, president of Marquette University, will give the homily and McGuire's old friend, U.S. Senator Herb Kohl, also will say a few words. There will be tears, but only because McGuire isn't around to tell the crowd to knock it off.

McGuire was too busy during life to waste much time thinking about death. When the legendary Adolph Rupp of Kentucky died,

McGuire didn't bother with the memorial service. "I bought him a bottle of bourbon that he liked," he said. When Utah coach Rick Majerus, a former Marquette player and assistant, faced septuplet coronary bypass surgery in 1990, McGuire never called. Why bother? If Majerus spun in, he spun in. A sobbing phone call wouldn't change fate.

"I don't go to funerals because I bought you a drink while you were alive," he said that day in '91. "Anyway, the crowd at a funeral is governed by the weather."

My ballpoint pen couldn't move fast enough across the notebook pages. McGuire never stopped talking. It was stream of unconsciousness stuff, something about "The most expensive thing is cheap labor," or, "It's only important to win in war and surgery," or, "Behind every bum on every street corner in America is a woman." He was the first basketball coach I'd ever met who used all twenty-six letters in the alphabet, not just the *X*s and *O*s. "I wasn't different," he said. "I was ahead of my time. I still am."

We drove around town in some late-model Buick, stopping once at a Waukesha mom-and-pop antique and doll shop. He tossed the car keys on the driver's side floor mat.

"You going to leave those there?" I said.

"Someone steals this car and they get the black plague," he said.

There on one of the store walls was a framed NBC-issued eight-by-ten glossy of McGuire in his network blazer. But you should have seen him that day as he puttered around the shop looking for toy soldiers: his hair was a mess and he was still recovering from a recent hernia operation.

"I only comb my hair if there are four people in the room, and if there are four people, I'm getting paid," he said.

McGuire walked away from Marquette twenty-four years ago with a 295–80 record, an NCAA championship, and an NIT championship (when it still meant something). Roundball — that's what he called it — was a moment, "a nice moment, but just a moment." That's probably why he gave away all two hundred watches he got for winning assorted games, including his 1977 NCAA Championship timepiece. He spent the rest of his life tooling around on his Harley, providing network TV with the best color analysis and post-game dances of all time, and traveling to Williston, North Dakota, for no other reason than to say he was there. McGuire would ask for directions to a city's bus depot, and then find the closest bar. "Good jukeboxes and sad, nostalgic country songs," he said.

McGuire died last Friday in the wee hours at age seventy-two. And even though he never let basketball define him as a person, he understood the imprint it made. "The best thing to happen to me is that it allowed me to be called 'Coach,'" he said in the Buick. "That's something non-negotiable."

Two things stick with me as I remember McGuire: that he was wrong about funerals and weather, and that those two Oklahoma State players are getting a hell of a coach.

ADAM SCHEFTER

Seeing the Light

FROM THE DENVER POST

THE HITS THEY HAVE TAKEN over the years are as different as the makeup of the two men.

Desmond Clark's hits have come on the football field, where he has developed into one of the Broncos' building blocks, among the best young tight ends in the game.

His father Paul's hits have come from crack cocaine pipes, in a maddening world only hard-core addicts can know.

The hits Paul Clark took on the streets of Lakeland, Florida, were an odd and disturbing juxtaposition. They were lively and deadly, at the same time. They cost him his savings, his marriage, his vision.

Even when his father was broken, little Desmond would wander Lakeland's streets, into its crack houses, just to visit the man who helped mold him.

Inside, they sat and talked and bonded, like any father and son. And eventually the conversation would come back to where they left off.

"He would tell me to hold that lighter right there for him," Desmond Clark said, sticking out his right hand and imitating the motion he used back in the day, from the time he was twelve years old until he was fifteen.

And young Desmond would. He would light the flame, touch it to his father's crack pipe, and watch Paul Clark's eyes open wider and wider, as if he were being supplied a rush of oxygen.

"Then once he faded off," Desmond said, "I faded out. Got myself out of there."

Until the next time. Desmond would return to visit his father regularly, as much a fixture in Lakeland's crack houses as any drug dealer. But any time any one of those dealers ever tried to approach Desmond about joining their team, as they inevitably did, Paul Clark stepped right in.

"I told them, 'Get away from him,'" Paul said. "They were not going to get near him."

Paul Clark recognized talents in Desmond that other children did not have. Desmond raced go-carts faster than anyone in the neighborhood, danced better than anyone not named Michael Jackson, worked harder than any person could expect. Which did not surprise his father.

Paul Clark always preached to his son what his grandfather had preached to him: if you don't work, you don't eat. So young Desmond would mow grass, lay tile, pick oranges, do anything to pad his pockets.

Eventually, part-time jobs turned into more regular ones. When Desmond advanced to Lakeland's Kathleen High School, he became a dishwasher in a Chinese restaurant, grasping the true meaning of overtime. When he enrolled at Wake Forest, he became a waiter in a steak house, with hands large enough to palm the restaurant's largest serving tray.

Desmond listened to his father, but he did not follow him. He did his own thing. And the jobs he held formed the foundation of the work ethic he drew upon to become Denver's top pass-catching tight end, the successor to Shannon Sharpe.

"I knew that boy was going to be somebody, and I always told him that," Paul Clark said.

Paul Clark was right. It's just too bad he never got a chance to see it.

From the moment he put a pinch of crack cocaine in his cigarette and smoked it in November 1984, Paul Clark was an addict.

"Thought that was the best thing I ever did," Paul Clark said. "Best high ever. It was. Hooked right away. Wanted to feel that effect over and over."

The cost, as exorbitant as it turned out to be, did not matter. Paul Clark found something that became his sustenance.

At all hours of any day, Paul Clark could be found in Lakeland's crack houses, inhaling the fumes that made his mind dance and his body come alive. Paul Clark was so high for so long he couldn't see the world around him changing.

He couldn't see how his wife, Rena, had no choice but to end their marriage and fend for the couple's five children on her own in a fatherless household.

He couldn't see how the long hours he used to put in laying tile to make money slowly changed into wasteful hours in which he smoked his earnings.

The last thing Paul Clark saw as he stood outside a crack house on Fifth Street in Lakeland on October 17, 1989, in another altered and hazy state, was a series of pellets fired from a shotgun. He recognized the sight.

Twice before, while he was on a high or coming down from one, Paul Clark had been shot. The first time came in 1983 in the right hand. The second time came in 1986 in the right leg, left middle finger, and groin area. Surgery was required to remove those bullets.

The batch of BBs were fired from the gun of a man whose bicycle Paul Clark said he had borrowed without permission. The man retrieved the bike from the crack house and took it home to get his shotgun and revenge. Once the pellets began flying, most lodged themselves in Clark's right eye. Others ricocheted off a tree and lodged themselves in his left eye.

Clark fell to the ground, bleeding and blinded. He was rushed to a hospital in Lakeland, then transported by helicopter to an eye trauma center in Tampa. There the determination was made.

Paul Clark truly could not see. Nor would he ever again.

To Paul Clark, Desmond always will look the way he did the last time he saw him in 1989. Desmond was a twelve-year-old, five-foot-ten, 150-pound boy, nowhere near the six-foot-three, 250-pound man he is today.

But then, Paul Clark also is different these days, too. On June 6, 1994, Paul Clark smoked crack for the last time.

"Had made up my mind to quit," Paul Clark said. "Had to. It wasn't my willpower that did it. It was that I was desperate to do anything I could to stop."

Since then, he has begun work as a part-time counselor for Narcotics Anonymous, helping people as helpless as he once was. On a recent trip to Denver, Paul Clark delivered a lecture at the Narcotics Anonymous on the west side of the city.

He has landed a job with Tropical Star, a seafood distribution company in Lakeland. During work days as regular as the one he once had when he was repairing homes and laying tile, Paul Clark makes boxes that transport the fish, always trying to ensure they are as sturdy as the life he believes he has rebuilt.

He remarried two years ago, settled into a new home in Lakeland, all while renewing a strong friendship with his former wife and her second husband.

"My problem is arrested," Paul Clark said. "But once an addict, always an addict. If I smoke that stuff again, I'll be out there again. That's why I go to meetings and try to give back. I give back so I can keep what I've got."

There is one other significant change in his life. His son has become a somebody, graduating to the NFL, giving Paul Clark a Sunday high better than any he ever has felt.

Each Sunday, Paul Clark is driven fifteen miles to Plant City, Florida, to his father Edward Buchanan's home, which is equipped with Direct TV and the capability to see every Broncos game. While the gathering watches Desmond, Paul Clark — a former high school defensive end and kicker — listens to each game and visualizes it in his mind.

And after each game, he calls his son and their conversations are instant replays.

"How many catches?" Paul Clark will ask.

Then, "How many yards?"

Then, "How many touchdowns?"

Lately, there are more and more. Clark already has established career highs, with 45 catches for 529 yards and 4 touchdowns. Sometimes, Paul Clark does more than hear about it. He feels it.

Last Sunday, he sat in the fourth level of Miami's Pro Player Stadium as the Broncos and Dolphins squared off. Midway through the third quarter, Paul Clark felt his neighbors stand, his section shake, and the cheers multiply. He didn't even have to ask his friends what had happened. He knew. Desmond had caught a four-yard touchdown pass.

"Makes me feel good, just being in the stadium with him," Paul Clark said.

"Makes me feel good having him there with me," Desmond Clark said.

This is what makes their bond as strong as muscle. As different as their histories and dispositions are, their blood is the same. They talk about everything. They hold back nothing. They do it regularly.

"They're so close, they're more like brothers than father and son," said Desmond's wife, Denise, who struggles to imagine the pictures from her father-in-law's former life. "They're truly pals."

Desmond's pal always is looking out for him even if he can't look out at him. For years, whenever Paul Clark would grab Desmond's arm to be walked around, he would always comment to his boy how little his arms felt.

Muscle up, he would instruct his son. Get bigger, he would order his boy.

Then last year, before another football season and during another visit in Denver, Paul Clark latched on to Desmond's arms and froze.

"Hold on," Paul Clark said, rubbing Desmond's biceps. "Your arms have a little size to them."

No doubt. The arms, not to mention the soul, are big enough to absorb any hit any defense dishes out.

RICK TELANDER

Making Their Points

FROM THE CHICAGO SUN-TIMES

ON TUESDAY, a young man named Dajuan Wagner scored one hundred points in a game, the first time a U.S. boys high school player had reached the century mark since 1979.

There was a lot of tongue-clucking about that display because, you know, not all of Wagner's one hundred points were needed.

Indeed, Wagner's school, Camden (New Jersey) High, beat Gloucester Township Technical School 157–67. So only eleven of Wagner's points would have sufficed for a victory.

Then we find out that on the same night, many miles away, a young man named Cedrick Hensley scored 101 points for Heritage Christian Academy of Texas City, Texas, in a 178–28 evisceration of Banff Christian School of Tomball, Texas.

Maybe it was Turn the Other Cheek Night for Banff. Who knows? But none of Hensley's points was necessary to send the Banff players home like flogged pilgrims.

Naturally, questions about sportsmanship came up. But they were dispelled like so many cattle gnats by Heritage Christian coach Jerome Tang.

According to the Associated Press, Tang urged Hensley to go for triple digits because, "He's having a surgical procedure done on Friday, and he will be out for about a week and a half."

Good thing Hensley wouldn't be out for a month. Tang might have had him go for three hundred.

"After he had fifty at the half," Tang said, "the kids said, 'We think we can get him one hundred.' They wanted to do this for him, and they sacrificed so that their teammate could accomplish something special."

Love that coach-speak.

Sacrifice. Something special.

But why go into the jargon at all?

Scoring one hundred points isn't that big a deal.

Hell, I've done it. Yes, I have.

Let me set the stage. It's the McGuane Park six-foot-and-under league in either 1974 or 1975. I'm playing for Henry's Sports & Bait Shop, a team made up of local Bridgeporters and a few of my football buddies from Northwestern. Our jerseys are reversible yellow and green and feature the proud logo of a man fishing in silhouette.

The old gym is so small that the games are four-on-four and the bench players have to stand. Spectators look in through the doorways. To take the ball out of bounds, you have to put your foot on the wall.

I'm a trifle taller than six-one, but I'm the shortest Henry's player on the floor at times. I don't want to name names, but Mark Krumptinger has to be six-two, and Frank Lutostanski is a whisker under six-three. But it's Bridgeport. There are various ways to measure.

We're playing Seemo's Schnozzles, and — how can I put this gently? — the Schnozzles are not in basketball shape. I'm pretty sure they are, well, let's say they've been visiting a tavern. Plus, they're all shorter than six feet.

At the half, Henry's is ahead something like 85–10, and we're all in double figures. What do we do to keep from being bored?

We look at the scorebook.

"Let's get somebody one hundred," somebody says.

I offer to be that person — my sacrifice, coach Tang — and away we go.

I had about thirty at the half, but now Henry's got serious. I didn't play defense, hovered at midcourt, took every outlet pass, and fired away. Nobody on Henry's shot except me, and every offensive rebound came flying back to me so that I felt like Kobe Bryant (who wasn't born yet) in his most orgasmic dream.

Still, I wasn't scoring fast enough, so I moved to the free-throw line. Then under the basket. Every now and then, a player would yell to the scorer, "What's he at?" It would take a while for the guy to calculate.

"Sixty-two."

Then later, "Seventy-nine."

By the time he said it, I had even more.

My lack of defense didn't matter. The Schnozzles, lurching and nauseous, were a team of self-checkers. They seemed to lose interest even in guarding me.

I don't want to say my arm got tired but it got numb. When the horn sounded, the scorer added up the little *X*s that ran all over the page.

A hundred and eight, he said. "Or 107."

Were there any snoopy press members around, wanting to know whether Henry's had poured it on in an ugly display of vanity, cheapness, and downright cruelty?

No.

Was there anybody there to ask me whether I felt big now, like a real man?

No.

Did the Schnozzles mind?

I don't think they knew.

In fact, if anyone was harmed, it was me.

"They ran the clock straight through at the end," said Joe Zigulich, one of my teammates. "You were robbed."

Did my life change because of hitting a hundred?

I think so, but I'm not sure how. Other than buying all the beers that night.

ART THIEL

No Angst in All-Star Ichiro

FROM THE SEATTLE POST-INTELLIGENCER

AFTER WATCHING HIM for just a half-season, here is the one true thing about Ichiro Suzuki, besides — but not apart from — his arm, speed, batting average, All-Star votes, faint sideburns, and right-sleeve tug:

Fearlessness.

As a rookie from a baseball nation that had never exported a position player, Ichiro walked over to major league baseball and put his foot on its throat.

Pedro Martinez, Yankee Stadium, cross-country travel, gut-bomb fast food, teammates with two new languages . . . none of it has mattered.

From the first game, Ichiro became the best player on the best team, a team chasing history as well as a championship. For an almost jockey-sized player who employs the one-hundred-foot single as his primary weapon, Ichiro's absence of apprehension has been a wonder but not much of a mystery — he's the first rookie in All-Star Game history to lead fan balloting.

Not that he was always cool.

In a recent clubhouse interview, via longtime interpreter Hide Sueyoshi, Ichiro remembered a time of baseball dread — his first All-Star Game in Japan in 1994.

"When I was first selected, I was barely recognized by fans," he said. "I remember starting to hit .400 just before the vote ended, and I barely made it as the third outfielder.

"I played left field, and the first batter up hit a fly ball to me. I was so nervous. I wasn't sure how I caught it, but I did.

"Back then, I wasn't sure of my abilities."

Nervous and unsure. Two qualities no major-leaguer has seen from him.

"Ichiro has answered every call," said Mariners manager Lou Piniella. "He's answered every question. He's been very focused. He plays as hard as anyone. And he's got great talent. He's a full package."

Talent wasn't as much a question as was his approach to the big, bad world of American ball. The conventional assumption was of a learning curve, an adjustment time, a graduation of expectations.

Wrong.

Right away, he was his own man, unflinchingly putting himself on his own spot.

He told Piniella he wasn't hitting third in the lineup, as the manager was considering. Nor would his unorthodox swing be altered for the allegedly more powerful major league pitchers. Nor would he demonstrate in spring training his ability to pull the ball to right field, despite Piniella's insistence, which led to this surprising retort on the field.

"I'm just setting 'em up," Ichiro said, referring to opposing pitchers. "No problem."

Teammate Al Martin was nearby and heard the exchange.

"I couldn't believe he said that," Martin told *Baseball Weekly*. "Come on. Nobody is that good. This isn't some little league. You just don't walk into your first spring training, hang around everyone, and set people up.

"I'm sorry, it doesn't work that way."

On the other hand . . .

Ichiro hit .336 in April, .379 in May and .348 in June. For most of the season he has been at or near the top of the AL leaders in hits, runs, average, at-bats, stolen bases, and singles that miss fielding leather by an inch. He is a threat to break one of baseball's longest-standing single-season records — the 257 hits of George Sisler in 1920.

So, contrary to Martin's conventional view, apparently it does work that way for a few players.

Or maybe one.

Another aspect of Ichiro's almost flawless transition has been how much more pleasant his day is at major league parks, where he is free of opponents' harassment.

"I can't even compare it," he said. "I mean, my feelings in coming to the ballpark are astronomically higher than when I was in Japan. I'm so happy to come here."

He said the difference is a long story. In Japan, some managers and players will harass Ichiro and top hitters as the pitcher releases the ball or as the batter begins a swing. Even catchers get into the act.

He recalled one episode in which former major-leaguer Troy Neel became so frustrated with the tactic that after a swing he reached back and grabbed the catcher, threatening to hit him.

"Here, players respect each other," Ichiro said. "At the plate, players on the other team do not bother the hitter. So far, I haven't seen anybody bother hitters. I hear my team cheering me, but I don't hear other players giving me a hard time.

"I understand why Troy was upset. There's a lot of harassment like that. In Japan, I had despair in going to the ballpark. As I got better, it got worse, but it depended on the opposing manager.

"That's just one of the ways I feel there is more respect for the game and for players here."

Ichiro is savoring his American experience. Though winning speaks for itself, pressure — from media as well as opponents — has lessened, believe it or not. Even though more than twenty credentials are issued to Japanese media for the average home game, Ichiro has arranged to speak only to one Japanese pool reporter after most games, in deference to the potential for clubhouse disruption.

Local reporters usually get a few minutes, but because translated quotes are often not as good, he is sometimes ignored. Ichiro understands and speaks more English than he lets on, but for the first year, language has been a useful buffer for someone who feels little need to further explain himself.

"As players, most of us want some of the spotlight, at least in Japan," he said. "From time to time, players get TV highlights and attention, and that's fine.

"But the media tend to overrate an individual player. In Japan, I got overrated. Other players were doing good jobs, but the focus was on me. I don't like to see that here."

Unfortunately for him, the individual and team successes have made him a national sports phenomenon in just three months. The media love phenoms, and Monday and Tuesday represent

Ichiro's first substantive introduction to the nation. He will be figuratively poked and prodded by writers who have not seen him in person, and other players will be eager to meet him for the first time.

What they will find, according to Yankees and AL All-Star manager Joe Torre, is beyond media rhetoric.

"A lot of times when you hear advance notice on players, they fail to live up to expectations," Torre said yesterday. "He goes far beyond his notices. He makes things happen for his team. He's a terrific defensive player, he runs the bases, and he'll have the home crowd for his first All-Star Game.

"I'm not supposed to give out my starting lineup yet, but I think I have a pretty good idea who's going to lead off."

As fellow All-Star Ivan Rodriguez, teammate of Texas' $252 million man, Alex Rodriguez, put it this week:

"Right now, he's the best player in the big leagues."

So the recognition is building toward what it was in Japan. However unsettling that may be to Ichiro, the virtues of Tuesday outweigh the liabilities.

"The All-Star Game is a stage for all the good players to get together," he said. "In terms of excitement, my first time selected in Japan, and the first time here, is on the same level. When I was first selected, I was so excited, I was overwhelmed.

"As years went by, I wondered what the significance was of the game. Many players declined to participate. But here, there are thirty clubs and so many good players, there's real value and significance."

So far, all of the forecasted obstacles — culture, food, travel, pitching — have been manageable, in part because Ichiro has no fear of any of it. But, he said, "there is no place to apply the word 'easy' in any of this."

His only problem?

"Day games. Usually, there is no pregame workout. I feel those days are difficult to prepare myself. I have to work out to prevent injuries."

A signal accomplishment of his half-season has been clubhouse survival. His locker is just a few stalls away from Jay Buhner, team wise guy.

As the designated abuser (albeit good-natured) of newcomers,

Buhner is a baseball staple who must be dealt with just as much as an earhole fastball from Roger Clemens. Ichiro quickly adapted.

"I just pretend to laugh," he said, "even though I don't understand the joke."

Ichiro smiled, something he does a lot more in the clubhouse than on the field.

He knows he gets set up in the clubhouse. He also knows he has set up the rest of major league baseball.

SCOTT OSTLER

Don't Go All Rasheed About This

FROM THE SAN FRANCISCO CHRONICLE

IN *Good Will Hunting,* Will's buddies give him a beat-up car for his twenty-first birthday. Will's best friend has been the group's wheel man. He plays off the gift, guy style, by telling Will, "I'm not going to Al Cowlings you around forever."

The reference being to O. J. Simpson's pal who chauffeured the Juice on the low-speed Bronco chase.

I hadn't realized how many sports-people references have crept into everyday conversation until I overheard two guys talking in a bar.

Pass me that bowl of bar snacks, dude. Don't Kobe 'em.

Don't have a Shaq attack, man. There's plenty. Say, how's your girlfriend?

She Tie Domi'd me.

No kidding? A blind-side cheap shot.

Yeah, she just went all Rasheed on me last night. Completely berserk. I had to eject her from my house. She was throwing things at me — bottles, candles, whatever. Fortunately, she was doing a Rick Ankiel.

What's she so 'Sheed off about?

She accused me of Al Davis-ing her.

That figures, knowing you. You just can't make a long-term commitment, can you?

Hell yes, I can. I'm an honorable guy. I just can't keep it. But what about her? She said she wanted to be my girlfriend for life, but couldn't commit to that unless I bought her a new car to prove I love her.

Sheffield city. Hey, is it true that she found out about you and the young chick in the hot tub?

Yeah, she laid a big Chmura trip on me. She doesn't realize the courage it took for me to come clean about that incident.

Courage? She found the Polaroids, dude. You're playin' out of control, Mr. Jason Williams [the Grizzlies guard].

You might be right. Still, it's a blow. It was great for a while, then another Mickelson finish. How's your girlfriend?

She played the George Karl card, whined that I didn't respect her, didn't give her enough attention. So we broke up a while back, but now she's Jordaning me.

Really? She's teasing you about coming back? That's good, right? She is a cutie.

She's also a Flutie.

You still have a Jones for taller women, eh?

Yeah, I guess you could say I have a "Too Tall" Jones.

How about that boss of yours? Still giving you a hard time?

Rod Smart.

He hate you, eh?

Yeah, ever since I started telling people I was bored with the job and probably would jump to another company the first chance I got.

Well, sure he's cranky if you're C-Webbing the man.

He gets on my nerves. He's a tyrant. Son of Steinbrenner. I'd like to Spre the dude.

Don't go there, girlfriend. If you Spre'd him, he'd just Bobby Knight you right back, and you'd both wind up with Merton Hanks neck. What's the deal, isn't he happy with your work?

He is, when I manage to show up. I've been late a lot, but it's not my fault. Why is it that scientists can put a man on the moon but they can't develop a reliable alarm clock?

Ah, so you been Isaiah Rider-ing. And bringing in high-quality alibis, I hope.

The best. My hamster died. I stopped to rescue orphans from a burning liquor store. Martians stole my sparkplugs. Original stuff. But every excuse I throw in this guy's direction, he Dikembes back at me. Today, he called me into his office and Tyson'd my ears. Said he was expecting more for all the money he's paying me, said I was A-Rodding him. He gave me a royal Aikman.

You gotta learn to Canseco that stuff, just let it bounce off your head and over the fence. Look, I sympathize with you, pal. I know that's a very hard job you've got.

Hard? On the hardness scale, it's between Shaq's free throws and Kobe's ear studs. If I ran into my boss right here in the bar, I'd Barkley his butt right through that window.

Maybe you should find another job. Have you checked out the want ads?

Can't. I never get my newspaper anymore. The delivery guy Knoblauchs the *Chronicle* onto my roof or into the puddle every day.

You're on a losing streak, dude. Maybe you should go the Tony Muser route.

Pray less and drink more? I'm thinking of giving that a try, old boy. Say, do you think you could give me a lift home? I'm a little tipsy.

I'm not surprised. We ordered about ten shooters and I didn't have any. You took all the shots. You Iverson'd me.

So Al Davis me.

No, I'm not going to sue you. I'm going to Al Cowlings your rear end home.

STEVE HUMMER

We All Have Some Inner Daly, but Most of Us Suppress It

FROM THE ATLANTA JOURNAL-CONSTITUTION

THERE IS A LITTLE John Daly in every male. Kings or tramps, no matter, little John calls out to us all at one time or another.

He is the voice inside that wants to tell the surgeon general to relax and enjoy some cool menthol satisfaction. It wants to says things like, "What this petting zoo needs is a good cigar bar."

The Daly within maintains that M&Ms have to be the perfect food, because they obviously contain twice the normal amount of Vitamin M.

He is the self-destructive impulse, the wild hair, the one-for-the-road reflex.

John Daly wears the Hippo brand name on his sleeve. His golf bag is emblazoned with the slogan, "Grip it and rip it." He and his caddie cupped enough cigarettes during Friday's long round to keep Belgrade supplied for a weekend. To this package we are inevitably drawn. He is the guilty pleasure we cannot deny.

The Daly Show is hot once again at Sugarloaf after his 3-under-69 opening statement. No matter that he has not won since the 1995 British Open or that he hasn't been among the top one hundred money winners on the PGA Tour since 1998, or that he missed sixteen cuts in twenty-six events last year. The least hint of success still draws the biggest, loudest throngs.

When he made his turn at 3-under, the course tipped his way. When he canned an eight-foot putt for birdie on his tenth hole — Sugarloaf's No. 1 — the hooting increased. When he hit the flagstick with his next shot, to the par-three No. 2, a little hoedown broke out.

"The fans have been great no matter where I've been," Daly said. "It's nice to play decent golf for them for a change. They've hung in there, through the ups and the downs. A lot of them relate to what I've been through. And I can relate to them. I think we have a sort of friendship."

For as much as Daly has abused himself, the fact that he is alive is reason to cheer. His trying to rebuild a career is an irresistible story. Daly might contend, he might shoot 90 today — there are no givens here. That's another part of the draw, the wild unpredictability to his game.

This has not be an altogether happy week for Daly. He is facing a Masters-free April, and feeling rather snubbed.

"Kind of makes me feel the two majors that I did win (PGA and British Open) don't seem to mean anything to committees and stuff anymore," he said. "That hurts my ego a little bit. I've always been gracious to the members and the people at Augusta. . . . It's my favorite tournament to play."

He just has to understand in the Masters rules there is no such heading as "Screw-up Exemption."

If he accomplishes nothing else this week, perhaps Daly can continue his trend of introducing some consistency to his game. His best finishes of ninth and eleventh so far this season represent a modest gain. Daly hasn't careened into such episodes as taking a 14 on the eighteenth hole at Pebble Beach (2000 U.S. Open) or six-putting from eight feet (1999 Memorial).

Just hold it together, big guy. Daly said he has even cut down his driver by an inch and a half to trade some distance for control. "When I get in the tee box, I feel like I'm going to hit a fairway. Last year, it was just hit it and hope I hit a fairway," he said.

"I've got to get myself in that position (to win) more in order to feel the heat and get used to it again. It's just been forever since that's happened."

You have to wish him well in the search for control, because for every man, it is a constant battle to suppress the Daly within.

STEVE RUSHIN

Cold Comfort

FROM SPORTS ILLUSTRATED

THE ALARM CLOCK beeps like a truck in reverse, and your heart begins to hammer the drum riff from "Wipeout," and your backpack hangs in rebuke from the bedpost, filled as it is with undone homework. Dread sets in until you see — through a crack in the curtains — a world outside covered in snow, as thick and muffling as fiberglass insulation.

So you bound downstairs to hear a radio anchor read the alphabetical list of school closings. The tension, as he nears the *N*s, is almost unbearable: "Maple Grove, Maple Plain, Maplewood" — it reminds you of a roller coaster ratcheting up a hill. Then it crests — he gets to *N* — and you hear "Nativity of Mary, closed." Instantly it's Mardi Gras and V-E Day and the Lindbergh parade all in one, and the flakes falling outside look like ticker tape.

You are a death-row inmate reprieved by the governor, and you'll relish every minute of this stolen Tuesday. You'll take your hockey skates in to be sharpened, the blades throwing off sparks like a welder's torch, and then carve up the neighbors' flooded backyard, your wrist shots made wicked by the boomerang curve of your Sher-Wood stick. You'll clear the ice every ten minutes by skating with a shovel in ever-tightening ovals — because your fondest desire, at age eleven, is someday to drive a Zamboni.

When you take off your skates, after hours of impersonating Mike Bossy, you'll feel a full foot shorter. Then you'll go inside and have hot cocoa warmed on the same stove-top burner on which you curved the Sher-Wood.

Your best friend will walk past your window dressed in his snowmobile suit, and you'll pop outside and pack a snowball and rear back with a windup like Juan Marichal's and peg him in the conk from sixty feet away. Then you'll duck behind a tree that looks — like every other tree on the block — as if it has been dipped in white chocolate. You will vow to build a fort, an impregnable igloo stocked with snowballs, from which you will conduct guerrilla raids on every other fort in the neighborhood, and by day's end you will rule your block like a raja.

After lunch your back yard will become Lambeau Field or Soldier Field or Rich Stadium in a whiteout. When your quarterback throws, with his unmittened hand, a bomb that you'll catch near the sideline, you'll high-step in moon boots into the end zone and then Nestea-plunge onto your back, and while lying there a moment to catch your breath, you will make a snow angel in celebration.

You will be so cold that you'll pull your parka hood with the fake-fur fringe up over your genuine replica Vikings helmet. (Come Sunday, while you're watching, from in front of the fireplace, some football game in Miami or Tampa or Los Angeles, you'll look at all those players and fans in their short sleeves and suntans and simply feel sorry for them.)

Back in the house, while your wet woolen socks are somersaulting in the dryer, Larry Bird will play Dr. J on the Nerf hoop that hangs from the back of your bedroom door. You will, of course, be both players. Dr. J will win this game of one-on-one because Bird's jumper too often hits the ceiling, whereas Dr. J can dunk at will. Still, it will go down to the final buzzer, which is the buzzer on the dryer that signals that your socks are ready. By now it will be mid-afternoon, and you'll be desperate to make the most of what little daylight remains.

So you'll fire a hair-dryer into your moon boots and — with newly toasted tootsies — you'll pull your sled, with the twin red runners and the steering bar, to the top of the tallest hill in town. You will stand atop that mountain of white, like a plastic groom on a wedding cake, and imagine that you're looking down the bobsled chute at Innsbruck. As you bomb headfirst downhill, your every nerve ending alive with feeling, you'll be certain of at least one thing in life: that the thirty minutes you spent ascending this hill was a pittance to pay for the breathtaking twenty seconds of descent.

When you finally heed your mother's call and head inside, at six o'clock, it will have long been pitch-dark. Your cheeks will glow red like the Christmas lights strung above your garage, and you'll remove your stocking cap to find that every hair on your head is standing on end. Your mom will say that it's static electricity. But you'll know better.

DAN NEIL

Big Night in Bithlo

FROM CAR AND DRIVER

THE MAYOR of Bithlo (pronounced *biff-low*) is fixin' to do some cuttin'. It's dark, the night falling out of the sky like poisoned buzzards. He lights a dazzling acetylene torch and proceeds to draw a molten line on the hood of a white 1977 Thunderbird. The mayor's entourage — his wife, his two barelegged kids — gather round to scorch their retinas.

We are standing in the potholed paddock of Orlando Speedworld, a bullring of a figure-eight track three-eighths of a mile in length and surrounded by sagging catch fences. Bithlo is seventeen miles east of Orlando, among the scrub pines and industrial mosquito farms. Some of the finest recipes for armadillo come from this part of the world.

Wes Railing has cut two holes the size of Crisco lids into the T-Bird's snout. "We got to chain down the hood," he says from deep within a beard, back there behind a lit Marlboro and out from under a camo hat. "Plus, we can shoot fire extinguishers through the holes." Oh, it's a safety procedure. See, to the untrained eye, all that sparking wet metal falling into the open carburetor looks dick-in-the-dirt dangerous.

Hanging limply from a broomstick on the back of the T-Bird is a Confederate battle flag with the promise, "The South Will Rise Again." The flag marks the grubby Suribachi around which tonight's activity swirls. On Friday nights from March to November, Orlando Speedworld runs raucous paint-swapping derbies, everything from super late model to sportsman to "dwarf" cars, which are asphalt sprint cars with nostalgic sheetmetal — and here in Bithlo they pronounce it *dwoff.* Tonight, however, the usual racing has stepped aside in favor of Speedworld's biannual — or twice a year, whichever comes first — Crash-O-Rama Night of Destruction.

Railing is a repeat winner and heavy favorite in several events, including the big draw, the twenty-lap figure-eight school-bus race. Also on tonight's card is a twenty-lap camper-trailer race, in which vehicles of every description — a blown Ford 4x4 pickup, a terminally ill Cadillac Cimarron, the mayor's Thunderturd — will race while towing trashed and rotting campers! A similar format attends the boat-trailer race, whose entries include a kiddy boat stolen from nearby Walt Disney World. Written on the fiberglass bulkhead is this:

"Keep dinner warm, bitch, I'm racing."

Oh, mama, I'm home.

On most Friday nights, says track owner Robert Hart, seats in the 6,000-capacity grandstand are easy to find. On Crash-O-Rama nights the place is an SRO sellout at $20 a ticket. Which means, theoretically, every living soul in Bithlo, a town of 4,834 population, plus some cousins from nearby Chuluota.

And it's easy to see why. For racing spectacle, F1 at Indy pales in comparison with Crash-O-Rama. No other motoring event can so thoroughly satisfy one's curiosity — what if I took a '77 Chrysler New Yorker and T-boned a camper really fast? Would that be cool?

By the end of this evening, the track infield will be knee-deep in the detritus of recreational lifestyle, including wet mattresses, cheap wood paneling, and . . . is that asbestos?

The evening's morally edifying finale will be a jet car, "The Green Mamba," burning a school bus to the ground. The jet car is chained to a bus that is half-buried in the ground. The jet's exhaust nozzle is pointed like a giant blowtorch into the bus's open emergency door, pouring a screaming pillar of flame into it. This is what they think of *Brown v. Board* in Florida. The display will churn up a monstrous cloud of toxic residue that will drift over the grandstands, further compromising the fans' iffy genetic status.

Track owner Hart, a cigar-chewing, Stetson-wearing big daddy, also owns the half-mile New Smyrna Speedway near Daytona Beach. But Crash-O-Rama is the malarial brainchild of C. A.

"Bucky" Buckman, erstwhile school-bus mechanic and Hart's sometime employee.

Bucky has his hands full. Overnight, a gang broke through the gate and stole the batteries out of the track's collection of school buses and siphoned all their gas. The "coordinator of all bus, boat-trailer, and demolition activity," Bucky has been working four days straight. His jeans and long-sleeved thermal underwear are caked with grease and his gray beard is sprouting like bread mold; he exhibits the classic signs of long-term homelessness.

Wes Railing makes a delicate adjustment before the camper race. Other events include the demo derby and the bus race.

"The hardest thing about this deal is getting them old buses to run," Bucky says behind glasses speckled like a trucker's windshield. Bucky and Hart staged their first Crash-O-Rama eight years ago, and at that time there were plenty of buses. "Back then we were paying $1,100 for used buses, just so we could total them," Bucky says. "Now they're getting kinda scarce."

Fortunately, participants who bring buses to the spectacle are inclined to donate the bus to the track once the race is over. So Bucky has a stable of recycled rent-a-rides. These old gladiators — Thomas Builts, Blue Birds, International Harvesters, most of them powered with gasoline V-8s — have been bashed and balled up, crumpled like big yellow milk cartons, and straightened out again. If they roll over, Bucky says, "we just pull 'em back on their wheels and fire 'em up again."

Those drivers who do not bring their own bus get assigned a bus. "If you can get it to crank," says Bucky, "it's yours to drive." In fact, for hotshoes like the mayor, Bucky actually pays $100 for their services. Which is, on balance, a hell of a lot more than most drivers net in Formula Atlantics. Winners take home $1,000, second place pays $500, and third is $300.

Railing — he's not actually the mayor but that's what people call him — isn't happy with the draw. "My bus ain't got no brakes," he wails. It turns out most buses don't have brakes.

Benjamin Craft drives a school bus for the Seminole County school system. He and an assistant — anybody remember the scary kid on the porch in *Deliverance?* — are applying Ferrari-yellow paint to "The Educator," a 1974 Blue Bird with a Chevy small-block for which he paid $300. "I got a little bit of an advantage," the ponytailed redhead says. "I know how these things corner, how to get them sideways," which must be terribly reassuring to the parents of Seminole County.

Craft's previous ride sulks in the weeds behind the track. Painted black with a big white "3" on the sides, "The Intimidator" was, says Craft, "full-race." Craft relocated the V-8 to a position ten feet behind the driver, making it mid-engined, and hooked it up to the Dana 60 rear axle using a Chevy-truck driveshaft. The bus was also equipped with a five-point harness.

"Hey, hey," the kid from the porch sputters, "you 'member when John mashed his nuts in the harness?"

"Own damn fault," says Craft. "Belts were too tight."

But the lead bus threads a gap, and the other buses rear-end one another accordion style. More buses fan out across the infield at full boogie, kicking up clods of dirt and clouds of dust, narrowly missing one another. Now the buses are forming scrimmages of five and six, intersecting at right angles at speeds not approved of by the Department of Education.

It can't last long. Buses are flying everywhere. A massive T-bone such as the Sizzler has never seen can be but moments away. As the pink "Heart of Love" bus comes off the eighteen-degree banking and dives toward the infield, it blows an outside tire. More tires blow. *Krr-aanggg.* . . . Two buses collide in the dusty haze, each sheering off a fender and bumper.

"This ain't as good as last year," Bucky says evenly, watching the mayhem while seeming to smoke five or six cigarettes at once. "We rolled some buses last year."

But it's definitely good enough, an edgy spectacle of the randomly dangerous, bizarre, and improbable. And that's just the nut scratching going on in the stands.

Seventeen laps into the twenty-lap heat, it looks like the fans screaming for bus blood might be disappointed. Then, Bus Armageddon. Butch Pierce, in the "red bus," has it floored, and Raybo, in the hobo death bus, the '57 International, isn't lifting. The night swims away as everyone gets tunnel vision, awaiting the impact. A crisp, orgasmic *krunch* ricochets off the pines as Butch's bus slams into Raybo's. Both buses leave the ground. The red bus's motor punches through the fire wall, landing well aft of the white line in a shower of hot oil and broken glass. The International's in-line six is knocked out of the engine bay and winds up sitting on the fender, dislodged like a broken molar. A toilet seat spins gracefully into the air.

In the microseconds that follow, two demolition-derby veterans from New York, Bob Genovese and Ken McNamee, plow into the disabled buses from both directions. The sound is like every elevator in Manhattan falling to the basement at the same time. The buses lunge and spin in a train-wreck spasm. They fill up with smoke.

The crowd is momentarily voiceless, then erupts in hoots, cheers, and rebel yells. Some even take the cigarettes out of their mouths.

And then it's over. Rusty Cruze, driving "America the Weird," wins the race and the $1,000 prize. The demolished buses' drivers walk wobble-kneed out to the start/finish line to congratulate him in front of the frenzied crowd.

The mayor's bus had stalled early, the victim of a fuel pump put in backward. "Sabotage," he says. He'll fare better in the boat-trailer and camper-trailer race. After these races, Orlando Speedworld looks like a trailer park in Homestead after Hurricane Andrew.

As the last toxic fumes from the jet-car bus burning waft over the crowd, the armadillos poke their heads out from their burrows and the crowd heads toward their pickup trucks, this edition of Crash-O-Rama seems an unqualified success, and by that I mean a complete disaster.

Man, I could go for a cucumber right about now.

DAN LE BATARD

Detour

FROM ESPN: THE MAGAZINE

SO MUCH GOT LOST in the translation.

Danny Almonte was untouched by the stench, like a rose growing implausibly in a sewer. American shame and outrage swirled noisily around him after his baseball triumph had been exposed as fraud, but Danny didn't understand the commotion, and still doesn't. He is a painfully shy kid, staring at the floor a lot, but when asked about his recent experiences with Little League Baseball Incorporated, he lifts his head, smiles, and says in Spanish, "It was so much fun and happiness." All of it? "All of it," he says.

All of it? How could all of it possibly have been fun and happiness when Danny's father was being threatened with arrest and Danny's coach was considering suicide? Well, somehow, the disgrace didn't translate. Maybe Danny is hiding safely behind all his naivete, and the fact that he doesn't speak a word of English. Maybe, after fourteen years of bouncing around too many homes of relatives, he is more perceptive and calculated than he ever shows, and figures that pretending to be the happy twelve-year-old ballplayer is a good way to keep his baseball-addicted father loving. But you aren't going to get anything like that out of him, not when he goes sheepish whenever asked about himself and then stares silently at the ground.

Asked what the best part of the past few months has been, his response is, "I forget." That's as deep as he'll go, or will allow you to go. He has let himself be protected, miraculously, by the language barrier in a way that leaves him looking like an unscathed infant cooing in the car seat after a wreck that killed everyone else. When the reporters tailed Danny to school in early September, asking in English, "Why did you cheat?" and, "Are you embarrassed?" it sounded like good noise to him, not unlike applause. And when the talking heads called him a liar and bully and cheat, as Bill Maher did on *Politically Incorrect,* all the accompanying footage revealed to Danny was that — look at me! — his strikeouts were on TV again. All he saw was that his arm — an arm that had struck out forty-six batters in three games, a one-hitter, a two-hitter, and a perfecto — had put him on the back pages of the tabloids and pushed Roger Clemens inside.

Never mind that his team had lost in the semis, or that, when his real age was finally revealed, it had to forfeit all of its wins. Danny was famous, not infamous, in his world, and all the attention, good and bad, was the same to him because the cameras staking out his apartment became indistinguishable from the boys asking for his autograph and the girls blowing him kisses. There is a certain exquisite symmetry in that — the boy's experience with Little League Baseball Inc. somehow remaining clean to him despite the adults who tried to soil it. All Danny lived was the New York parade, not the litter afterward, which makes his oxymoronic view of this mess much like the game he pitched to produce it — flawed, certainly, but technically perfect.

"He still doesn't know there is anything bad about this," his father, Felipe, says in Spanish. It's a warm November Monday, and he's whispering so Danny, in the other room of this tiny Bronx apartment they're sharing with Danny's coach, can't hear him. Danny, meanwhile, is eating McDonald's fries while flipping between Ludacris, Stone Cold Steve Austin, and Britney Spears on TV, and listening to a friend talk about how rapper Fat Joe grew up across the street and sometimes returns by limo. This is what Danny knows of America, or cares to know, and, as Fat Joe might say, it's all good.

"Danny has no wounds, no scars, no nothing," Felipe says. "When the controversy would come on Spanish TV, someone would change the channel or turn it off. We'd . . ." Danny walks into the nearby kitchen. His father stops talking, waiting for him to leave. "If he knew how bad the press was, he'd be wrecked," Felipe whispers. "He'd need a team of psychologists. But he never felt any suffering." A family friend, seated on the couch, says, "None of the crap ever touched Danny. God doesn't let the crap touch the children." Amen, brother.

The adults, though, are another matter entirely.

Cheating is cheating, in any language, but you should know Danny's story isn't quite as black-and-white as either of his birth certificates — just as you should know the sacred symbol of Americana he assaulted, Little League Baseball Inc., is as much about green as it is about red, white, and blue.

Yes, Danny was nearly four months past his fourteenth birthday at the start of an international twelve-and-under championship, but lost amid the shouts of "Cheat! Fraud! Ringer!" was that Danny's father wasn't forging records with the intent of winning a children's tournament. Felipe was doing what a lot of poor baseball fathers do in the Dominican Republic — being creative with age to make his son more attractive to pro scouts. This is simple math: a sixteen-year-old with an eighteen-year-old's fastball is going to be worth more. Felipe did the same thing with his older son, the one you've never heard of. Felipe was trying to win himself and his kid an American future, not an American trophy.

Baseball is more than a game in their Dominican; it is an escape. The impoverished island's chief exports are sugar, cocoa, and ballplayers, so age discrepancies are as prevalent as hunger. Desperation is such that veteran scouts tell of older brothers using the identities of little brothers or of dead people. UNICEF estimates nearly 25 percent of Dominican children over five lack proper birth certificates,

"I thought that number would be even higher," says Al Avila, VP of scouting for the Florida Marlins. "It goes the other way, too. Parents have children and can't afford to feed them, so they add age to make them sixteen [the legal signing age] and get them a better life. It isn't easy to tell if a prospect is seventeen or twenty-four when he's malnourished."

Danny, for his part, still thinks he is twelve, at least until April, his next birthday. Either that, or he is a very good liar. He says he is twelve, and everyone close to him says he genuinely believes it. "A lot of kids over there don't know their age," says Avila, and that's why there was confusion even when it came to, say, Braves shortstop Rafael Furcal, who said he was nineteen even as HBO revealed documents that said he was twenty-two. Danny has never celebrated a birthday. That's not abnormal among the poor in his country. Would you have known how old you were at six if your parents or the cake's candles didn't tell you? And if not at six, would you at twelve or fourteen or sixteen, if keeping track wasn't important where you come from? Wouldn't you say you were sixteen or eighteen if you thought it might get a rich American team to feed you? In the Dominican, you are often as old as your parents say you are. Danny's father told Danny he was twelve. Felipe hasn't gotten around to telling him otherwise.

Because friends and parents softened questions they translated from English to protect him, Danny never did understand why so many people were asking about his age. Hadn't he told them a thousand times he was twelve? Danny's shyness and monosyllabic answers allowed for no give-and-take in interviews, so the assumption was that Danny must have known how old he was and was therefore lying. "How could a fourteen-year-old possibly not know how old he is?" was the thought, and it didn't allow for just how much could get lost in that translation. "Danny and I are both very timid," Felipe says. "The interviews never came out the way I meant. I don't know anything about this country. Where I'm from, we do things in pencil, not computers."

Dominican kids are sometimes registered many years after birth, if at all, and Felipe says he registered Danny at seven, give or take. In March 2000, Felipe had Danny's birth certificate altered so Danny could more or less be born again. You can look at this deception two ways. Felipe was being an overbearing Little League dad, living vicariously through his son, trying to win at any cost, even if it meant cheating. Or he was a poor father trying to help his kid. Either way, we ought to acknowledge there is an either way. "I live to find an opportunity for my child," Felipe says. "We live very humbly in my country, and there are more opportunities for youth in this country. If I could, I'd bring my whole family here, but I can't yet."

So Felipe accompanied Danny to the States in June, and Danny lived with his Little League coach, one of Felipe's best friends since childhood, after Felipe returned home, because there was a big, televised tournament here that might get Danny noticed. Danny didn't immediately register in school, which is not that uncommon for Latin kids new to this country who don't speak English and are here without their parents. But the notion that later developed was that Danny was shipped in as a mercenary specifically to win the World Series against younger kids. Felipe adamantly says this isn't so. He says he wanted his kid in America because it is the best place for a kid, and points out Danny would be back in the Dominican now, far away from this mess, if winning the World Series had been all that brought him here.

For all the shame that ravaged Felipe afterward, there was only one time he wept throughout this ordeal. It wasn't when he saw himself called a lying, terrible father by the tabloids and television. And it wasn't when he heard a Dominican official threaten Felipe with a prison term for falsifying government documents. (Felipe says now, "If I'm arrested, I will go tranquilly. My heart will not beat one beat faster because I know I was trying to create opportunities for my son.") No, the one and only time Felipe cried was back in the Dominican on August 18, as he watched his boy on television throw that perfect game against Apopka, Florida.

"I softened," he said. "Such a grand feeling. Big. I felt something big."

But, Felipe, wasn't your pride diluted by knowing your son was striking out younger kids — sixteen of eighteen he faced? Felipe looks at you as if you'd asked if he arrived here by flying saucer.

"No," he says.

He had, spectacularly, gotten his son noticed. And anyway, he figured there was no shortage of overage kids in that tournament whose parents had tried to do the same thing, though not nearly as well.

The coach is obsessed. Rolando Paulino's apartment is filled with so many trophies, plaques, commendations, and team pictures that there is no space for anything else. He has lineup cards tucked away, some of them more than two decades old, and he can tell you from memory every player on his team in 1983. Paulino, thirty-seven, has a stepson but likes to say he has 450 kids, roughly the number in the Bronx league that bears his name.

"He can go to a room in the back of this apartment and tell you I was three-for-five with two runs scored on the second Saturday of May, twenty-two years ago," says Felipe, a teammate of Paulino's as a kid. "You think I'm kidding? I'm not."

Paulino has done a lot of good work, helping countless kids in a rugged neighborhood, and that's why so many local parents and politicians have supported him despite his recent travails. They have seen him go door-to-door for donations. They have watched him pay umpires out of his own meager salary as a sportswriter for a Spanish-language newspaper, and borrow money from his mother to buy catching equipment. They know that, in a league where a mother coaches against her son because there are so many kids who want to play and so few adults to coach them, Paulino is coaching six of the thirty-six teams.

But Paulino has been banned by Little League Baseball Inc. for life now, as has Felipe, a stain that has left him close to ruin. He lost almost thirty pounds in the weeks after the Almonte allegations surfaced. His wife, Carmen, would wake and find him sitting in the dark. In one breath, he says, "I don't need or care about Williamsport. Williamsport has never bought me one bat or ball." In the next moment, though, he shows the five letters he's sent to Williamsport, trying to get his name cleared.

As he sits in his living room now, surrounded by his trophies, he keeps looking over his shoulder to make sure Carmen, cooking dinner, won't hear what he's about to say. "I was so depressed I thought about taking my life, but I wouldn't give them the pleasure," he whispers. On the TV there is news of American Flight 587, which crashed this morning going from New York to the Dominican. All around Paulino in this panicked neighborhood, televisions flicker with flames and plane pieces, and phone calls are made to make sure that friends weren't — or were — on that flight. But Paulino isn't much in the mood for perspective. "I'd rather die in a plane crash, quick, than suffer what I did," he says.

Paulino says, ad nauseam, that he didn't know Danny was overage, that he relies on parents to be honest. This has caused some tension between Paulino and Felipe. "If there is anybody who has a right to be mad at Danny and his father, it is me," Paulino says. "Look at what has happened to me because of them." Still, Paulino is letting Danny live with him indefinitely, since Felipe returned to the Dominican shortly after these interviews (where he was not jailed).

Paulino loves kids too much to hold a grudge against even the one who tarnished him. And he loves winning with them, too, perhaps too much. Paulino organized his first tournament in the Dominican when he was fifteen, selling sacks of rice to raise money, getting visas so his players could travel and teams from elsewhere could play there, and persuading a church to pay for hotel costs. Before 2001, the only other time he'd been to the Little League World Series was in 1987, when he took a Latin American team also rumored to have overage players. (A year later, a Paulino team was banned from a Puerto Rican tournament for lacking the proper documents for some players.)

To cover the expenses for that 1987 World Series team, Paulino used the entire inheritance left him by his father. Paulino was twenty-three. "Money never mattered like baseball did," he says. Adds Felipe, who runs his own league in the Dominican, "What we have is a sickness without cure. I feel bad, nauseous, when I don't go to the field. I get so uncomfortable when games are rained out that I go out there and get wet anyway, just to be near the field. If drugs are this addictive, I understand drug addicts."

Few teams of Dominican players before the one that represented the Bronx this summer had been checked so thoroughly because few Dominican teams before this one had such success. "It's just because he has kicked everybody's ass that people complained," says Red Sox superstar and Dominican native Pedro Martinez. "He comes from the mountains, goes to New York, gets the opportunity to play, and then he gets all the crap America has to offer just because he does good."

Here was a team of dark-skinned kids from a poor neighborhood, blowing through suburban teams from air-conditioned America, and Paulino wonders aloud why nobody looked at how old the white kids were. Little League officials admit there have been Anglo players bigger and better than Danny whose credentials have never been questioned. Paulino heard rumors that one of the kids in this year's tournament had a *child,* and points out, correctly, that the tournament is set up so foreigners beat each other up for the right to play an American team guaranteed a spot in the finals. (League officials say, since 96 percent of all Little Leaguers play here, the format is designed to ensure that a non-U.S. team reaches the finals.) "Florida was the team from the United States, not us," Paulino says. "We didn't have the blond hair, the blue eyes, and the perfect English. This never happens if we have those things."

He says he encountered prejudice in Williamsport, fans from other teams wondering why so many Bronx parents were waving that "communist" Dominican flag. He could hear it when his team's parents were blowing whistles, beating drums, and waving flags, so he went out and bought a big American flag and draped it from his team's dugout.

"Did you hear what Turk Wendell said?" Paulino asks, and now he is going to that back room, searching for the words. What Wendell said was, "I thought it was kind of funny. Here's a kid playing in the Little League World Series for an American team, holding an American flag, and he can't speak English? No way." But Paulino is looking for the exact quote, and brings a garbage bag full of newspapers back and dumps it on the living room floor, headlines spilling out in a jumble. "Danny's Dad Faces Arrest." "Danny's 14! Coach a Big-Time Cheat." Paulino pushes past all this and stumbles on a photo of a Japanese player towering over his teammates.

"Look at this giant," Paulino says. "Are they going to Japan to find out *his* age? They aren't going to Japan, and Japan isn't letting them in if they do go. But in the Dominican, everyone can be bought. Americans get what they want on a platter."

He continues to rummage and read, rummage and read, rummage and read for a half-hour, looking for that Wendell quote. He is trying very hard to find a paragraph of prejudice amid this mountainous mess of his own making that sits right at his feet. He never does find it.

How dare they? That was the tone, wasn't it, inflated with indignation? "How dare they make winning that important?" we asked . . . after these kids played in games attended by 42,000 fans, including the president . . . and were broadcast on international television . . . and, despite a third-place finish, were launched into a whirlwind that included a parade . . . and ringing the bell on Wall Street . . . and getting the key to the city from Rudy Giuliani . . . and receiving calls from Ken Griffey, Jr., and Randy Johnson . . . and meeting the Yankees . . . and receiving an all-expenses-paid trip to Disney World (revoked after the forfeit). "How dare they make winning that important?" we asked . . . after we had made winning that important.

Or hadn't you noticed? The way a ball bounces reverberates pretty enormously here, and that's how it came to be that the headlines coming out of New York just a few days before the Twin Towers crumbled were somehow about the birth certificate of a kid on a Little League team.

Danny suddenly became a symbol for something, the way Latrell Sprewell and John Rocker and Rodney King and Elián González had. We needed a face to put on this sports-run-amok issue, needed a face to go with overbearing parents who break the ump's jaw and fight in the stands, and Danny's would do just fine. Didn't much matter that the face of Danny's father or coach would have been more appropriate, didn't much matter that the face of the kid that kept appearing over the TV anchor's shoulder might have been innocent in more ways than one. These Dominicans had spray-painted the Norman Rockwell painting, see?

But Little League is Big Business. Its annual budget is nearly $15 million. The World Series brings in $13 million to the Williamsport economy every year. The games have been televised since 1963. The kids give press conferences. Little League has a dozen corporate sponsors, and more than one hundred licensing agreements that allow companies to use Little League's name on its products for a fee, after Little League has tested the products in its own lab.

There is the illusion of quaint, old-time America in Williamsport, with the $1.25 hot dogs and 50-cent sodas, the volunteer umps and tickets given away and never sold (though sometimes scalped). But this is hardly the first time parents have ruined it for the kids. Crowds used to boo the Taiwanese team that won fifteen championships in twenty-two years, a team that practiced during school hours, had its education paid for by Taiwan's first lady, and had a stamp issued to commemorate it. As far back as 1972, a fight so large broke out among fans that police had to be brought in by helicopter to calm people swinging four-foot sticks and throwing rocks.

Innocence lost? Doesn't something have to be innocent first before its innocence can be lost?

Danny? He's sponsored now, too. A Bronx dentist has become his "adviser," setting him up with Fred Cambria, a $40-an-hour pitching coach who used to work in the Padres organization. The arrangement is promising enough that Danny's father turned down Hall of Famer Juan Marichal's offer to pay for Danny's expenses and baseball grooming back in the Dominican. Says Felipe:

"In the end, despite everything, the vocational mission of the coach is working. His player is advancing. The mission of the father is working. The son is advancing."

Cambria has Danny doing a total of 500 different reps of special exercises a day and never allows him to throw curveballs. It is impossible to project potential for someone this young, but one major league scout says, "Teams will be following his progress. What he did was extraordinary for his age, whatever his age was. He would be less extraordinary if he pitched against kids his own age, but still pretty extraordinary. He has a very good arm." Says Cambria: "His mechanics were terrible, and he has nothing in the way of muscle, but he's throwing in the mid-seventies from a big-league distance, which is terrific for his age. You don't see this kind of loose, fluid arm with this kind of terrific movement on the ball very often."

Danny is attending English classes from 8:00 to 9:00 A.M. and then again from 3:00 to 6:00 P.M. after school, but Cambria still can't speak to him. He has a catcher translate, uses a lot of hand gestures, and adds, "I try to have a big smile on my face so he knows when he's doing very well."

Ah, yes, a big smile. It translates. After everything else, the big smile is all he sees.

PETER RICHMOND

Flesh and Blood

FROM GQ

ONE BY ONE, day by day, they'd glide to the witness stand, this procession of improbable women, a spangled harem of them, drifting into the courtroom and out again, leaving the scent of their perfume and the shadow of their glitter and the echo of their cool. Week in, week out, they never stopped coming.

That was the extraordinary thing. How many there were. The final count stopped short of thirty — that was the number of photographs of women Rae was said to keep in a box at home — but there were more than enough of them to make each and every morning worth my springing out of bed for, worth walking down to the courthouse for, worth getting frisked at the doorway for: in the hope that a new one might illuminate the somber courtroom with its smoked-glass view of the jailhouse across the street.

And sure enough, in the middle of a gray day of testimony filled with the babble of a psychologist or the grunt of a jail guard or the platitudes of a coach, out of the blue Rae's attorney would suddenly say, "The defense calls Dawnyle Willard," and next to me the TV guy would arch an eyebrow at the local columnist — who's this one? what's the angle? lover? friend? cleaned his apartment? helped him jump bail? — and they'd both shrug, because no one had heard of Dawnyle Willard.

Then everyone would turn to the back of the courtroom to get a look at the newest entrant, because we just knew she was going to be beautiful. And honestly, she just about always was.

Dawnyle certainly was. Stately, slim, a dancer. Former girlfriend, now confidante. Wept on the stand, at the pure goodness of the man.

Amber was cool, slim, and fiery and a favorite among those of us who spoke of such things during breaks in the action, although Starlita was easily the most exotic; she looked like an African princess dropped into a southern murder trial. Michelle was the pretty little girl next door. Monique was innocently cute. Tnisha, Rae's current squeeze, was . . . well, a tad young looking. But she was pretty enough for you to understand why Rae would nod at her each day when, sandwiched by grim bailiffs, he left the courtroom — nodding as if to say, Hey, babe, don't worry: *you're* the one now. And I swear, she believed it.

Sometimes, though, Rae nodded at the woman in the front pew. She was there every day. By some measures, she was the most handsome of all: high forehead, piercing eyes, coiffed and jewelried to the highest. Some newcomers to the courtroom thought she was another female friend. But this was Rae's mother, Theodry Carruth, anchoring the Cult of Rae from the center of the home-team bench.

Really, there was no other way to think of them — other than as a cult — at least not after the mother of one of Rae's former girlfriends took the stand near the end of the trial, and the *mother* was gorgeous. Not only was she beautiful, but get this: after her daughter testified against Rae, the mother testified glowingly *for* Rae.

And then, as she left the stand, she looked right at Rae — a man facing the death penalty for taking out a hit on a pregnant woman — looked right into his eyes and, all sweet and wet, mouthed the words *I love you*.

As the weeks passed and the women came and went, I would look over at Rae and stare at his profile, which never changed, because Rae never changed expressions, even during the closing argument, when the lead prosecutor played the 911 tape of Cherica Adams's moans: sounds from beyond the grave, all sputtering utterances, atonal syllables so skin-crawling that throughout the courtroom shoulders heaved in sobs. But Rae's face flinched not at all. Animated and emotional and expressive as the women were — weaving and looping their tales of his goodness and his charity — Rae remained a well-tailored sphinx.

And so, day in, day out, I'd ask myself a question. Not what they all saw in him; the first look at Rae explained that: this baby face, the contours all smooth and rounded, the outward downslant of his eyebrows giving him this puppy-dog-swatted-with-a-newspaper look. Girls loved to take care of Rae even before he became a millionaire. No, the question I kept asking myself was this: If Rae Carruth loved women so much, why did he keep threatening to have them killed? How, if he gathered women around him like a cocoon, if he thrived on them and fed on them and drew sustenance from them, could a man get to a point in his life where he routinely considered disposing of them? And how could such a man wind up finding a home — even flourishing — in the National Football League?

Well, because he really didn't like women at all. (He liked to fuck them, and he liked their attention, and he liked the *idea* of them, but he didn't like them.) And because he was accustomed to violence. And because he was making a living in a league in which a man and his basest instincts are encouraged to run wild. Well, he was until recently, anyway; Rae doesn't play football anymore. He's in prison up in Nash County, where he won't have to worry about women and women won't have to worry about him, and as his crime swiftly seeps into the background noise of the culture, we're already starting to act as if we didn't have to worry about Rae Carruth anymore. As if the whole episode were an aberration.

Of course, it's anything but. Take even a cursory look at how Rae Carruth went from first-round NFL draft pick to ward of the state of North Carolina, serving a quarter century of hard time for conspiring to commit the most horrific crime in the history of professional sports, and the question is not how it could happen but when is it going to happen again.

Football is a violent sport, growing far more violent and mean and attitudinal every year, and it has been played by men who have traditionally been violent against their women. This has been the case since Jim Brown, the greatest running back ever to play the game, garnered the first of a half-dozen charges of violence against women, ranging from spousal battery to rape to the sexual molestation of two teenage girls. Brown, who has never been convicted of a single charge, begat O. J., the second-greatest running back, who, at this writing, continues to seek out Nicole's true killers. O. J. begat Michael Irvin of the Dallas Cowboys, who, prior to one of his frequent cocaine-sex bacchanals a few years back, cavity-searched one of his girls a little too hard for the liking of her cop boyfriend, who then took out a hit on Irvin. It wasn't just Irvin who dodged a bullet that time. It was the NFL, which retired Irvin with pomp and circumstance.

This year, of course, Super Bowl MVP and murder defendant Ray Lewis, who has twice been accused — but not convicted — of hitting women, commanded headlines and earned full forgiveness at the hands of a most understanding media machine. Wearing a Giants uniform in the same Super Bowl was Christian Peter, a man accused of so many crimes against women in college that public outcry forced the Patriots to drop him within days of drafting him in 1996. Lost in the shuffle but not forgotten, Corey Dillon and Mustafah Muhammad and Denard Walker contributed, each in his own way, to this long-standing tradition. On the day he ran for a record 278 yards, Cincinnati's Dillon, now arguably the game's best running back, was facing charges of striking his wife; after the season, he plea-bargained to avoid trial. His uniform was sent to the Hall of Fame, where it now keeps company with the memorabilia of Brown and Simpson. As for Walker, he played for Tennessee last year after being convicted of hitting the mother of his son. He then declared himself a free agent and was courted by several teams until the Denver Broncos anted up a cool $26 million. Muhammad, a cornerback with Indianapolis, led his team into the playoffs last year after being convicted of hitting his wife. And let's not forget the domestic-assault conviction of Detroit's Mario Bates or former Packer Mark Chmura's troubles surrounding his dalliance with his seventeen-year-old baby-sitter.

And what about the more subtle misogyny embodied by the late and revered Derrick Thomas of the Kansas City Chiefs, who was killed in a car wreck two years ago? He left behind seven kids by five women, and no will — thus no guarantees of money or consideration for any of the children or any of the women.

The NFL claims it is doing more than ever to educate its recruits. Its preseason three-and-a-half-day symposia are supposed to make its rookies duly aware of their newfound responsibilities to their fans and their leagues and the kids who put their posters on the wall: To avoid the sleaze joints. Steer clear of the hucksters. Grow up quick.

But what is it really doing? When the NFL parades its first-round draft picks to a podium on national television and slathers them in their first frosting of celebrity, its message effectively and immediately neutralizes all the good-behavior seminars. On that day, the commissioner is not only handing each of the players a guarantee of several million dollars; he is also giving them the whispered assurance that the league likes them just the way they are. No need to grow up too fast.

Ultimately, the league refused to ban Ray Lewis and his brutal peers because it needed them on the playing field, and that mandate speaks more loudly than a lecture about good citizenship — especially to a remarkably immature kid like Rae. After all, little boys don't like little girls, and what was Rae Carruth other than an overgrown boy, a bundle of muscle and fiber jerry-rigged to play a game? Of course, most kids grow out of that stuff. It's the rare one who is allowed to harbor his playground sexism until it blossoms into monstrosity.

He came from the place so many seem to come from; only the details vary from kid to kid. Rae didn't grow up with his biological father. As a child, Rae split time among several houses, including his mother's, set in a neighborhood of squalor and dismay on the south side of Sacramento — on an avenue where vandals routinely set cars aflame — and her sister's place in a nicer part of town, absent the bars on the windows. Even then, even before he was showered with privilege, Theodry worried about the sharks and the vultures preying on her son, "the guppy."

This is how she describes him. This is why she describes herself as "the piranha" when it comes to protecting her son. To know Rae Carruth and to understand the course he chose to take, to divine the nature of his particular rebellion — because isn't that what all our adolescent contrarinesses are? rebellion against what was lacquered onto us beforehand? — you must first know Theodry Carruth. There is a hardness and a strength to her, and they seem like the same thing; she seizes the space she is in and commands it from on high.

But if one may be tempted to call Rae's mother domineering, one ought not to, because she will not tolerate being described as overbearing, and she will tell you so. Describe her instead, she warns in a voice that brooks no argument, as simply having been raised by a southern mother, and then say she is raising her son thusly.

Theodry Carruth's vigilance over her only son's upbringing paid off, at least in the short run: Rae's grades at Valley High School were solid, he stayed out of trouble, and big colleges came calling. In 1992 Rae went off to the University of Colorado. Back on the infernal block on Parker Avenue, Theodry Carruth turned one of the rooms into a miniature shrine where family and friends gathered to sit in mock stadium chairs and watch Rae's games from Boulder. It was called the Rae of Hope room. Neighborhood kids would set it on fire a few years later.

At Colorado, Rae's coach Bill McCartney was a demagogue. On the field, McCartney was known for teams that played hard and thuggishly. Off the field, he was known for the conversation he'd had with God. One day God told McCartney to found the Promise Keepers. Soon thereafter, at McCartney's urgings, tens of thousands of fathers and husbands took to gathering in football stadiums across the land to beat their chests and flagellate their souls and collectively recommit to their gender. The subtext of the Promise Keepers was a patently sexist one, of course: portraying women as worthy beings but regarding them, ultimately, as secondary, as biblical chattel.

But beneath the roar of McCartney's fire and brimstone, his daughter was getting pregnant by two different football players in four and a half years — the first, the star quarterback, wanted her to abort the fetus; the second sired his child during Rae's freshman year. This only proved that when you climb too high in the pulpit, it's easy to ignore the funky stuff going on under your nose. Especially if you're a member of the sinning crowd: McCartney himself quit on his Colorado contract after Rae's third autumn in Boulder. Broke his promise, if you will.

Rae's college athletic achievements were legendary — in one game alone, he had seven receptions for 222 yards and three touchdowns. In 1997 he entered the hallowed fraternity of first-round draft picks under the watchful wink of the NFL. The Carolina Panthers took him as their first selection, number twenty-seven overall. Like all rookies, he would be instructed on how to behave. But like his first-round peers, he knew what had actually just happened: he'd been ushered into a land of entitlement, where the only promise he'd really be held to was the promise he'd shown thus far on the playing field.

The Panthers gave him a four-year contract worth $3.7 million and a $1.3 million signing bonus, and it wasn't so much the amount of money that was stunning but the ease with which it came. Within days of being signed, Rae got a check for $15,000 in the mail from a trading-card company. Just for being Rae. How sweet was that?

He immediately signed it over to his seventeen-year-old girlfriend in Boulder, Amber Turner, and told her to go ahead and set up house for them in Charlotte. Amber was a stylish and precocious beauty, a high school senior. (Even as a fifth-year college senior, Rae's tastes still tended toward postadolescence.) His girlfriend in high school, Michelle, had been a sophomore when he was a senior, and she'd just turned eighteen when Rae got her pregnant on a visit back home from college. He'd waffled about whether or not to have the baby from day to day. Michelle wasn't surprised at his indecision. She says she knew him as a man of many moods. He could be a real joker, or he could be a cipher, or he could even be, in the dark moments, the Devil himself.

Amber Turner knew about the baby back in Sacramento. Amber also knew Rae said the boy might not be his, and even if it were his baby, he said, there were ways to fix the blood tests.

And what of the parents? Amber's mother had no problem with Amber setting up house with Rae in a distant city, right out of high school. She loved Rae, too. He was polite and civilized and kind. He called her Mrs. Turner even after she said he could call her Barbara.

Rae's mom, Theodry, was pleased, too — pleased that her only son would be living in a southern town with family values. But it wasn't family values that Rae found in Charlotte. It was what all young, wealthy, transplanted men find there, these strangers in a strange land: nightclubs, comedy clubs, strip clubs. Charlotte is full of gentlemen's clubs, peopled by men who are anything but. On the high end, there's the Men's Club, Charlotte's topless palace nonpareil.

The Men's Club, planted right off the interstate, like everything else in a town laid down like a new quilt of plywood and Sheetrock, is a sumptuous palace of fiction. What the Men's Club lacks in poetry it makes up for in excess. The red-felt pool tables are illumined by hanging lamps ensconced in blue glass. The lobby boutique is filled with expensive clothes for men and women. The kitchen will serve you a fillet medallion sautéed in a mushroom demiglace.

In the center of the place, beyond the sunken bar, is the main stage. But the dancers are not the only attraction; above the stage looms a huge television screen, like Oz's mask, eternally tuned to ESPN, so that the allure of even the most seductive sirens competes with huge images of men being tackled and talking heads blathering about blitzes. In a very real sense, the women at the Men's Club are just another product, with this exception: there is nothing real about them. The tattoos on the soft planes south of the hipbones are frosted over with pancake makeup. Their names are as false as their chests. They are stage actors. They are not meant to be the stuff of reality.

This, of course, explains why Rae sought them out. Because they seemed to be less than real women yet possessed of the necessary female attributes. So that considering their feelings was a less complicated process.

Despite a terrific rookie season on the field — Rae earned a starting position at wide receiver and finished with an impressive forty-four receptions — Rae's home life soon proved rocky. Amber went home after that first season. He found her too possessive: she was jealous of all his other female friends. And there would be many female friends. There was Starlita, whom Rae had so charmed in a barbershop one day that before she'd finished having her hair done, Rae had taken her young son down the street for pizza. Soon Starlita thought Rae was the best thing in Jacobe's life. Rae was worried that Starlita was turning her son into a mama's boy. (Rae always harped on that. And what was Rae if not a mama's boy?) There was Fonda Bryant, who kept a picture of her son on her desk at a radio station Rae visited one day, and before long the boy was spending nights at Rae's. Rae was exactly what the boy needed; Rae was firm about staying away from alcohol and drugs, firm about making sure the boy did his homework. When they played, Fonda couldn't tell who was the kid and who was the adult.

And yet Rae hardly ever visited his own child. He gave Michelle grief about breast-feeding the kid and hugging him so much — he worried she was making Little Rae soft. So Michelle sued him for child support: a judge granted her $5,500 a month. She offered to lessen it if Rae would come home and visit more. He promised. He didn't. In the meantime, Amber went back to Charlotte for a quick visit. She got pregnant. As Rae's responsibilities and missteps threatened to collide, as his little-kid appetites met his stunted ability to cope with adversity, he began to consider a solution both novel and bizarre on the surface but certainly logical in the context of a man who regards his women as disposable and dispensable: any time he'd get a woman pregnant, he'd threaten her with death.

He didn't carry out all the threats, of course. He was a joker. He just talked about it a lot — about having Michelle and Amber killed.

Like the time Michelle called him in March 1998. She'd been unsuccessful in persuading Rae to come back home to visit their son. Rae had another idea. He suggested the two of them fly east to Charlotte. Fine, she said. I'll rent a car and see the sights while you play with your son.

"Don't be surprised if you get in a fatal car accident," Rae answered, according to Michelle. He spoke very quietly, nearly in a whisper.

"What did you say?" asked Michelle.

"It was a joke," Rae said.

"It's not funny," Michelle said.

"That's why it didn't work out," he said. "You never know when I'm joking."

Back in Charlotte one day, Rae got off the phone, turned to Amber, and said, as she recalls it, "Would it be messed up if I had somebody, you know, kill Michelle and my son? Or just my son, so that I wouldn't have to pay her any money? Or if she just got in, like, a car accident, or something happened to her, I could have my son and I wouldn't have to pay her money?"

He said it jokingly. Amber had overheard him talking about the same thing to a friend. Yeah, she said. It'd be messed up, Rae.

So some months later, when Amber called from Boulder to say she was pregnant after her five-day visit and Rae insisted she get an abortion, insisted he was not going to have any more kids by women he had no intention of being with, well, how could Amber be surprised when he said what he said to her?

"Don't make me send someone out there to kill you," Amber remembers him saying. "You know I would."

This one didn't sound funny at all. She had the abortion. Barbara Turner hadn't raised her daughter to be no fool.

Cherica Adams worked in the Men's Club boutique. She also danced under an alias at a different bar — over on the stages of the Diamond Club, a slightly more frayed entry in the topless-club genre, a place where a dancer is likely to be visiting from her home club in Buffalo for the long weekend, to pick up a couple of bucks, leaving the two-year-old back with her grandmother. Cherica Adams was a very attractive, baby-faced young woman who moved with a glittery crowd and felt equally at home backstage at a Master P concert or courtside at the 1998 NBA All-Star Game in Madison Square Garden, where several players, including Shaquille O'Neal, came by to say hello to her.

They never really dated, Rae and Cherica. They had sex a few times. Rae was also having sex with an exotic dancer who was having an affair with Charles Shackleford, a former Charlotte Hornet who happened to be married with three children, but it was Cherica whom Rae got pregnant, in March 1999 — exactly one year after he and Amber conceived their second child.

Rae was ambivalent about this one. On the one hand, he kept a new set of baby furniture in a storage facility under his name and took Cherica to Lamaze classes. On the other hand, it was at a Lamaze class that Rae first learned Cherica's last name.

Rae's second season had been a disappointment. He'd broken his foot after a forty-seven-yard catch, and he'd missed most of the year. When Cherica got pregnant, his world began to close in.

He was taking grief from teammates and friends about letting a stripper use him, about her boasting all over town that she was carrying Rae Carruth's baby and wasn't going to have to work anymore. By now Rae's circle of male friends had expanded. Tired of the slick jocks in the Panthers' locker room, he was glad to finally meet some people who were real. This new coterie included a man named Michael Kennedy, who had dealt crack, and a man named Van Brett Watkins, who had once set a man on fire in the joint and stabbed his own brother. Watkins, too, had unusual ways of showing love to his women. He'd once held a meat cleaver to his wife's face.

Frequently injured, no longer a starter, Rae had by now become that singularly sorry football phenomenon: a first-round draft pick gone bust. Taxes and agents had taken half the bonus. He'd invested in a car-title-loan scam that had promised the trappings of easy living — and lost his money. He'd hired former wide receiver Tank Black, later indicted on fraud charges, to manage his money. He'd signed a contract on a new house, but he'd had to pull out when he couldn't get the financing, and the owners had sued him.

And he had hired Van Brett Watkins, for $3,000, to beat up Cherica Adams so she'd lose the baby, but Watkins hadn't delivered.

He was tired of being victimized, tired of having these women sucking out his sperm, tired of being rewarded for all his kindness by predators and gold diggers. Tired of taking the ragging. Panicked at the money situation.

So Rae did the only thing he could do, the only option they'd left him.

It's as dark as Charlotte gets, the two-lane stretch of Rea Road a few miles north of the movie theater where Cherica and Rae went that night, in separate cars, and it's so silent, so still in the hour after midnight on a weekday, that if you stop your car in the dip in the road and kill the engine, you can imagine yourself back in the South when the farmland was creased by rambling stone walls and the woods were thick with kudzu.

There are houses here, a few of them, a light or two winking through the trees, but none has a clear sight line to the spot. No one could have known the exact location, even if anyone had been looking, even if someone had been awake and heard the hush of tires on pavement down the road.

No one could have seen Rae's Ford Expedition slowing down in front of Cherica's BMW, blocking her path. No one could have seen Michael Kennedy's rented Nissan Maxima pulling up alongside Cherica.

But they'd have heard the five distinct cracks of the .38, when Watkins sent five metal-jacketed bullets through the tinted glass of the driver's window of the BMW. Four of them hit their target, burrowing through Cherica Adams's lung, bowel, stomach, pancreas, diaphragm, liver, and neck, one of them passing within an inch of her fetus, leaving behind two distinct clusters of star bursts in the glass.

They'd have heard Rae's car pull forward and disappear up Rea Road, and Kennedy making a U-turn to go the other way, and Cherica's BMW weaving down a side street until it crawled to a stop on someone's lawn and she bled out her life onto the front seat. They'd have heard the moans. They *did* hear the moans, in fact; the woman who lives in the house where Cherica ended up that night told me she'd never forget the moans. But she wouldn't give me her name, and she wouldn't open the door more than a few inches, just far enough to flick out her cigarette ashes.

But she did remember one more thing: how after Cherica repeated Rae's license-plate number to the 911 operator, after she pleaded with the operator to save her life, Cherica had had the presence of mind to carefully place the cell phone back on the dashboard.

One other detail of the scene escaped the woman's notice. The way Rae looked back at Watkins, the shooter, in his rearview mirror. As Watkins remembered it, for the briefest moment, their eyes met.

Cherica was conscious when the ambulance arrived at the hospital. Unable to speak, she motioned for a notepad and described the way Rae slowed down in front of her. "He was driving in front of me," she wrote. "He stopped in the road. He blocked the front."

Cherica gave birth to a son named Chancellor, who survived. Then the mother went into a coma from which she never awoke.

Nine days later, at dawn on Thanksgiving, police investigators drove to Rae's house in the Ellington Park subdivision. They rang the doorbell. Rae came to the door naked. A woman was in the bedroom. They arrested him. He made bail. Three weeks later, when Cherica died, and Rae now faced first-degree-murder charges, he skipped town.

They found him lying in the coffin-dark trunk of a gray '97 Toyota Camry in the parking lot of a $36-a-night motel in Tennessee, surrounded by candy bars and two water bottles filled with urine and a cell phone and a couple thousand in cash. His mom had turned him in: Theodry had given him up to the bail bondsman. When FBI agents popped the trunk, Rae kept his eyes closed, and he didn't move.

Soon he opened his eyes, raised his hands, and climbed out. This seemed curious at the time, but it doesn't seem curious anymore.

Knowing Rae as we do now, we know that he simply reasoned thusly: if he didn't see them, then the agents weren't there at all.

Michelle Wright watched the trial on television, watched as Candace, Starlita, Dawnyle, Monique, Fonda, and Amber took the stand, and told Little Rae about all the pretty women.

"How many girlfriends did my dad have?" Little Rae asked his mother.

"I don't know, Rae," she answered. "I'm learning just like you."

"But you can't marry that many women, can you?"

"No," said Michelle. "You can't."

The creak of the knee braces Rae wore beneath his pants to keep him from fleeing was the only sound in the courtroom when he was led in to hear the verdicts, one day shy of his twenty-seventh birthday. Out the smoked windows in the back of the courtroom, black clouds huddled on command and great Gothic spills of water tumbled out of the southern sky as Judge Charles Lamm pronounced the verdict of a jury of Rae's peers: guilty of three of four counts, including conspiracy to commit murder. Innocent of first-degree murder.

The weeping of the women on Cherica Adams's side of the courtroom was immediate and audible and joyous. In a state with no parole, a murder-conspiracy conviction means that Rae will be off the streets for decades. He'll serve nineteen years minimum, twenty-four maximum.

Rae took the news of the verdict the way he'd taken everything for seven straight weeks: with no discernible emotion or expression. Just, as the bailiff led him for the last time past his women, a slight nod — at Tnisha, whose expression was confused, and at Theodry, who was already steeling herself to be strong, and at the rest of the women, who were looking toward him with whatever expressions they could muster.

Rae seemed, if anything, distracted, as if it had just occurred to him for the first time: the only intimate adulation he'd get for the next quarter century would be from men. The women were finally out of his life.

GARY SMITH

Higher Education

FROM SPORTS ILLUSTRATED

THIS IS A STORY about a man, and a place where magic happened. It was magic so powerful that the people there can't stop going back over it, trying to figure out who the man was and what happened right in front of their eyes, and how it'll change the time left to them on earth.

See them coming into town to work, or for their cup of coffee at Boyd & Wurthmann, or to make a deposit at Killbuck Savings? One mention of his name is all it takes for everything else to stop, for it all to begin tumbling out. . . .

"I'm afraid we can't explain what he meant to us. I'm afraid it's so deep we can't bring it into words."

"It was almost like he was an angel."

"He was looked on as God."

There's Willie Mast. He's the one to start with. It's funny, he'll tell you, his eyes misting, he was so sure they'd all been hoodwinked that he almost did what's unthinkable now — run that man out of town before the magic had a chance.

All Willie had meant to do was bring some buzz to Berlin, Ohio, something to look forward to on a Friday night, for goodness' sake, in a town without high school football or a fast-food restaurant, without a traffic light or even a place to drink a beer, a town dozing in the heart of the largest Amish settlement in the world. Willie had been raised Amish, but he'd walked out on the religion at twenty-four — no, he'd peeled out, in an eight-cylinder roar, when he just couldn't bear it anymore, trying to get somewhere in life without a set of wheels or even a telephone to call for a ride.

He'd jumped the fence, as folks here called it, become a Mennonite and started a trucking company, of all things, his tractor-trailers roaring past all those horses and buggies, moving cattle and cold meat over half the country. But his greatest glory was that day back in 1982 when he hopped into one of his semis and moved a legend, Charlie Huggins, into town. Charlie, the coach who'd won two Ohio state basketball championships with Indian Valley South and one with Strasburg-Franklin, was coming to tiny Hiland High. Willie, one of the school's biggest hoops boosters, had banged the drum for Charlie for months.

And yes, Charlie turned everything around in those winters of '82 and '83, exactly as Willie had promised, and yes, the hoops talk was warmer and stronger than the coffee for the first time in twenty years at Willie's table of regulars in the Berlin House restaurant. They didn't much like it that second year when Charlie brought in an assistant — a man who'd helped him in his summer camps and lost his job when the Catholic school where he coached went belly-up — who was black. But Charlie was the best dang high school coach in three states; he must've known something that they didn't. Nor were they thrilled by the fact that the black man was a Catholic, in a community whose children grew up reading tales of how their ancestors were burned at the stake by Catholics during the Reformation in Europe more than four hundred years ago. But Charlie was a genius. Nor did they cherish the fact that the Catholic black was a loser, sixty-six times in eighty-three games with those hapless kids at Guernsey Catholic High near Cambridge. But Charlie. . . .

Charlie quit. Quit in disgust at an administration that wouldn't let players out of their last class ten minutes early to dress for practice. But he kept the news to himself until right before the '84 school year began, too late to conduct a proper search for a proper coach. Willie Mast swallowed hard. It was almost as if his man, Charlie, had pulled a fast one. Berlin's new basketball coach, the man with the most important position in a community that had dug in its heels against change, was an unmarried black Catholic loser. The only black man in eastern Holmes County.

It wasn't that Willie hated black people. He'd hardly known any. "All I'd heard about them," he'll tell you, "was riots and lazy." Few had ever strayed into these parts, and fewer still after that black stuffed dummy got strung up on the town square in Millersburg, just up the road, after the Civil War. Maybe twice a year, back in the 1940s and '50s, a Jewish rag man had come rattling down Route 39 in a rickety truck, scavenging for scrap metal and rags to sell to filling stations thirty miles northeast in Canton or sixty miles north in Cleveland, and brought along a black man for the heavy lifting. People stared at him as if he were green. Kids played Catch the Nigger in their schoolyards without a pang, and when a handful of adults saw the color of a couple of Newcomerstown High's players a few years before, you know what word was ringing in those players' ears as they left the court.

Now, suddenly, this black man in his early thirties was standing in the middle of a gym jammed with a thousand whites, pulling their sons by the jerseys until their nostrils and his were an inch apart, screaming at them. Screaming, "Don't wanna hear your shoulda-coulda-wouldas! Get your head outta your butt!" How dare he?

Worse yet, the black man hadn't finished his college education, couldn't even teach at Hiland High. Why, he was working at Berlin Wood Products, the job Charlie had arranged for him, making little red wagons till 2:00 P.M. each day. "This nigger doesn't know how to coach," a regular at the Berlin House growled.

Willie agreed. "If he wins, it's because of what Charlie built here," he said. "What does he know about basketball?"

But what could be done? Plenty of folks in town seemed to treat the man with dignity. Sure, they were insular, but they were some of the most decent and generous people on earth. The man's Amish coworkers at the wood factory loved him, after they finally got done staring holes in the back of his head. They slammed Ping-Pong balls with him on lunch hour, volleyed theology during breaks, and dubbed him the Original Black Amishman. The Hiland High players seemed to feel the same way.

He was a strange cat, this black man. He had never said a word when his first apartment in Berlin fell through — the landlord who had agreed to a lease on the telephone saw the man's skin and suddenly remembered that he rented only to families. The man had kept silent about the cars that pulled up to the little white house on South Market Street that he moved into instead, about the screams in the darkness, the voices threatening him on his telephone, and the false rumors that he was dating their women. "They might not like us French Canadians here," was all he'd say, with a little smile, when he walked into a place and felt it turn to ice.

Finally, the ice broke. Willie and a few pals invited the man to dinner at a fish joint up in Canton. They had some food and beers and laughs with him, sent him on his merry way, and then . . . what a coincidence: the blue lights flashed in the black man's rearview mirror. DUI.

Willie's phone rang the next morning, but instead of it being a caller with news of the school board's action against the new coach, it was him. Perry Reese, Jr. Just letting Willie know that he knew exactly what had happened the night before. And that he wouldn't go away. The school board, which had caught wind of the plot, never made a peep. Who was this man?

Some people honestly believed that the coach was a spy — sent by the feds to keep an eye on the Amish — or the vanguard of a plot to bring blacks into Holmes County. Yet he walked around town looking people in the eyes, smiling and teasing with easy assurance. He never showed a trace of the loneliness he must have felt. When he had a problem with someone, he went straight to its source. Straight to Willie Mast in the school parking lot one night. "So you're not too sure about me because I'm black," he said, and he laid everything out in front of Willie, about racism and how the two of them needed to get things straight.

Willie blinked. He couldn't help but ask himself the question folks all over town would soon begin to ask: Could I do, or even dream of doing, what the coach is doing? Willie couldn't help but nod when the black man invited him along to scout an opponent and stop for a bite to eat, and couldn't help but feel good when the man said he appreciated Willie because he didn't double-talk when confronted — because Willie, he said, was real. Couldn't help but howl as the Hiland Hawks kept winning, forty-nine times in fifty-three games those first two years, storming to the 1986 Division IV state semifinal.

Winning, that's what bought the black man time, what gave the magic a chance to wisp and curl through town and the rolling fields around it. That's what gave him the lard to live through that frigid winter of '87. That was the school year when he finally had his degree and began teaching history and current events in a way they'd never been taught in eastern Holmes County, the year the

Hawks went 3–18 and the vermin came crawling back out of the baseboards. Damn if Willie wasn't the first at the ramparts to defend him, and damn if that black Catholic loser didn't turn things right back around the next season and never knew a losing one again.

How? By pouring Charlie Huggins's molasses offense down the drain. By runnin' and gunnin', chucking up threes, full-court pressing from buzzer to buzzer — with an annual litter of runts, of spindly, short, close-cropped Mennonites! That's what most of his players were: the children, grandchildren, and great-grandchildren of Amish who, like Willie, had jumped the fence and endured the ostracism that went with it. Mennonites believed in many of the same shall-nots as the Amish: a man shall not be baptized until he's old enough to choose it, nor resort to violence even if his government demands it, nor turn his back on community, family, humility, discipline, and orderliness. But the Mennonites had decided that unlike the Amish, they could continue schooling past the eighth grade, turn on a light switch or a car ignition, pick up a phone, and even, except the most conservative of them, pull on a pair of shorts and beat the pants off an opponent on the hardwood court without drifting into the devil's embrace.

The Hawks' Nest, Hiland's tiny old gym, became what Willie had always dreamed it would be: a loony bin, the one place a Mennonite could go to sweat and shriek and squeal; sold out year after year, with fans jamming the hallway and snaking out the door as they waited for the gym to open, then stampeding for the best seats an hour before the six o'clock jayvee game; reporters and visiting coaches and scouts sardined above them in wooden lofts they had to scale ladders to reach; spillover pouring into the auditorium beside the gym to watch on a video feed as noise thundered through the wall. A few dozen teenage Amish boys, taking advantage of the one time in their lives when elders allowed them to behold the modern world, and sixteen-year-old cheerleaders' legs, would be packed shoulder to shoulder in two corners of the gym at the school they weren't permitted to attend. Even a few Amish men, Lord save their souls, would tie up the horses and buggies across the street at Yoder's Lumber and slink into the Nest. And plenty more at home would tell the missus that they'd just remembered a task in the barn, then click on a radio stashed in the hay and catch the game on WKLM.

Something had dawned on Willie, sitting in his front-row seat, and on everyone else in town. The black man's values were virtually the same as theirs. Humility? No coach ever moved so fast to duck praise or bolt outside the frame of a team picture. Unselfishness? The principal might as well have taken the coach's salary to pep rallies and flung it in the air — most of it ended up in the kids' hands anyway. Reverence? No congregation ever huddled and sang out the Lord's Prayer with the crispness and cadence that the Hawks did before and after every game. Family? When Chester Mullet, Hiland's star guard in '96, only hugged his mom on parents' night, Perry gave him a choice: kiss her or take a seat on the bench. Work ethic? The day and season never seemed to end, from 6:00 A.M. practices to 10:00 P.M. curfews, from puke buckets and running drills in autumn to two-a-days in early winter to camps and leagues and an open gym every summer day. He out-Amished the Amish, out-Mennonited the Mennonites, and everyone, even those who'd never sniffed a locker in their lives, took to calling the black man Coach.

Ask Willie. "Most of the petty divisions around here disappeared because of Coach," he'll tell you. "He pulled us all together. Some folks didn't like me, but I was respected more because he respected me. When my dad died, Coach was right there, kneeling beside the coffin, crossing himself. He put his arm right around my mom — she's Amish — and she couldn't get over that. When she died, he was the first one there. He did that for all sorts of folks. I came to realize that color's not a big deal. I took him for my best friend."

And that man in Willie's coffee clan who'd held out longest, the one given to calling Coach a nigger? By Coach's fifth year, the man's son was a Hawk, the Hawks were on another roll, and the man had seen firsthand the effect Coach had on kids. He cleared his throat one morning at the Berlin House; he had something to say.

"He's not a nigger anymore."

The magic didn't stop with a nigger turning into a man and a man into a best friend. It kept widening and deepening. Kevin Troyer won't cry when he tells you about it, as the others do. They were brought up to hold that back, but maybe his training was better. He just lays out the story, beginning that autumn day ten years ago when he was sixteen, and Coach sat him in the front seat of his Jeep, looked in his eyes, and said, "Tell me the truth."

Someone had broken into Candles Hardware and R&R Sports and stolen merchandise. Whispers around town shocked even the whisperers: that the culprits were their heroes, kids who could walk into any restaurant in Berlin and never have to pay. They'd denied it over and over, and Coach had come to their defense . . . but now even he had begun to wonder.

A priest. That's what he'd told a few friends he would be if he weren't a coach. That's whose eyes Kevin felt boring into him. How could you keep lying to the man who stood in the lobby each morning, greeting the entire student body, searching everyone's eyes to see who needed a headlock, who needed lunch money, who needed love? "Don't know what you did today, princess," he'd sing out to a plump or unpopular girl, "but whatever it is, keep it up. You look great."

He'd show up wearing a cat's grin and the shirt you'd gotten for Christmas — how'd he get into your bedroom closet? — or carrying the pillow he'd snagged right from under your head on one of his Saturday morning sorties, when he slipped like smoke into players' rooms, woke them with a pop on the chest, then ran, cackling, out the door. Sometimes those visits came on the heels of the 1:00 A.M. raids he called Ninja Runs, when he rang doorbells and cawed "Gotcha!" tumbling one family after another downstairs in pajamas and robes to laugh and talk and relish the privilege of being targeted by Coach. He annihilated what people here had been brought up to keep: the space between each other.

His door was never locked. Everyone, boy or girl, was welcome to wade through those half dozen stray cats on the porch that Coach gruffly denied feeding till his stash of cat food was found, and open the fridge, grab a soda, have a seat, eat some pizza, watch a game, play cards or Ping-Pong or Nintendo . . . and talk. About race and religion and relationships and teenage trouble, about stuff that wouldn't surface at Kevin Troyer's dinner table in a million years. Coach listened the way other folks couldn't, listened clean without jumping ahead in his mind to what he'd say next, or to what the Bible said. When he finally spoke, he might play devil's advocate, or might offer a second or third alternative to a kid who'd seen only one, or might say the very thing Kevin didn't want to hear. But Kevin could bet his mother's savings that the conversations wouldn't leave that house.

Coach's home became the students' hangout, a place where they could sleep over without their parents' thinking twice . . . as long as they didn't mind bolting awake to a blast of AC/DC and a 9:00 A.M. noogie. There was no more guard to drop. Parents trusted Coach completely, relied on him to sow their values.

He sowed those, and a few more. He took Kevin and the other Hawks to two-room Amish schools to read and shoot hoops with wide-eyed children who might never get to see them play, took the players to one another's churches and then to his own, St. Peter, in Millersburg. He introduced them to Malcolm X, five-alarm chili, Martin Luther King, Jr., B. B. King, crawfish, Cajun wings, John Lee Hooker, Tabasco sauce, trash-talk fishing, Muhammad Ali.

And possibility. That's what Coach stood for, just by virtue of his presence in Berlin: possibility, no matter how high the odds were stacked against you, no matter how whittled your options seemed in a community whose beliefs had barely budged in two hundred years, whose mailboxes still carried the names of the same Amish families that had come in wagons out of Pennsylvania in the early 1800s — Yoders and Troyers and Stutzmans and Schlabachs and Hostetlers and Millers and Mullets and Masts. A place where kids, for decades, had graduated, married their prom dates, and stepped into their daddies' farming or carpentry or lumber businesses without regard for the fact that Hiland High's graduating classes of sixty ranked in the top ten in Ohio proficiency tests nearly every year. Kevin Troyer's parents didn't seem to care if he went to college. Coach's voice was the one that kept saying, "It's your life. There's so much more out there for you to see. Go places. Do things. Get a degree. Reach out. You have to take a chance."

The kids did, more and more, but not before Coach loaded them with laundry baskets full of items they'd need away from home, and they were never out of reach of those 6:00 A.M. phone calls. "I'm up," he'd say. "Now you are, too. Remember, I'm always here for you."

He managed all that without raising red flags. He smuggled it under the warm coat of all that winning, up the sleeve of all that humility and humor. Everyone was too busy bubbling over the eleven conference titles and five state semifinals. Having too much fun volunteering to be henchmen for his latest prank, shoving Mr. Pratt's desk to the middle of his English classroom, removing the ladder to maroon the radio play-by-play man up in the Hawks' Nest loft, toilet-papering the school superintendent's yard and then watching Coach, the most honest guy in town, lie right through all thirty-two teeth. He was a bootlegger, that's what he was. A bootlegger priest.

"Kevin . . . tell the truth."

Kevin's insides trembled. How could he cash in his five teammates, bring down the wrath of a community in which the Ten Commandments were still stone, own up to the man whose explosions made the Hawks' Nest shudder? How could he explain something that was full of feeling and empty of logic — that somehow, as decent as his parents were, as warm as it felt to grow up in a place where you could count on a neighbor at any hour, it all felt suffocating? All the restrictions of a Conservative Mennonite church that forbade members to watch TV, to go to movies, to dance. All the emotions he'd choked back in a home ruled by a father and mother who'd been raised to react to problems by saying, "What will people think?" All the expectations of playing for the same team that his All-State brother, Keith, had carried to its first state semi in twenty-four years, back in 1986. Somehow, busting into those stores in the summer of '91 felt like the fist Kevin could never quite ball up and smash into all that.

"I . . . I did it, Coach. We. . . ."

The sweetest thing eastern Holmes County had ever known was ruined. Teammate Randy Troyer, no relation to Kevin, disappeared when word got out. The community gasped — those six boys could never wear a Hawks uniform again. Coach? He resigned. He'd betrayed the town's trust and failed his responsibility, he told his superiors. His "sons" had turned to crime.

The administration begged him to stay. Who else was respected enough by family court judges, storekeepers, ministers, and parents to find resolution and justice? Coach stared across the pond he fished behind his house. He came up with a solution both harder and softer than the town's. He would take Randy Troyer under his own roof, now that the boy had slunk back after two weeks of holing up in Florida motels. He'd be accountable for Randy's behavior. He'd have the six boys locked up in detention centers for two weeks, to know what jail tasted and smelled like. But he would let them back on the team. Let them feel lucky to be playing basketball when they'd really be taking a crash course in accountability.

Kevin found himself staring at the cinder-block wall of his cell, as lonely as a Mennonite boy could be. But there was Coach, making his rounds to all six lost souls. There was that lung-bursting bear hug, and another earful about not following others, about believing in yourself and being a man.

The Berlin Six returned. Randy Troyer lived in Coach's home for four months. Kevin walked to the microphone at the first pep rally, sick with nerves, and apologized to the school and the town.

Redemption isn't easy with a five-foot-eleven center, but how tight that 1991–92 team became, players piling into Coach's car every Thursday after practice, gathering around a long table at a sports bar a half-hour away in Dover and setting upon giant cookie sheets heaped with five hundred hot wings. And how those boys could run and shoot. Every time a twenty-footer left the hands of Kevin Troyer or one of the Mishler twins, Nevin and Kevin, or the Hawks' star, Junior Raber, Hiland's students rose, twirling when the ball hit twine and flashing the big red 3s on their T-shirts' backs.

Someday, perhaps in a generation or two, some Berliner might not remember every detail of that postseason march. Against Lakeland in the district championship, the Hawks came out comatose and fell behind 20–5, Coach too stubborn to call a timeout — the man could never bear to show a wisp of doubt. At halftime he slammed the locker-room door so hard that it came off its hinges, then he kicked a crater in a trash can, sent water bottles flying, grabbed jerseys, and screamed so loud that the echoes peeled paint. Kevin and his mates did what all Hawks did: gazed straight into Coach's eyes and nodded. They knew in their bones how small his wrath was, held up against his love. They burst from that locker room like jackals, tore Lakeland to bits, and handily won the next two games to reach the state semis. The world came to a halt in Berlin.

How far can a bellyful of hunger and a chestful of mission take a team before reality steps in and stops it? In the state semifinal in Columbus, against a Lima Central Catholic bunch loaded with kids quicker and thicker and taller and darker, led by the rattlesnake-sudden Hutchins brothers, Aaron and All-Stater Anthony, the Hawks were cooked. They trailed 62–55 with thirty-eight seconds left as Hiland fans trickled out in despair and Lima's surged to the box-office windows to snatch up tickets for the final. Lima called timeout to dot its *i*'s and cross its *t*'s, and there stood Coach in the

Hiland huddle, gazing down at a dozen forlorn boys. He spoke more calmly than they'd ever heard him, and the fear and hopelessness leaked out of them as they stared into his eyes and drank in his plan. What happened next made you know that everything the bootlegger priest stood for — bucking the tide, believing in yourself and possibility — had worked its way from inside him to inside them.

Nevin Mishler, who would sit around the campfire in Coach's back yard talking about life till 2:00 A.M. on Friday nights, dropped in a rainbow three with twenty-seven seconds left to cut the deficit to four. Time-out, calm words, quick foul. Lima's Anthony Hutchins blew the front end of a one-and-one.

Eleven seconds left. Junior Raber, whose wish as a boy was to be black, just like Coach, banked in a driving, leaning bucket and was fouled. He drained the free throw. Lima's lead was down to one. Time out, calm words, quick foul. Aaron Hutchins missed another one-and-one.

Nine ticks left. Kevin Troyer, who would end up going to college and becoming a teacher and coach because of Coach, tore down the rebound and threw the outlet to Nevin Mishler.

Seven seconds left. Nevin turned to dribble, only to be ambushed before half-court by Aaron Hutchins, the wounded rattler, who struck and smacked away the ball.

Five seconds left, the ball and the season and salvation skittering away as Nevin, who cared more about letting down Coach than letting down his parents, hurled his body across the wood and swatted the ball back toward Kevin Troyer. Kevin, who almost never hit the floor, who had been pushed by Coach for years to give more, lunged and collided with Anthony Hutchins, then spun and heaved the ball behind his back to Junior Raber as Kevin fell to the floor.

Three seconds left. Junior took three dribbles and heaved up the impossible, an off-balance thirty-five-footer with two defenders in his face, a shot that fell far short at the buzzer . . . but he was fouled. He swished all three free throws, and the Hawks won, they won — no matter how many times Lima fans waiting outside for tickets insisted to Hiland fans that it couldn't be true — and two days later won the only state title in school history, by three points over Gilmour Academy, on fumes, pure fumes.

In the aisles, people danced who were forbidden to dance. The plaque commemorating the crowning achievement of Coach's life went straight into the hands of Joe Workman, a water and towel boy. Kevin Troyer and his teammates jumped Coach before he could sneak off, hugging him and kissing him and rubbing his head, but he had the last laugh. The 9:00 A.M. noogies would hurt even more those next nine years, dang that championship ring.

Someone would come and steal the magic. Some big-cheese high school or college would take Coach away — they knew it, they just knew it. It all seems so silly now, Steve Mullet says. It might take Steve the last half of his life to finish that slow, dazed shake of his head.

Berlin, you see, was a secret no more by the mid-1990s. Too much winning by Coach, too many tourists pouring in to peer at the men in black hats and black buggies. Two traffic lights had gone up, along with a Burger King and a couple dozen gift shops, and God knows how many restaurants and inns with the word *Dutch* on their shingles to reel in the rubberneckers. Even the Berlin House, where Willie Mast and the boys gathered, was now the Dutch Country Kitchen.

Here they came, the city slickers. Offering Coach big raises and the chance to hush that whisper in his head: Why keep working with disciplined, two-parent white kids when children of his own race were being devoured by drugs and despair for want of someone like him? Akron Hoban wanted him. So did Canton McKinley, the biggest school in the city where Coach had grown up, and Canton Timken, the high school he attended. They wanted to take the man who'd transformed Steve Mullet's family, turned it into something a simple and sincere country fellow had never dreamed it might be. His first two sons were in college, thanks to Coach, and his third one, another guard at Hiland, would likely soon be, too. Didn't Steve owe it to that third boy, Carlos, to keep Coach here? Didn't he owe it to all the fathers of all the little boys around Berlin?

Coach had a way of stirring Steve's anxiety and the stew of rumors. He would walk slow and wounded through each April after he'd driven another team of runts to a conference crown, won two or three postseason games, and then yielded to the facts of the matter, to some school with nearly twice as many students and a couple of six-foot-five studs. "It's time for a change," he'd sigh. "You guys don't need me anymore."

Maybe all missionaries are restless souls, one eye on the horizon, looking for who needs them most. Perhaps Coach was trying to smoke out even the slightest trace of misgivings about him, so he could be sure to leave before he was ever asked to. But Steve Mullet and eastern Holmes County couldn't take that chance. They had to act. Steve, a dairy farmer most of his life, knew about fencing. But how do you fence in a man when no one really understands why he's there, or what he came from?

Who was Coach's family? What about his past? Why did praise and attention make him so uneasy? The whole community wondered, but in Berlin it was disrespectful to pry. Canton was only a forty-five-minute hop away, yet Steve had never seen a parent or a sibling of Coach's, a girlfriend or even a childhood pal. The bootlegger priest was a man of mystery and moods as well as a wide-open door. He'd ask you how your grandma, sister, and uncle were every time you met, but you weren't supposed to inquire about his — you just sensed it. His birthday? He wouldn't say. His age? Who knew? It changed every time he was asked. But his loneliness, that at last began to show.

There were whispers, of course. Some claimed he'd nearly married a flight attendant, then beat a cold-footed retreat. A black woman appeared in the stands once, set the grapevine sizzling, then was never glimpsed again. Steve and his pals loved to tease Coach whenever they all made the twenty-mile drive to Dinofo's, a pizza and pasta joint in Dover, and came face to face with that wild black waitress, Rosie. "When you gonna give it up?" she'd yelp at Coach. "When you gonna let me have it?"

He'd grin and shake his head, tell her it would be so good it would spoil her for life. Perhaps it was too scary, for a man who gave so much to so many, to carve it down to one. Maybe Jeff Pratt, the Hiland English teacher, had it right. Loving with detachment, he called it. So many people could be close to him, because no one was allowed too close.

A circle of women in Berlin looked on him almost as a brother — women such as Nancy Mishler, mother of the twins from the '92 title team, and Peg Brand, the school secretary, and Shelly Miller, wife of the booster club's president, Alan. They came to count on

Coach's teasing and advice, on his cards and flowers and prayers when their loved ones were sick or their children had them at wit's end, and they did what they could to keep him in town. "I wish we could find a way to make you feel this is your family, that this is where you belong," Peg wrote him. "If you leave," she'd say, "who's going to make our kids think?" The women left groceries and gifts on his porch, homemade chocolate-chip cookies on his kitchen table, invited him to their homes on Sundays and holidays no matter how often he begged off, never wanting to impose.

But they all had to do more, Steve decided, picking up his phone to mobilize the men. For God's sake, Coach made only $28,000 a year. In the grand tradition of Mennonites and Amish, they rushed to answer the community call. They paid his rent, one month per donor; it was so easy to find volunteers that they had a waiting list. They replaced his garage when a leaf fire sent it up in flames; it sent him up a wall when he couldn't learn the charity's source. They passed the hat for that sparkling new gym at Hiland, and they didn't stop till the hat was stuffed with 1.6 million bucks. Steve Mullet eventually had Coach move into a big old farmhouse he owned. But first Steve and Willie Mast had another brainstorm: road trip. Why not give Coach a couple of days' escape from their cornfields and his sainthood, and show him how much they cared?

That's how Steve, a Conservative Mennonite in his mid-forties, married to a woman who didn't stick her head out in public unless it was beneath a prayer veil, found himself on Bourbon Street in New Orleans. Standing beside Willie and behind Coach, his heartbeat rising and stomach fluttering as he watched Coach suck down a Hurricane and cock his head outside a string of bars, listening for the chord that would pull him inside.

Coach nodded. This was the one. This blues bar. He pushed open the door. Music and smoke and beer musk belched out. Steve looked at Willie. You could go to hell for this, from everything they'd both been taught. Willie just nodded.

They wedged into a whorl of colors and types of humanity. When Steve was a boy, he'd seen blacks only after his parents jumped the fence, became Mennonites, and took the family in their car each summer to a city zoo. Nothing cruel about blacks was ever said. Steve's parents simply pulled him closer when they were near, filled him with a feeling: our kind and theirs don't mix. Now there were blacks pressed against his shoulders, blacks on microphones screaming lust and heartache into Steve's ears, blacks pounding rhythm through the floorboards and up into his knees. People touching, people gyrating their hips. You could go to hell for this. Steve looked at Willie as Coach headed to the bathroom. "I can't take this," Steve said.

"It's Coach's time, bub," Willie said.

Coach came back, smelled Steve's uneasiness, and knew what to do. "Liven up," he barked and grinned. They got some beers, and it was just like the Hawks' radio play-by-play man, Mark Lonsinger, always said: Coach stood out in a room the instant he walked in, even though he did everything to deflect it. Soon Coach had the folks nearby convinced that he was Black Amish, a highly obscure sect, and Steve, swallowing his laughter, sealing the deal with a few timely bursts of Pennsylvania Dutch, had them believing the three of them had made it to New Orleans from Ohio in a buggy. Before you knew it, it was nearly midnight, and Steve's head was bobbing, his feet tapping, his funk found deep beneath all those layers of mashed potatoes. You know what, he was telling Willie, this Bourbon Street and this blues music really aren't so bad, and isn't it nice, too, how those folks found out that Mennonites aren't Martians?

When they pulled back into Coach's driveway after days filled with laughter and camaraderie, Steve glanced at Willie and sighed, "Well, now we return to our wives."

"You're the lucky ones," said Coach. "Don't you ever forget that."

Steve realized something when they returned from the road: it wasn't the road to ruin. He felt more space inside himself, plenty enough room for the black friends his sons began bringing home from college for the weekend. He realized it again the next year, when they returned to Bourbon Street, and the next, when they went once more, and the one after that as well. "Some things that I was taught were strictly no-nos . . . they're not sins," Steve will tell you. "All I know is that it all seemed right to do with him."

Funny how far that feeling had fanned, how many old, deep lines had blurred in Berlin, and what occurred in a dry community when Coach overdid it one night four years ago and tried one last time to leave. "I screwed up," he told school superintendent Gary Sterrett after he got that second DUI, fourteen miles up the road in Sugar Creek. "You need to take my job."

What happened was sort of like what happened the time the ball rolled toward the Hawks' bench in a game they were fumbling away that year at Garaway High, and Coach pulled back his leg and kicked the ball so hard that it hissed past a referee's ear and slammed off the wall, the gym hushing in anticipation of the technical foul and the ejection. But nothing happened. The two refs had such enormous respect for Coach, they pretended it away.

He apologized to every player and to every player's parents for the DUI. Steve never mentioned it. The community never said a word. It was pretended away.

They've combed through the events a thousand times, lain in bed at night tearing themselves and God to shreds. There were clues, after all, and it was their job to notice things Coach was too stubborn to admit. They thought, when he holed up in his motel room for three days in Columbus last March, that it was merely one of his postseason moods, darker than ever after falling one game shy, for the third straight year, of playing for the state title. They thought he was still brooding two months later when, preoccupied and suffering from a cold he couldn't shake, he started scrambling names and dates and getting lost on country roads.

It all came to a head one Saturday last June, when he climbed into another rented tux because Phil Mishler, just like fifty or sixty kids before him, had to have Coach in his wedding party. At the reception, Coach offered his hand to Tom Mullet and said, "I'm Perry Reese, Jr., Hiland High basketball coach." Tom Mullet had been Hiland's assistant athletic director for ten years.

Phone lines buzzed that Sunday. People began comparing notes, discovering new oddities. On Monday night two of Coach's best friends, Dave Schlabach and Brian Hummel, headed to Mount Hope and the old farmhouse Coach had moved into just outside Berlin, the only house with lights in a community of Amish. They found him shivering in a blanket, glassy-eyed and mumbling nonsense.

Their worst possible fears . . . well, it went beyond all of them. Brain tumor. Malignant. Inoperable. Four to eight months to live, the doctors at Canton's Aultman Hospital said. You can't bring down a sledgehammer faster than that.

Jason Mishler, Coach's starting point guard the past two years, was the first kid to find out. He stationed himself in the chair beside Coach's bed, wouldn't budge all night and most of the next day. His cousin Kevin Mishler, from the state championship team, dropped his vacation on Hilton Head Island, South Carolina, and flew back. Dave Jaberg, who had played for Hiland a few years before that, dropped the bonds he was trading in Chicago and drove for six hours. Junior Raber was on the first plane from Atlanta. Think a moment. How many teachers or coaches would you do that for?

The nurses and doctors were stupefied — didn't folks know you couldn't fit a town inside a hospital room? Coach's friends filled the lobby, the elevator, the halls, and the waiting room. It was like a Hiland basketball game, only everyone was crying. Coach kept fading in and out, blinking up at another set of teary eyes and croaking, "What's new?"

What do people pray for when doctors don't give them a prayer? They swung for the fences. The Big M, a miracle. Some begged for it. Some demanded it. A thousand people attended a prayer vigil in the gym and took turns on the microphone. Never had so much anger and anguish risen from Berlin and gone straight at God.

Steroids shrank the tumor enough for Coach to return home, where another throng of folks waited, each telling the other tales of what Coach had done to change his life, each shocked to find how many considered him their best friend. When he walked through his front door and saw the wheelchair, the portable commode, the hospital bed, and the chart Peg Brand had made, dividing the community's twenty-four-hour care for Coach into six-hour shifts, he sobbed. The giving was finished. Now all he could do was take.

Go home, he ordered them. Go back to your families and lives. He called them names. They knew him well enough to know how loathsome it was for him to be the center of attention, the needy one. But they also knew what he would do if one of them were dying. They decided to keep coming anyway. They were family. Even more in his dying than in his living, they were fused.

They cooked for him, planned a trip to New York City he'd always dreamed of making, prayed and cried themselves to sleep. They fired off e-mails to churches across the country, recruited entire congregations who'd never heard of Coach to pray for the Big M. Louise Conway, grandmother of a player named Jared Coblentz, woke up three or four times a night, her heart thumping so hard that she had to drop to her knees and chew God's ear about Coach before she could drop back to sleep. People combed the Internet for little-known treatments. They were going to hoist a three at the buzzer and get fouled.

Coach? He did the strangest thing. He took two radiation treatments and stopped. He refused the alternative treatments, no matter how much people cried and begged and flung his own lessons in his face. Two other doctors had confirmed his fate, and damned if he was going to be helpless for long if he could help it. "Don't you understand?" he told a buddy, Doug Klar. "It's okay. This is how it's supposed to be."

He finally had a plan, one that would make his death like his life, one that would mean the giving wasn't finished. He initiated a foundation, a college scholarship fund for those in need, started it rolling with his $30,000 life savings and, after swallowing hard, allowed it to be named after him on one condition: that it be kept secret until he was dead.

He had no way to keep all the puzzle pieces of his life in boxes now; dying shook them out. Folks found out, for instance, that he turned forty-eight last August. They were shocked to meet two half-sisters they'd never heard of. They were glad finally to see Coach's younger sister, Audrey Johnson, whose picture was on his refrigerator door and who was studying to be a social worker, and his younger brother, Chris, who helps run group homes for people who can't fend for themselves and who took a leave of absence to care for Coach.

It turned out that Audrey had made a couple of quiet visits a year to Coach and that the family had gathered for a few hours on holidays; there were no dark or splintering secrets. He came from two strict parents who'd died in the '80s — his dad had worked in a Canton steel mill — and had a mixed-race aunt on one side of the family and a white grandfather on the other. But there were never quite enough pieces of the puzzle for anyone to put them together on a table and get a clean picture.

Coach's family was shocked to learn a few things, too. Like how many conservative rural white folks had taken a black man into their hearts. "Amazing," said Jennifer Betha, his half-sister, a supervisor for Head Start. "And so many loving, respectful, well-mannered children around him. They were like miniature Perrys! Our family was the independent sort, all kind of went our own ways. I never realized how easy it is to get to Berlin from Canton, how close it is. What a waste. Why didn't we come before?"

Coach had two good months, thanks to the steroids. Berlin people spent them believing that God had heard them, and that the miracle had come. Coach spent the months telling hundreds of visitors how much he cared about them, making one last 1:00 A.M. Ninja Run, and packing his life into ten neat cardboard boxes.

The first week of August, he defied doctors' orders not to drive and slipped into the empty school. Gerald Miller, his buddy and old boss at the wagon factory, found him later that day at home, tears streaming down his cheeks. "Worst day of my life," Coach said. "Worse than finding out about this thing in my head. I cleaned out my desk. I can't believe it. I'm not gonna teach anymore. I'm done."

In early September the tumor finally had its way. He began slurring words, falling down, losing the use of his right hand and leg, then his eyesight. "How are you doing?" he kept asking his visitors, on blind instinct. "Is there anything I can do for you?" Till the end he heard the door open and close, open and close, and felt the hands, wrapped around his, doing that, too.

On the day he died, November 22, just over a week before the Hawks' first basketball game and seventeen years after he first walked through their doors, Hiland looked like one of those schools in the news in which a kid has walked through the halls with an automatic weapon. Six ministers and three counselors walked around hugging and whispering to children who were huddled in the hallway crying or staring into space, to teachers sobbing in the bathrooms, to secretaries who couldn't bear it and had to run out the door.

An old nettle digs at most every human heart: the urge to give oneself to the world rather than to only a few close people. In the end, unable to bear the personal cost, most of us find a way to ignore the prickle, comforting ourselves that so little can be changed by one woman or one man anyway.

How much, in the end, was changed by this one man? In Berlin, they're still tallying that one up. Jared Coblentz, who might have been the Hawks' sixth man this year, quit because he couldn't play for anyone other than Coach. Jason Mishler was so furious that he quit going to church for months, then figured out that it might be greedy to demand a miracle when you've been looking at one all your life. Tattoo parlors added Mennonites to their clientele. Junior Raber stares at the RIP with a P beneath it on his chest every morning when he looks into the mirror of his apartment in Atlanta. Jason Mishler rubs the image of Coach's face on the top of his left arm during the national anthem before every game he plays at West Liberty (West Virginia) State.

The scholarship fund has begun to swell. Half the schools Hiland has played this season have chipped in checks of $500 or $600, while refs for the girls' basketball games frequently hand back their $55 checks for the pot.

Then there's the bigger stuff. Kevin Troyer has decided that someday, rather than teach and coach around Berlin, he'll reverse Coach's path and do it with black kids up in Canton. Funny, the question he asked himself that led to his decision was the same one that so many in Berlin ask themselves when they confront a dilemma: What would Coach do? Hard to believe, an outsider becoming the moral compass of a people with all those rules on how to live right.

And the even bigger stuff. Like Shelly and Alan Miller adopting a biracial boy ten years ago over in Walnut Creek, a boy that Coach had taken under his wing. And the Keims over in Charm adopting two black boys, and the Schrocks in Berlin adopting four black girls, and the Masts just west of town adopting two black girls, and Chris Miller in Walnut Creek adopting a black girl. Who knows? Maybe some of them would have done it had there never been a Perry Reese, Jr., but none of them would have been too sure that it was possible.

"When refugees came to America," the town psychologist, Elvin Coblentz, says, "the first thing they saw was the Statue of Liberty. It did something to them — became a memory and a goal to strive for your best, to give your all, because everything's possible. That's what Coach is to us."

At the funeral, just before Communion, Father Ron Aubry gazed across St. Peter, Coach's Catholic church in Millersburg. The priest knew that what he wanted to do wasn't allowed, and that he could get in trouble. But he knew Coach, too. So he did it: invited everyone up to receive the holy wafer.

Steve Mullet glanced at his wife, in her simple clothing and veil.

"Why not?" she whispered. After all, the service wasn't the bizarre ritual they had been led to believe it was, wasn't all that different from their own. Still, Steve hesitated. He glanced at Willie Mast. "Would Coach want us to?" Steve whispered.

"You got 'er, bub," said Willie.

So they rose and joined all the black Baptists and white Catholics pouring toward the altar, all the basketball players, all the Mennonites young and old. Busting laws left and right, busting straight into the kingdom of heaven.

ELIZABETH GILBERT

Near Death in the Afternoon

FROM GQ

AT FIRST THERE WERE ONLY three old men outside the bullfighting plaza, offering scalped tickets and opinions about the matadors. Then came the children, chasing each other around in the shade. Then came the vendors, selling ice cream and icons. Then the older residents gradually began streaming from their homes, greeting each other on the sidewalks with kisses and embraces, walking together toward the plaza in loud, animated groups.

By midafternoon, the first buses had arrived, pouring out bullfighting fans from the Basque region, with their binoculars and their goatskins of wine. Behind the plaza, grooms began unloading horses and preparing them for the bullfight, draping them in protective armor and riding them in circles. Then the transport trucks arrived with the most sacred cargo of all — the six bulls themselves, hidden away in the darkness within. The air was filling now with the smells of manure, livestock, and sweat. . . .

There is not much to the sleepy northern town of Haro, and even within Spain most people have never heard of it. But today something was different. The legendary young matador El Juli was coming to fight, and as the hours passed, the town stirred and filled, growing slowly into its own importance. Bullfights generally don't begin in Spain until seven o'clock, an hour that this most nocturnal of nations still refers to as afternoon. By that time, the sun was low enough in the sky to be almost tolerable and the entire population of northern Spain, it seemed, was crowding into the old bullfighting arena.

Most of these people had never seen the young matador fight in a live performance. Still, having followed the development of El Juli's career for years, they felt comfortable discussing his merits with expert authority. They generally agreed with one another that El Juli was a true prince of Spain, the brightest hope for bullfighting's future. Some of the older aficionados were not so sure, arguing that El Juli was too young to be judged, too much of a show-off, not yet in total control of his emotions, as a noble matador needs to be. One old man scoffed at the whole cult of El Juli, saying, "He is nothing but a boy, nothing but a little bonbon for the ladies," at which his wife laughed and called him jealous.

The boy in question was just eighteen years old — *is* just eighteen years old. He is small, fair-haired, extremely attractive, profoundly intelligent and arguably the best living bullfighter on the planet. His name is Julián López, but he is more widely known across Spain as El Juli, which translates literally as "the Juli" — something akin to calling a man named James "the Jim."

The Spanish also call him the Mozart of bullfighting, since he began to garner fame as a mere child. He was only nine years old when he entered El Batán, the national bullfighting academy in Madrid (over the strong objections of his father — a failed matador, who had lost an eye in the ring years earlier). But El Juli could not be deterred, and his teachers at the academy — from the first time they ever saw him move — knew immediately that he had the markings of real genius. They were astonished by his physical grace, by his perfect instincts, and by his utter absence of fear.

"It was as though he had landed here from another galaxy," they would later say.

They put the boy before his first bull calf when he was only ten and then marveled as El Juli fought flawlessly, sinking his sword into the back of the bull's neck in one unhesitating, fluid motion. Watching that sword disappear, El Juli's teachers were so shaken by a sense of destiny, they may as well have been watching the young Arthur pull his sword from a stone — the exact same fateful and dramatic gesture, played in reverse.

By the time El Juli was twelve, his teachers felt they had nothing more to offer him; he already knew all he needed to become a great matador. His father, too, had realized that his son was born to fight bulls. Unfortunately for the young prodigy, though, strict European child-labor laws forbid boys to fight professionally until the age of sixteen. Luckily, however, the Mexican government doesn't get fussy about such nonsense, so El Juli's family moved him to Mexico, where he became — by fourteen — the most popular matador in Latin America.

In 1998, El Juli finally returned to Europe like a beloved prince coming out of exile, facing his first bull as a professional just after his sixteenth birthday. He confirmed in that ring (and has confirmed in every ring since) the rumors that had been swirling about him for years — that he is indeed the stuff of legend. Invariably, he fights with poise, brilliance, speed, honor, and perfect intuition. But his most distinguishing characteristic remains his unshakable courage. El Juli faces a bull with such fearlessness that you might guess he doesn't know it's possible to be injured by such an animal. But of course, he does know this. And not just because he knows the whole bloody history of all those fine Spanish matadors trampled and impaled and crippled and killed in the ring, either. El Juli knows the danger of bullfighting *personally,* having been — before that afternoon in Haro — seriously gored four times, including once through the face. In one memorable fight in the South of France, he took a bull's horn straight through the thigh. His men rushed to his assistance, but he pushed them away, reportedly saying, "If you really want to help me, get out of here, I have a bull to kill."

At one minute before seven, there were still spectators crowding into the hot, airless stairwells of the old Haro plaza, pushing for their seats. But at exactly seven, the trumpets sounded (in a nation where *nothing* starts on time, the bullfights always start on time) and the arena doors were sealed closed. Anyone stuck in the stairwells was out of luck as all the world's humanity cleaved into a division between *inside* and *outside,* between those who would now collectively participate in this ancient ritual and those who would not. The vast universe narrowed to this small circle of sand.

El Juli stepped into the ring, and the day was shredded by cheers. Dressed in the classic matador's "suit of lights," he positively shimmered in the sun. He looked impossibly young, impossibly small. Standing just shy of five feet seven, he couldn't have weighed more than 140 pounds. His legs looked strong enough, but his arms seemed thin. His hands were not large. His shoulders were narrow. He had a soft mouth and wide eyes, and it was quite possible to look at his face and imagine that this boy had never even shaved.

The bull plowed into the ring and was met with the same welcoming response. The contrast between the enormous bulk of the bull and the physical smallness of the young matador made for a jarring mismatch. A Spanish fighting bull is a terrifying opponent — half a ton or so of muscle and bone and horn and vengeance, packed on a frame that can spin like a cat and outsprint a horse. With a head harder than bedrock and neck muscles thicker than radial tires, a bull has only one point of vulnerability on its body — a tiny soft spot located just between the shoulder blades into which the matador must slip a sword to make his kill (moving *over* the bull's head and horns to do so, making this the most dangerous moment of the fight).

El Juli, on the other hand, appeared to be made of nothing but soft spots. And his matador's costume, it should be said, was not lending him any protection, either. An American football player wouldn't dream of squaring off against a 250-pound human linebacker without enough protective gear to help him survive a fall from a ten-story building, yet here was young El Juli, calmly facing down a murderous 1,500-pound bull, wearing a bejeweled jacket, elegant britches, pink silk stockings, and the daintiest little black ballet slippers you ever saw.

With perfect composure, El Juli raised his hat toward the crowd, circled once in salutation, accepted the adoration of Haro and then immediately drew the bull past him in one, two, three, four, five quick passes. The cape in his hands looked at times like a lion trainer's whip, at times like a flamenco dancer's fan, both commanding and delicate. He wrapped the cape around his torso like a sari and twirled, pulling the bull along with him in a tight spin. Then he reversed and spun himself and the bull in the opposite direction. The crowd was clapping in rhythm, voices calling for *música! música!,* and upon this demand the band started playing a fiery *pasadoble* as El Juli led this bull into the dance of its life.

Had you never seen a bullfight before, had you never *heard* of bullfighting before, you would have still recognized immediately that you were watching something extraordinary in this boy. Just as there are certain stage actors who are so magnetic that you must always watch them, even when they are not the center of the dramatic action, it was impossible not to stare — riveted — at El Juli, even when he was standing perfectly still. Indeed, it was his episodic stillness during this bullfight that was perhaps the most compelling thing about him. El Juli did not move until he needed to move. He never flinched unnecessarily, never wasted a gesture, never second-guessed a physical choice. From the first moment the bull thundered across the sand in Haro, El Juli stood motionless to face it, hips slightly forward, arms relaxed, regarding his animal in a calm state of contemplation, appearing to ask only: *Well, then . . . what have we here?*

Also impressive was the quiet command El Juli exerted over the other men (far, far older men) in the ring who formed his support team — the picadors and *peones* and *banderilleros* who participate in the killing of the bull, their roles as ritualized in this ancient ceremony as the roles of altar boys at a High Mass. With a nod, with a simple word, he set the strategy, demonstrating a stately self-assurance unfathomable in a teenager.

Now, as El Juli signaled, it was time for the picador to do his job. The picador is a horseman with a long lance who lures the bull into attacking his horse and then administers the first wound of the day to the animal — stabbing into the hump of muscle behind its head. Like everything else in bullfighting, this is both a savage and a delicate operation. With all the might it could summon, the bull slammed into the side of the horse, who was blindfolded, whose ears were stuffed with newspaper, whose flanks were draped in protective Kevlar gear, who had no idea what on earth was happening, only that it was horrifying. If the bull is strong enough, it can often topple over both horse and rider in this moment, trapping the man under the terrified animal, ultimately goring both. It's an extremely dangerous process and one that the matador must orchestrate well if all is to proceed safely. But as El Juli's picador — the sixty-seven-year-old Salvador Herrero, a man of legendary courage himself — has always said of his teenage boss, "I only pay attention to the most intelligent man in the ring. And that man is always El Juli."

El Juli gave the signal, the picador moved in, the bull slugged into the horse, the horse leaned into the bull's attack, and the picador rose up in the saddle and stabbed his lance down into the bull's back, looking like a harpooner going after a rising whale. Salvador Herrero delivered the ideal wound — deep enough to anger the animal and focus its attention, but not so deep as to "kill" it by injuring its spinal cord or sapping all its strength. Then El Juli was flitting at the bull faster than a jackrabbit, drawing the bull away from the horseman, using his own nimble body as a lure, coaxing the animal, whose back was now glistening and purple with blood, to the center of the ring.

Now El Juli seemed to be playing with the bull, both chasing and being pursued by it as he set three pairs of steel darts into the animal's back to further agitate it. At one point, he and the bull charged headlong toward each other so fast and determined — the ultimate game of chicken — that it seemed inevitable they would collide in a ball of hair and bone and curses and death, but El Juli dodged and twisted at the last instant (*after* the last instant is actually how it appeared) and the bull scarcely missed him. Outraged, the bull took off after El Juli with a concentrated fury, chasing him toward the wall and damn near pinning him against it, bellowing in frustration when El Juli leaped over the five-foot barricade with all the practiced agility of a gymnast leaping onto a pommel horse.

Tossing his body lightly back into the ring again, El Juli received a riotous ovation from the crowd. He let himself grin widely for a moment, pumping his fist once in the air and tossing his chin up in a brief and cocky acknowledgment of his own audacity. Then, immediately, he took up his red fighting cape and all his elegant composure — all his perfect matador-ness — returned.

Quiet and poised, El Juli stood in the center of the ancient arena in Haro, watching his animal. This bull was in the last minutes of its life. It was tired and injured and dazed. The two gazed at each other. Heaving for breath, tongue swollen, back shimmering metallic with blood, the bull looked far more tranquil than the furious, thrashing beast that had first entered the ring. But it was, in fact, a much more dangerous animal now. The pain and the exhaustion had brought a clearer focus, a realization that it was fighting for its life. This is the point in a bullfight when bulls start killing matadors. This is the point in a bullfight when bulls start *aiming.*

El Juli called to the bull. His voice — high and ringing — echoed against the silent stones of the arena.

"Venga, toro!" he shouted. Come, bull!

It was a provocation, accompanied by a quick snap of the cape. The bull charged like an entire battalion of infantry, headed straight for the matador. El Juli stood his ground and then pivoted lightly on one heel, opening his body like a well-oiled door on a hinge, allowing the bull to miss him by centimeters.

"Venga, toro!" El Juli shouted again, spinning and setting his feet once more, twitching the cape almost imperceptibly. The bull charged again, this time passing so close that its horn seemed in danger of snagging a sequin from El Juli's jacket, of pulling a thread loose.

"Venga, toro!" El Juli shouted in that chiming voice again. When the bull passed this time, El Juli leaned far into its massive bulk, reaching out with one arm and caressing the bull's body as it passed, the way a man will let his arm linger luxuriously across the body of a woman he is waltzing with. El Juli was no longer letting this bull pass so close that they were almost touching; now they *were* touching on each pass. He was brushing so tightly against the animal, in fact, that his torso was soon soaked with the bull's blood. *"Venga, toro!"* he shouted again.

The Spanish say of El Juli that his head is a computer, that this baby-faced teenage boy holds the entire history of bullfighting inside his brain. They say that he has a quality called *raza,* which means breeding, nobility, refinement, grace. They also say, however, that he is *fogoso* — a word with its root in fire, a word that is often translated as fierce but can mean explosive. And it's this dichotomy that was making El Juli's performance in Haro so electric — the powerful alternation between stillness and eruption, the sudden transformation of a prince into a pugilist, the blurring instant when *raza* becomes *fogoso.*

The bull charged once more. This time El Juli met the charge down on one knee, setting his stance in such a manner that it would be impossible for him to move quickly out of the way. He set himself there like bait but with all the confidence of one who knows just where to drop, of one who knows just where the bull is going to pass, of one who inexplicably knows the future. The bull thundered by, and El Juli rippled his cape over its face.

The bull spun, and El Juli leaped back to his feet. He beckoned the animal toward him, then raised his arm like a traffic cop as though to say *Stop.* And the bull did stop, just like that, pulled itself to a halt only inches in front of the matador. They looked at each other. El Juli seductively drew the tip of his sword down the bull's face, lightly tracing the beautiful line from horn to horn, like a lover learning the curves of a loved one's body with the tip of a finger. The kill would be coming soon, and it was almost as though El Juli wanted to memorize the animal one last time, to cherish its singularity. The bull did not move. Then — astonishingly — El Juli turned his back on the animal and strolled away from it, unconcerned and undefended. The bull did not stir.

The crowd roared, came to its feet in wonder. An elderly woman high up in the arena smiled and nodded in the warmest satisfaction.

"You see?" she said to the dumbfounded American tourist seated beside her. "We Spaniards may never have stepped on the moon, but look how bravely we walk the earth."

It is an indefensible position to state that human beings have the right to torture and kill another species for entertainment. Who among us, for instance, would not intervene in horror if we came upon a group of boys in an alleyway tormenting a stray dog — cutting it with knives and taunting it and terrifying it — merely for their own amusement? All across Europe today are people who protest bullfighting as archaic and inhumane. To such people, there is no difference between the slow and systematic killing of a bull in a ring and the torture of a defenseless stray dog in an alleyway.

Of course, a Spanish fighting bull is far from defenseless. These bulls are warriors, descendants of the massive prehistoric bison of Europe — animals whose portraits are preserved (etched in their own blood, the first evidence of Western art) on the walls of caves in rural France. These are creatures whose destiny has always been tied to man in violent and sacrosanct ways. Their ancestors were hunted out of northern Europe, ritually sacrificed in ancient Greece, worshiped as deities in Asia Minor, and bred for fearsomeness by medieval Spanish feudal lords for just this purpose — to be killed in public by a man in a ring on a hot afternoon.

And perhaps it's important to clarify here that a bullfight is indeed a fight. No Spanish fighting bull is ever asked to go down without having first been given the opportunity to eviscerate the matador, or puncture the man's lungs, or see to it that his attacker never walks again. Which is more of a chance than your average veal calf ever gets to even out the scales of justice. Still, animal rights activists want to know what entitlement we have as human beings to put another creature through agonizing torment for our own entertainment, and that question is — when posed as such — indeed indefensible. Except that it doesn't take into account another, larger question, which is whether bullfighting is entertainment at all.

The Spanish have certainly never thought so. They have never categorized bullfighting as a sport. For the last seven centuries of Spanish history, bullfighting has instead hovered in a mystical dimension located somewhere between the world of art and the world of religion. Articles about bullfights are not even published in the sports sections of Spanish newspapers but instead appear in the cultural and arts pages, right next to essays about opera and ballet and theater and literature.

Matadors may be athletic, but they have never been seen as athletes. The first bullfighters were medieval Spanish knights, who practiced fighting bulls to prepare themselves and their horses for battle against Moorish invaders. The knights made these practice sessions public so the nervous populace could be reassured that their defenders were brave, and matadors ever since have carried on their shoulders the responsibility of embodying Spanish bravery and defending Spanish culture. Which explains the pride of the old woman in Haro as she witnessed El Juli's courage in the ring. His performance restored her confidence that her country was still safe — maybe not from invading Moors this time, but from invading American tourists, from globalization, from the shock of losing the familiar Spanish peseta to the newly minted homogeneous euro, from the bloodless international threat of soccer (which her grandchildren now vastly prefer to bullfighting), from the cancerous spread of the Internet, from the loss of one's very identity. . . .

And then there is the religious aspect of bullfighting. Its codes and etiquette have developed over centuries until every moment of a bullfight has been thoroughly ritualized and every gesture of the matador has become a deliberate metaphor, often sacred in nature. One of the most profound moves a matador can make in the ring, for instance, is to flutter the cape over the bull's face as it passes by him. This is called the veronica — named for Saint Veronica, who wiped the suffering face of Christ with a cloth as he passed her on his torturous journey toward death up Calvary Mountain.

Of course, just because bullfighting has a sacred and complicated cultural history does not mean that it cannot also be savagely inhumane. Bullfights are often just that. To see a clumsy bullfight is to witness an almost unwatchable violence. You will sometimes see an awkward matador attempt to sink his sword six, seven, eight, nine times into the back of a bull, ripping the animal apart without killing it, making you feel ashamed to be a human participating in this horror. A botched bullfight is a prolonged and dreadful act of butchery. You can no more understand the mystical richness of bullfighting by watching an inadequate matador than you can understand the mystical richness of human dance by watching the gesticulations of a drunken oaf. Instead, watch El Juli.

El Juli faced the bull in the center of the Haro plaza. He was speaking to the bull again but quietly enough now that the crowd could not hear him. El Juli inched slowly toward the bull. His face was filled with unspeakable tenderness as he approached the animal the way you might approach a child who had hidden under a table in tears: gentle, coaxing, head tilted to one side. The bull, heaving for breath, watched the matador's approach. There was no resistance in the bull's body, nor was there total defeat.

The two of them were in some distant place of their own now. They had just spent twenty minutes participating in each other's destinies with such grace that it would appear they had become partners, that they had colluded to draw the utmost beauty and boldness out of each other. Now the bull dropped its head toward El Juli in a gesture that was impossible to see as anything other than sentient acceptance, a gesture that appeared to say: *I understand. This time I am the butt and you are the matador. Proceed.*

El Juli lifted up on his toes, tensed like a diver preparing to let his body fly, drew back his sword, and called to the bull one last time. One last time the bull charged toward him and the young matador struck faster than a cobra — there was a flash of gold, and then he spun away from the bull and opened his arms, and his sword had vanished, buried already to the hilt in the bull's heart.

The bull wove, swaying on its feet like kelp swaying in a tidal current. El Juli stood before it with one arm extended, reaching out as though to help the animal along, persuading it toward death, reassuring it that this was right and timely and good. The young matador's face was respectful. His eyes never left the bull's eyes, and his lips moved in what could have been prayer. He presided over this bull to its very last breath, almost seeming to accompany the animal along, dipping his knees somewhat as the bull took one last step and then buckled down to the sand, folding gracefully into death.

It did not feel like a killing, it felt like an *offering*.

There was awed silence. Then came a flare of raucous cheers. Then came the unanimous waving of handkerchiefs (which symbolized the audience's respect), then came the cascading of the bullring with flowers (which expressed the audience's love), then came the awarding of both the bull's ears to the smiling young matador (which honored the boy's excellence). Then came the part where El Juli was carried in triumph from the bullring on the shoulders of the very strongest men in the village of Haro.

Lifted as such, hoisted high into the air and elevated like a true hero, the boy now appeared to be extraordinarily tall. Taller than any two men put together. Taller than anyone in Spain.

The Plaza de Toros de las Ventas in Madrid is the holy temple of Spanish bullfighting. The fans there are famously critical. They accept nothing but the best and are sometimes bored by that. Anything less than a passionate demonstration of perfection in the plaza is met with jeers, whistles, sarcasm, disdain, and a rain of seat cushions thrown into the ring, aimed at the offending matador's head. The audience's famously gladiatorial-style demand to be thrilled and stirred often pushes bullfighters to take more dangerous risks than they can manage, just to appease the masses. Either the bull will kill you in Madrid, it has been said, or the crowd will.

El Juli had promised the press that after the great performance in Haro, he would deliver the fight of his life in Madrid. But before he got his chance to dazzle that afternoon, two other matadors had to fight in the great arena (the youngest matador always goes last), and those fights were dreary and disappointing. Victor Puerto suffered the woeful humiliation of actually tripping in the ring and dropping his cape, then having to clownishly scramble out of the bull's way. The cranky Madrid audience was so disgusted by this clumsy show it almost turned into a lynch mob.

"Lord, have mercy on me, you and the king of Spain!" one man groaned, as poor Victor Puerto attempted again to make the kill, only to have his sword bounce off the bull's back and hit the sand.

The second fight was no more impressive. Rivera Ordóñez came out and fought a stiff and lackluster bull in a stiff and lackluster style, nearly putting the crowd to sleep in the hot afternoon sun. "Holy God, get it over with!" one heckler jeered as Ordóñez took five awkward attempts to kill this resigned and tired old bull. When the bull finally went down, an aficionado high in the stands stood up and shouted, "That bull died of boredom! Now bring on El Juli already!"

Indeed, the sudden appearance of El Juli in the ring snapped the audience right to attention. Dressed all in gold and silver, he glittered with promise. And then came the bull. It was a perfect bull, black and glossy as oiled granite, carrying all its power in a heavily muscled chest and intimidating head. And when this massive animal stormed with rage and lethal intent into the Plaza de Toros — bellowing, tossing its horns, and pawing the earth like a veritable caricature of a bull — the audience of 23,000 restless and jaded aficionados caught its collective breath, held still for one shared instant, and then detonated into awed applause.

Madrid — who never approves of anything — approved of this bull.

El Juli started the fight with a dancer's grace, twirling the bull around the ring as effortlessly as the wind twirls a kite on a string, commanding both the animal and the audience with a regal ease. At first, El Juli used only his most elegant passes and smoothest swirls of the cape, but as the bull became more determined to murder him and as the audience's adrenaline rose, El Juli kicked up his strategy to pure aggression. Suddenly, the pretty flourishes were gone, and El Juli was all brio and challenge and *you-want-a-piece-of-me?* fury. He stampeded at the bull, snarled at it, taunted it, smacked its ass as it drove by him, defying it to say something back to his face. This was no longer a dance, this was a boxing match.

The whole crowd was white-knuckled and breathless now, seeming to rock and ebb with the waves of this match, every heart beating as a single heart within the stiff, old stone rib cage of the great Madrid arena. With each pass, the bull got closer and more outraged and El Juli got closer and more daring and the audience's gasps got louder and more astonished — *did he really just* do *that?* — and the boy stuck out his chest that was spattered with the bull's blood and thrust that cocky chin of his up even higher in the air and planted his feet in the sand like a conquistador claiming his rightful ground, because he was ready to triumph over the entire known universe.

That's when the bull caught him.

The bull caught him on a sweeping pass, plunging a horn straight through the young matador's thigh in one unspeakable motion. Time stopped. Then the bull snatched the best matador in Spain off the ground by that impaled leg — very much the same way you might pull a pickle out of a barrel with a long fork — and jerked El Juli into the air. Then the bull dropped El Juli to the ground and yanked its horn out of his leg. The boy made one attempt to stir, but the bull caught him again, this time scooping up under him like a pitchfork and tossing him up onto its head and horns. The bull thrashed wildly, and the matador's limbs, so graceful and coordinated just heartbeats earlier, were now snapping and twisting through the air, horribly distorted, grotesquely rag dolled as the bull whipped its colossal neck. Then El Juli was down and the bull was driving hard with hooves and horn and head, digging with livid focus into the matador's body, pulverizing him.

The attack lasted no more than thirty seconds. It took only that long for El Juli's men and the other matadors to get themselves into the ring and lure the bull away. The bull took off after someone else's flashing cape and — astonishing! a miracle! — El Juli pulled himself up from the sand and actually stood. His ornate and bejeweled clothes were torn and soaked with blood. A section of his thigh muscle was hanging out through a hole in his leg. He made a gesture as though to push away the men who were running forward to help him, and then he collapsed on the hot yellow sand of the great Madrid arena, broken and small, face-down in his own blood.

In a flash of capes and a whirl of gold, El Juli's men surrounded him, lifted him, carried his limp body out of the ring on their shoulders at a full sprint, rushing him toward the surgeons who are always on hand in the arena's infirmary. El Juli's beloved older brother was running alongside him, sticking his fingers in El Juli's mouth, trying desperately to keep the boy's windpipe clear of blood. Their father ran close behind, weeping and praying, his face twisted in dreadful fear.

Then El Juli and his people were gone, and the matador Rivera

Ordóñez stepped into the ring and picked up the bullfight just where El Juli had left off. There was no further pause. There never is. This is the custom. The bullfight must continue, the bull must be killed, the ritual must be fulfilled, no matter what the outcome. At first, the traumatized audience paid little attention to Ordóñez and the bull, still shaken from El Juli's attack, but as Ordóñez continued to fight — showing considerably more competence and gravity than he'd demonstrated earlier in the ring — the audience slowly quieted and focused back on the action. Ordóñez finished the ceremony, killing in one clean stroke the bull that had attacked El Juli. The audience applauded warmly and then waited for the next fight to begin.

During the pause between fights, there was concerned talk of El Juli, but nobody was overanalyzing the event. Certainly, nobody suggested that El Juli had made any kind of error or had brought the accident on himself. On the contrary — everyone agreed he had been fighting flawlessly. So what had gone wrong? What happened? When the weathered old men in the stands were asked their opinion, they merely shrugged.

"What happened?" one of them said. "What happened is that a man stepped into a ring with a bull."

The only way to learn what had become of El Juli was to head down to the arena's infirmary after the bullfight was over and receive the news. There, tacked beside the infirmary door, was posted a handwritten report from a doctor announcing El Juli's condition. Like medieval villagers reading a bishop's proclamation, crowds of Madrid aficionados gathered around that little note, their faces tilted upward in the dying light, looking as grave as figures in a religious fresco, whispering word back to the masses.

The scrawling cursive announced in pencil that El Juli was gravely but not mortally wounded. He had been gored in the thigh to a depth of twenty centimeters, but no arteries had been severed. There was no major nerve damage. There were serious concussions to his head and chest. He had been transferred to intensive care following emergency surgery.

It seemed that the attack had looked worse than it actually was. Reassured, the crowd dispersed. Outside, it was 10:00 P.M. and only now beginning to get dark. A beggar with one arm was pleading with the exiting crowd to compensate him for his misfortune. Two nuns left the ring arm in arm, heads bowed, talking about the day's events. A young man in a green uniform pushed a broom over the cobblestones, sweeping up the ticket stubs and programs of the day, casting his long shadow across the plaza. Another young man pushed a beautiful dark-haired girl up against the exterior wall of the arena, and they began to kiss each other fiercely. She was gripping him hard enough to crack his spine; he was driving her body into the warm brick wall; they were devouring each other's mouths as the entire arena emptied out around them.

The next afternoon, El Juli welcomed newspaper and television reporters to the hospital. The journalists found him there in his private room, sitting up in his hospital bed, dressed in a neat white polo shirt. There was a crisp white sheet pulled up to his waist and an airy white pillow behind his head. With the white-on-white effect of the bedding and the shirt, young El Juli looked positively angelic. His leg wound was hidden under the sheets. He seemed very calm. Also proud. The morning newspapers had reverently lauded his Madrid appearance after all, pronouncing that despite the attack, "There was only one name in the Plaza de Toros yesterday afternoon. And that name was Julián López."

El Juli addressed reporters from his hospital bed with the dignified composure of a man three times his age. He used formal grammar and spoke with the faint Andalusian accent of his father's people. When asked if he would be afraid to return to the ring after such an accident, El Juli replied, "One is likely to be gored many times in this profession. One must accept the risk or not be a bullfighter."

When asked what qualities a matador must have to be truly brilliant, he replied, "One must have love for the bulls, as well as great ambition."

El Juli went on to explain that one must also have faith in oneself. One must not allow for distraction. One must nurture a true spiritual connection to the bulls. One must have respect for the great matadors of the past. One must always leave the arena with one's head up, proud and determined, no matter what the outcome.

The interview was coming to a close, and El Juli had not yet once referred to himself in the first person. It was all about this mysterious, all-inclusive nonperson called "one." It was as though he recognized that his business of goring was not really about him. He was merely a participant in some ageless ritual that had preceded him by centuries. He was not even El Juli but the living embodiment of bullfighting itself.

Only to the final question did he respond in the personal. This was when he was asked whether he had ever considered the remote possibility of doing something else with his life. Something, perhaps, a little less deadly.

El Juli let that sentiment hang in the air for a moment and then replied, with a leveling coolness, "If I could not fight bulls, my life would make no sense."

TOM SCOCCA

Blood Sport

FROM BALTIMORE CITY PAPER

IDLY, LAST WEEK, I watched Beethavean Scottland get beaten into a coma. It was June 26. I was looking for the score of the Red Sox game, switching to ESPN2 to check the ticker after the Blue Jays finished off the Orioles. There at the top of the screen was Tuesday Night Fights, Jones vs. Scottland.

Scottland. I'd seen Bee Scottland once or twice, at Michael's Eighth Avenue in Glen Burnie, a good southpaw, bold and active. He wore a wild black-and-gold loincloth/trunks combination, with a B on the front flap, and he fought like he dressed. He had hand speed and stamina and enough power to make his victories interesting without making them easy. The hall buzzed when he was in the ring, with the memory of past action and the promise of more to come.

"The attraction with Bee is always in the performance he delivers," promoter Scott Wagner said the next day, afterward. He kept his verbs in the present, with Scottland unconscious and under the knife in New York's Bellevue Hospital with a subdural hematoma and secondary brain swelling. Scottland's first fight came on Wagner's first Ballroom Boxing card at Michael's, in February 1995. It was a four-round decision over Stan Braxton, the first of twenty career wins.

When I began watching Scottland's latest bout, I didn't know that there would never be a twenty-first. It was the ninth round on June 26, live from the deck of the decommissioned U.S.S. *Intrepid,* docked in the Hudson River, and Scottland was moving and hitting, outboxing the bigger and taller George Jones. I picked up fragments from the announcers: Jones, the undefeated up-and-comer, dominant all night but now getting tired; Scottland, hanging in and trying to rally. "He is a very courageous, bighearted fighter," Wagner would say the next day.

What I didn't know. I didn't know Scottland was fighting up out of his class, battling a light-heavyweight after his scheduled super-middleweight bout on June 21 at Michael's had fallen through. I didn't know that Jones's short record was deceptive, that he was a thirty-two-year-old ex-con, not some raw kid.

And I didn't know how bad the early going had been, how the ringside doctor told the ref, "I don't think he should take any more shots," after the seventh round. An overlay on the screen showed the punch count, lopsided in Jones's favor, but I looked right through it. Jones's hands were drooping; Scottland was tagging him. The announcers were caught up: here comes the final round, they said. The most exciting three minutes in sports. One of them, inspired, said something about William Wallace, punning on Scottland's name.

William Wallace died by inches, his guts pulled from his living body. Whatever carried Scottland through the ninth left him in the tenth. Jones got his wind back and started hitting again. Scottland bobbed and clinched, still fighting, but there was something wrong and numb in his eyes. Yet he kept going, ducking, weaving, taking more shots. With thirty-seven seconds left, the TV guy started to say it would be a moral victory if he finished on his feet. A moral victory.

Halfway through the sentence, Jones hit Scottland with a crunching right hand to the skull. A knockout punch. And still, some last thing resisted. Beethavean Scottland steadied himself, blindly and uselessly, and held his head up. Held his head up for nothing more than to take a final blow, the left hand, darkness inescapable. He fell.

It was a stupid and brutal thing, and quite expectable. If you see enough boxing, something terrible is going to happen in front of you. Thirty-nine years ago, well before I was born, my father watched Emile Griffith kill Benny "Kid" Paret on television. It did not make him stop watching the fights. Paret got pinned in the corner, stuck upright and helpless in the gap between the top and middle ropes, and Griffith hit him eighteen times in a row.

Boxing went to four ropes after that, so no one else could get trapped.

There's always a lesson. Scottland should not have been fighting a light-heavyweight. The doctor should have had the conviction to step in and stop things outright after the seventh. The ref should have remembered the doctor's advice and stopped it in the tenth before Scottland got in trouble again. Boxing is endlessly reformable, and endlessly in need of reform.

The clearest response, morally, is to reject the sport. Boxing is wrong. It is wrong to hurt other people in the name of entertainment and spectacle. The *Afro-American*'s Sam Lacy, the wisest sportswriter alive, believes this. My mother believes this. My own ambivalence has blood on it, not theoretically but in fact. It has Bee Scottland's blood on it.

I could try to wash the blood in mystification. Joyce Carol Oates has written that she doesn't regard boxing as a sport. She is fascinated by it as a ritual, something that "inhabits a sacred space predating civilization." Which I suppose it is, but it is a sport, too, and it is a sport more like other sports than we take it to be.

No sooner was Scottland down than the announcers were trying to defend boxing. Thirteen kids died last year playing high school football, they said, over and over, as if it were an invocation against evil. Boxing is a contact sport, and people get hurt in contact sports.

This is a glib line to take while a man's brain is bleeding, but it is true in an important way. You cannot draw a line to exclude boxing without excluding football. Boxers are deliberately trying to hurt each other? So are football players. The difference between Tony Siragusa and a boxer is that Siragusa has a 150-pound weight advantage over the man he wants to injure, and his target isn't trying to defend himself. Football is grotesque and savage.

And the savagery takes a toll. Steve Young, Troy Aikman, Al Toon — all forced from the game by repeated, malicious head injuries. Nor should we stop with the brain. Look at Johnny Unitas, with his chronic limp and his ruined right arm. Johnny Unitas's body was broken for your pleasure.

You cannot separate it from his heroism. We watch sports to see excellence, and we see excellence in extremity. Every quarterback who takes a hit and gets up, wincing, to play on — all are testing the limits of health, and possibly life. That's what athletes do, in all sports. The marathon reenacts a feat that killed the first person who did it; marathoners die to this day. Past the bounds of human endurance is where the good stuff happens: Pete Sampras puking on his shoes, Willis Reed limping onto the Garden floor, Greg Louganis wiping away the blood and diving for a gold medal. They kept fighting, we say, admiringly. And that, horribly, is exactly what Bee Scottland did.

STEVE FRIEDMAN

"It's Gonna Suck to Be You"

FROM OUTSIDE

THE FIRST TIME HE TRIED IT, the vomiting started after 67 miles, and it didn't stop until six hours later. The last time, his quadriceps cramped at mile 75, so he hobbled the last quarter of the course. But Kirk Apt is a resilient, optimistic, obsessive — some might say weird — man who describes experiences like being trapped on an exposed peak during a lightning storm as "interesting," and that is why he's here, in Silverton, Colorado, cheerfully tucking into a plate of pancakes, eggs, and bacon at 4:00 A.M., discoursing on the nature of fun while he prepares to take on, yet again, the most punishing 100-mile footrace in the world.

It's called the Hardrock Hundred Endurance Run, even though it's actually 101.7 miles long, and is known to the small and strange band of people who have attempted it as the Hardrock 100. Or, simply, the Hardrock. In 1992, the first year of the race, just 18 of 42 entrants finished. Today, nearly half of the 118 men and women who set off into the mountains will quit or be told to stop. Based on medical opinion, history, and statistical probabilities, death for one or two of them is not out of the question.

Apt could not look more pleased. "Enjoy yourself," he says to a fellow racer, a man staring fearfully at a strip of bacon. "Have fun," he blithely exhorts another, a pale woman clutching a cup of coffee, clenching and unclenching her jaw. Apt says "have fun" frequently enough to sound creepy. Even among other Hardrockers — many of them sinewy scientists from New Mexico's Los Alamos National Laboratory who tend to describe themselves with staggering inaccuracy as "mellow" — the thirty-nine-year-old massage therapist from Crested Butte, Colorado, is known as Mr. Mellow.

It's race day, the first Friday after the Fourth of July (the 2001 Hardrock will start on July 13), and Mr. Mellow is working over his pancakes at a worn wooden picnic table inside a café hunkered at the northern end of the only paved road in town. Silverton, population 440, is encircled by peaks, nestled at 9,305 feet in a lush mountain valley in the southern San Juans, at least an hour by way of the most avalanche-prone highway in North America from fresh vegetables, a movie theater, or a working cell phone. If you didn't know about the fifteen feet of snow that falls here every winter, or the unemployment rate that's four times the state average, or the knots of bitter, beery ex-miners who gather at the Miner's Tavern toward the southern end of the paved road most every night to slurrily curse the environmentalists they blame for shutting down the mines and trying to ban snowmobiles downtown, you might think that Silverton was quaint.

Outside, the sky is a riot of stars, the air clean and cold and so thin it makes you gasp. Inside the café, it's warm and cozy, a perfect place for Mellow to break bread with Terrified.

"The most important thing about the race," Apt says, "is to remember to make sure to enjoy yourself." Yes, there can be crippling cramps and hair-raising lightning bolts — big smile — but there are also remote, deserted vistas, long and lonely treks up mountains and across ridgelines, precious hours spent alone among old-growth forest and fresh wildflowers.

It sounds cleansing. If you didn't know about the dozens of unusually fit people who every midsummer collapse into near-catatonic, weeping blobs of flesh, their faces and hands and feet swollen to grotesque balloons because entire clusters of the racers' capillaries are breaking down and leaking (more on that later), you might think the Hardrock was fun.

Apt unfolds his six-foot-one, 168-pound frame from the café's picnic bench. Broad-shouldered, long-legged, clear-eyed, and, above all, mellow, he strides out of the emptying restaurant. He won the Leadville 100 in 1995, and though he's completed six Hardrocks, he's never finished first. Maybe this will be the year. Maybe not.

Big, big smile.

"How lucky are we?" he says.

*

Five minutes before six, the sun still not up, the competitors are turning in small circles on the gravel road outside Silverton Public School, taking in the surrounding peaks, scanning the distance for answers to questions most people never even consider. "Will I be hospitalized before sunset?" for example. They will spend the next day and at least one sleepless night in the deepest backcountry, almost constantly above 10,000 feet, climbing, sliding, wading, hiking, staggering, limping, and occasionally running. (Unlike other 100-mile racers, the fastest and most fit of the Hardrockers will jog no more than 60 percent of the course.) They will face five mountain passes of at least 13,000 feet and one 14,000-foot peak. Those who complete the loop will climb and descend 66,000 feet (more than would be involved in climbing and descending Mount Everest from sea level, as the race organizers like to point out). A large number of racers will vomit at least once. One or two might turn white and pass out. The slower runners will almost certainly hallucinate.

One of the most horrifying Hardrock visions is often all too real. It occurs when a race official informs a racer that he or she is moving too slowly to finish within the prescribed 48 hours. Getting "timed out," whether at mile 75 or at the finish line itself, is a bitter experience. Just ask Todd Burgess, a thirty-two-year-old newspaper-page designer from Colorado Springs. Five-foot-ten and 175 pounds, Burgess is cheerfully cognizant of his limitations and aspires only to finish and to enjoy himself along the way. So last year he snapped pictures, meandered in the wildflowers, gamboled through the old growth. But toward the end of the race, he saw that unless he hurried, he wasn't going to make it. He sprinted. He stumbled. He panicked. And when he crossed the line at 48 hours, three minutes, and 35 seconds — which means that, officially, he didn't finish at all — another racer told him, "It's gonna suck to be you for the next year."

It was a cruel thing to say, but, as it turns out, somewhat prophetic. For Burgess, the last year has been one filled with doubts, fears, and horrific training sessions — 12-hour runs and 50-mile practice races and Sunday-morning sleep-deprivation workouts. While it has sucked to be him, it would suck more to be timed out again this year.

It's been said that recovering alcoholics and bulimics and drug addicts are disproportionately represented among Hardrockers, which is tough to confirm, but it makes sense if you consider that addictive tendencies and compulsive behavior would come in handy with the training regimen. It's also been said that full-time Silvertonians tend toward the same kind of ornery optimism and obsessive, clannish, and sometimes perversely mellow brand of masochism exhibited by many of the racers. That's equally difficult to nail down, but having spent the better part of two winters here, I can vouch for the general soundness of the theory. It's no surprise that Silvertonians and Hardrockers tend to get along.

A few dozen townspeople have awakened early this morning to see the racers off, partly because three Silvertonians are entered, including one of the Hardrock's most popular hard-luck cases, fifty-two-year-old Carolyn Erdman, who has tried and failed three times to finish. Also at the starting line is the only Silvertonian ever to complete a Hardrock, Chris Nute. Nute, thirty-three, will be pacing Erdman the second half of the race. He is not entered this year largely because of his wife, Jodi, thirty, who is with him for the start and whom no one has ever accused of being mellow, especially when it comes to the Hardrock.

The year Chris Nute ran the Hardrock "was the only time I ever thought we might get a divorce," Jodi says. "I couldn't understand wanting to do that. The training time sucked. And it made me feel out of shape. It totally gave me a fat complex. I had a [terrifying] vision of the future: that I was going to be married to an ultrarunner."

Dawn. Race director Dale Garland yells, "Go!" and about fifty Hardrock volunteers and spouses and Silvertonians watch as Apt, Burgess, Erdman, and their fellow racers jog and walk down a gravel road, turn southeast, and then head into the mountains — and toward the cold and dark and pain.

Some 100-mile races are more famous. Many are more popular. Most have more corporate sponsors. None approach the Hardrock's brutality.

"This is a dangerous course!" warns the Hardrock manual, a fantastic compendium of arcane statistics, numbingly detailed course descriptions, grave warnings, and chilling understatement. When it comes to the temptation to scale peaks during storms, for instance, the manual advises, "You can hunker down in a valley for two to four hours and still finish; but if you get fried by lightning your running career may end on the spot."

Though a forty-four-year-old runner with a history of high blood pressure, Joel Zucker, died of a brain aneurysm on his way to the airport after completing the race in 1998, no one has perished during a Hardrock. But, according to the manual, "It is our general opinion that the first fatality . . . will be either from hypothermia or lightning!" (A Hardrock-manual exclamation point is rare as a Sasquatch sighting; one suspects typographical error, grim subject matter notwithstanding.)

"There's a reasonable chance somebody could die," says Tyler Curiel, forty-five, a Dallas-based doctor specializing in infectious disease and oncology who's run eleven 100-milers and "fifty or sixty" ultras (any race longer than 26.2 miles). "I've fallen into ice-cold water, almost been swept away by a waterfall, walked six hours alone at high elevations in boulder fields," he says of his Hardrock experiences. "Had I sprained an ankle then, I might have been dead. I almost walked off a 2,000-foot cliff in the middle of the night once. Two more steps, and I would have been dead for sure. And I'm fairly competent. So, yeah, there's a reasonable chance."

By late afternoon, after ten hours of climbing and sliding and "EXPOSURE" (the manual lists dehydration, fatigue, and vomiting as "minor problems," so racers tend to take capitalized nouns seriously), the fleetest and most fit of participants are a good five hours from being halfway finished. At this juncture — the fifth of thirteen aid stations, Grouse Gulch, mile 42.4 — one would expect the appropriate emotion to be grim determination. So it comes as something of a shock to onlookers when a slender young man named Jonathan Worswick skips through a light rain, down a narrow, switchbacking trail, and across a stream into Grouse Gulch at 4:27 P.M. He is smiling. The thirty-eight-year-old runner from England is on pace for a course record.

The Hardrock old hands are unimpressed. These are retired runners, longtime observers of ultrarunning, in demeanor and worldview much like the leathery old men who hang around ballparks in Florida and Arizona, sneering at the fuzzy-cheeked phenoms of spring and their March batting averages. The old hands have seen young studs like Worswick before. Seen them tear up the first half of the course, only to be seized later by fatigue, cramps, nausea, and a despair so profound they can't even name it. Besides, the promising dawn has turned into a chilly, wet afternoon. And this is Grouse Gulch. Dangerous things happen at Grouse Gulch.

It doesn't look dangerous: a wooden yurt twelve feet in diameter, a canvas elk-hunters' shelter with three cots and a propane heater, and a telephone-booth-size communications tent where a radio operator hunches over his sputtering equipment, all hugging the west bank of the fast-flowing Animas River.

But if you've just trekked more than 40 miles, climbed 14,000 feet, and descended 10,000, confronted Up-Chuck Ridge ("ACROPHOBIA"), which is nearly three times as steep as the steepest part of the Pike's Peak marathon, tackled the 14,048-foot Handies Peak ("Snow fields, altitude sickness, fantastic views"), where through a freezing rain you looked out upon the world and pondered the sleepless night (or nights) and the long hours that lie ahead, and now you are staggering down rocky switchbacks through pellets of freezing rain . . . well, then Grouse Gulch is danger itself. And nothing is more menacing than its banana pudding.

If there is some Higher Power watching over Hardrockers, urging them on, then surely there is a corresponding demon, tempting them to stop. What the fiend wants is for them to taste the pudding. Not the oatmeal, or soup, or mashed potatoes, or individually prepared breakfast burritos (meat or vegetarian) — though all are tempting. No, the pudding, whose scent floats along the riverbanks and up the mountain slopes as easily as the Sirens' lethal song wafted over the wine-dark sea.

The pudding itself is creamy, smooth, not quite white, not quite brown. (The recipe is absurdly prosaic: one large package of Jell-O instant vanilla pudding mixed with four cups whole milk and three fresh bananas; makes eight servings.) But for the weeping runner who has been slogging up and down talus slopes and through marshes for fifteen hours or so, the pudding . . . for that person, the pudding whispers to them.

"Stop," it whispers. "Rest." The rush of the river blends with the hushed static from the radio equipment, but the pudding won't shut up. "Don't go on," it whispers. "Have some more pudding."

Worswick wolfs a vegetarian burrito — he won't even look at the pudding — and leaves ten minutes after he arrives. Fourteen minutes later, Kirk Apt strides across the bridge, looks around the aid station, sits down, changes his socks, and frets. Things are taking too long; he's wasting precious minutes. By the time he is ready to go, Mr. Mellow is thoroughly agitated. When he leaves Grouse Gulch, he starts too fast, realizes he's too "amped up," and has to breathe deeply in order to regain the calm he regards as essential.

Apt spends less than ten minutes at Grouse Gulch.

Todd Burgess had planned to be here by 6:00 P.M., but at 10:00 he is still struggling down the mountain, thighs burning, tentative, taking baby steps, fearful of falling.

He enters Grouse Gulch at 10:12 and leaves at 10:28.

Carolyn staggers in at 10:30, loses sight in her left eye, then leaves at 10:36, two minutes ahead of her planned 43-hour pace.

Others — swifter, more accomplished, less tortured — are not so strong. Scott Jurek, twenty-seven, who two weeks ago won the Western States 100-miler, hits Grouse Gulch at 6:05 P.M. and takes a rest. He will not go on. Eric Clifton, who has won thirteen 100-milers since 1989, walks into the aid station two minutes later, and also stops for good.

Soaked and cold and exhausted, other racers hear the rushing river and the steady drizzle and the devilish gibberings of the Pudding Master, and they feel the propane heat, and then they cast their weary eyes on the cots, soft as dreams.

Twenty-three Hardrockers quit at Grouse Gulch.

Vomiting, cramping, collapsing, whimpering hopelessly before the devil's pudding, and/or surrendering to that despair so profound that it's difficult to name, are all variations, in Hardrock parlance, of bonking. Typically, when a runner bonks, he or she also quits the race, as Apt did when he couldn't stop puking in 1992. Sometimes a runner bonks and keeps going, and even finishes, as Apt did when his quadriceps cramped and he trudged the last 25 miles of the course in 11 hours in 1999. To continue after bonking earns a runner enormous respect among fellow racers, most of whom have bonked at some point in their running careers. These people appreciate speed, but they revere grit.

When male Hardrockers bonk, they tend to quit. This is accepted wisdom among the racers, as is the fact that women bonkers, in general, do their best to finish. A racer can bonk without timing out, and he can time out without bonking. All things being equal, it's better to have bonked before being timed out than the other way around. Non-bonking runners who are timed out — especially late in a Hardrock — suffer the fate of Todd Burgess (it sucks to be them).

The Ouray aid station, at mile 58 and an elevation of 7,680 feet, would provide an excellent place to quit. Though there is no pudding of any sort here, nor heated tents with cots, next to the aid station is a parking lot, and next to that, a highway. Silverton is less than an hour's drive away, in a heated car.

But there will be no quitting here for Jonathan Worswick, who arrives at 7:42 P.M., still leading, and leaves at 7:56. Not for Kirk Apt, who arrives at 8:20 and leaves at 8:27 — "psyched," he says, "but in a relaxed, calm way."

Neither will there be any quitting for Todd Burgess, who trundles toward the aid station the next morning at 5:14. His pacer, Fred Creamer, urges Burgess to run the last mile or so to the aid station, but Burgess wants to conserve his energy until he eats something. He's sure that a meal will give him the boost he needs for the second half of the course. In Ouray he takes a bite of warm roast turkey, a long pull of Gatorade, and vomits.

Creamer asks Burgess if this has ever happened to him during a race, and when Burgess says no, Creamer considers ending their journey. But Burgess says he feels great. He does feel great. Creamer feels grave concern. They continue.

Like Burgess, Erdman approaches Ouray in the predawn darkness, moving fast enough to finish in less than 48 hours, but just barely. No one — not the aid station volunteers and not pacer Chris Nute — entertains the slightest suspicion that she might quit in Ouray. Not that they wouldn't welcome such an event.

Erdman entered the race for the first time in 1997, when she was forty-eight, eight years after she quit smoking and one year after she and her husband left their cattle farm in Wisconsin and moved to Silverton. Nute paced her that year, and she made it 85 miles before race organizers told her that she was moving too slowly and that she was done.

In 1998 she entered again. Four weeks before the event she ran a 50-mile warm-up race in Orem, Utah. Three miles into it she fell and scraped her left knee. There was blood, and a little pain, but she thought it was no big deal. By the time she finished, she could see her patella; she was shocked at how white it was. The doctor in the emergency room told her she was lucky he didn't have to amputate the limb. She spent a week in the hospital with intravenous antibiotics. Surgeons operated on her twice.

In '99 she was timed out at mile 92.

Erdman has long gray hair that she wears in a braid, the lean body of someone half her age, and brown eyes that sparkle with an intensity peculiar to religious leaders and Hardrockers. She runs ten miles a day, more in the midst of Hardrock training, through rain, snow, and blistering sun. Her dedication has unified Silvertonians — like many residents of small mountain towns, notoriously resistant to unification unless it involves railing against silent black helicopters and the craven jackbooted federal thugs who claim the choppers don't exist. But they're worried about her. Will she endure too much, just to finish? What if she doesn't finish?

Nute knows that Erdman would sooner end up on an operating table than quit, and that's one reason he's agreed to pace her. They're friends. He wants her to finish, but he also wants her to live.

After thirteen minutes at the station, they walk along the Uncompaghre River out of Ouray and onto a dirt road, which they climb steadily through thick forest. The air is moist with dew and sweet with pine; birds are starting to sing. Though Erdman is falling further behind her 43-hour pace, and hasn't slept for a full 24 hours and won't for another 24, the approaching dawn invigorates her — for about two hours. Then she wants to take a nap.

Not a good idea, Nute tells her.

Leafy undergrowth and lush, grassy ground beckon. Just a few minutes lying in that pillowy green would be so nourishing, so healing. It would make her go so much faster.

Really not such a smart thing to do, Nute says.

She pleads. She whines. She begs.

Pacers are valuable precisely because they warn their charges not to surrender to their worst temptations — like gobbling fistfuls of ibuprofen and taking ill-advised naps. But Nute is also Erdman's friend, not to mention a fellow Silvertonian. Okay, he says, one nap. They settle on seven minutes.

She nearly cries with happiness. She spreads her jacket, makes a pillow of her pack, and lies down in a perfect leafy spot. But it's not perfect enough. She picks everything up, moves to another leafy spot, and lies down again. Nute watches, looks at his watch; eight minutes have passed. She doesn't like the position of the pillow, so she adjusts it. Then she adjusts her jacket. Then her body. Three adjustments later, she sighs. It is a pitiable little sound.

"Go!" she chirps to Nute, who is sitting down, staring at her. "Start timing."

This is when Nute starts to worry.

Back in Silverton, Jodi Harper Nute is worried, too. She has watched over the past week as Chris has helped with various Hardrock tasks, handing out literature, signing in runners, helping pace Carolyn. Jodi watched him chat with other runners. She watched him study the course map. She watched him huddle with the old hands, doubtless revering grit.

And what she feared has come to pass. Just last night Chris told Jodi he wants to race again. (The couple has since moved to Durango, where less snow makes it easier to train.)

"Goddammit," Jodi says. "I can't believe this." Pause. "Yes, I can. I was wondering why I've been so pissy the past few days. Now I know why. Goddammit."

While Jodi worries, Hardrockers trudge 10.4 miles and 5,420 feet up to Virginius Pass (elevation 13,100 feet), then 5.3 miles and 4,350 feet down into the aid station at Telluride. They have traveled 73.7 miles and have another 28 to go. Soon they'll have to tackle Oscar's Pass, 6.5 miles away and 4,400 feet higher. "Basically," says Jonathan Thompson, editor of *Silverton Mountain Journal,* the local biweekly, "straight up a friggin' mountain."

After Oscar's ("Acrophobia, exposure, cornice"), surviving runners will face Grant Swamp Pass, the most difficult climb of the course, a murderously steep scramble over boulders and loose scree ("rock and dirt that will slide back down the hill with each step you take"). It would be daunting on a day hike.

Erdman has been awake, racing, for 31 hours. It's now one in the afternoon, and after she wolfs a slice of pepperoni pizza, she and Nute leave town, climbing, straight into the zone where Hardrockers too proud, too foolish, or too dense to quit often get themselves in danger. In 1998, as two-time Hardrock champion Dave

Horton was ascending Grant Swamp Pass, a melon-size rock dislodged by a runner above fell and struck his right hand. "A little later," Horton, fifty-one, wrote in his account of that race, "I noticed that my glove was soaked through with blood." After finishing (of course), he realized that it was a compound fracture.

Many runners ignore puffy faces, hands that have ballooned like boxing gloves, feet like clown shoes, telling themselves it's merely a lack of sodium or some low-level kidney failure. Probably not fatal. They'll try to ignore the moist rattling they hear with every breath. Chances are the swelling and rattling are the result of damage to the body's capillaries. High-altitude races tend to starve capillaries of oxygen, which makes them leak fluid, which pools in the racers' hands and feet. "The danger," says Curiel, the doctor from Dallas, "is that one of the largest capillary networks is in your lungs, and when those capillaries start leaking, you have difficulty breathing. Pulmonary edema. In a really bad case, your lungs can fill up with water and you'll drown."

Digestive problems barely merit consideration. Jonathan Worswick left Ouray still in the lead but vomiting every few miles and suffering stomach cramps and diarrhea. Mr. Mellow stalked him during the climb, enjoying the view, confident in his uphill power, even more confident that Worswick had expended too much energy too early. Just before passing Worswick and crossing Virginius Pass, Apt recalled later, "a mental shift occurred for me. I knew I was in this race, and really had a good shot at winning."

Worswick overtook him on the downhill to Telluride, but Apt was having fun. Just after beginning the brutal assault on Oscar's, Apt told his pacer he wanted to "get after it." Minutes later they blew by Worswick, who was too sick to fight anymore. He bonked. But he continued.

Burgess hasn't puked since Ouray, and though by midafternoon he's suffering fatigue, muscle soreness, chills, and a slight loss of motor coordination, he's still in the race.

Erdman? She regained her sight near Telluride. But three miles later, she begins to gasp.

She turns to Nute. "I'm not going to make it," she says.

Nute knows she might well be speaking the truth. He's been monitoring his watch, worrying as Erdman has slowed to a 40-minute-mile stagger. He's been despairing that she'll never make it out of the next aid station, Chapman, at 83.1 miles, before the cutoff time. But Erdman is the one who inspired Nute to run his first and, depending on Jodi, possibly only Hardrock. Plenty of people have told Erdman to stop. Nute's not going to be one of them.

"Let's sit down for a minute," Nute says. "Let's just process this. Let's do the math."

But what calculus of the spirit can take into account years of training, hours alone, broken bones, and the taunting of the devil's pudding? Has an equation yet been written so elegant that it can encompass impossible dreams?

They sit, and they sit some more. They peer upward, above tree line, where the skies are black with monstrous storm clouds. Lighting crashes.

Erdman does the math. Instead of a number comes a word.

"All I can think," she says, "is why?"

She doesn't bonk, and she isn't timed out. But after 77 miles, Erdman drops out of her third and — she says — final Hardrock.

Ten miles from the finish, Todd Burgess forgets how to walk a straight line. Counting, he decides, will solve the problem. If he can put eight steps together, one ahead of another, without wavering, and name the number of each step, he won't swerve into the wilderness and be lost forever. He is sure of this. He counts aloud for an hour.

When he steps onto the abandoned rail bed that will take him the last two miles to Silverton, Burgess can see the gentle, aspen-covered hill ahead. Once he climbs that, he'll be able to look down into the town. He'll be able to see the finish line below. He knows he's going to make it. Only one thing can stop him.

He knows it's a silly fear, most likely the result of exhaustion and chills. If he knew about leaking capillaries, he might ascribe his anxiety to that. But Burgess's attempts at rationality won't banish a dreadful notion, born of sleep deprivation, or cellular rioting, or the desperate, fearsome need to finish under 48 hours:

"This would be a terrible time for a nuclear bomb to fall."

Burgess isn't the only one losing his mind. Gigantic june bugs wriggle from the soil and onto the damp and wobbly legs of Hardrockers unlucky enough to find themselves on the course after dusk on the second day of the race. Ghostly condominiums waver on top of mountain passes. Severed elk heads bob in the arms of grinning aid-station volunteers.

It's probably not capillary leakage. The visions seem to visit the slower runners, the ones who have been awake the longest.

"We know that people who have been sleep deprived have been noted to have visual, auditory, as well as tactile hallucinations," says Dr. Clete Kushida, director of the Stanford Center for Human Sleep Research. "They can also suffer irritability, as well as changes in memory, focus, and concentration. And psychomotor deficits."

That's one way of putting it.

After 40 hours, phantom Texans in ten-gallon hats walk beside the sleepiest Hardrockers at 13,000 feet, drinking beer and laughing. Grass turns to snow, rocks morph into Chevy Suburbans, plants transmute into Gummy Bears and bows. Before he died, Joel Zucker saw Indians.

Burgess finishes at 47 hours, 41 minutes, and three seconds, the fifty-eighth of sixty finishers (none of them Silvertonians). Then he sits on the ground.

Race Director Dale Garland walks to Burgess and asks if he would mind turning off the digital clock when it hits 48 hours. "I think this is good therapy," Garland says.

Burgess sits next to the clock and stares at it. At 48 hours he pushes a button, but the clock keeps going. Burgess keeps sitting, staring at the running numbers.

Jonathan Worswick finishes sixth, at 30 hours, 46 minutes, 16 seconds.

Kirk Apt wins in 29 hours and 35 minutes — beating the course record by more than 35 minutes. His legs tremble, and he weeps. Some onlookers get teary, too, even a few of the old hands. They don't like to talk about it, but they know that some of the fastest finishers are the most patently competitive, the loudest, the least liked, and the most likely to quit when outright victory seems impossible. Then there's Apt, who bonked and walked the last 25 miles of the course last year, enjoying the scenic vistas and the lonely ridgelines. Cramped. Limping. Having fun.

Local newspaper reporters gather round the champion. It's almost noon, clear and sunny. Apt tells one note-taker that he consulted a nutritionist before this year's Hardrock and that his "homemade goos" (various combinations of blendered hard-boiled egg, potato, tofu, avocado, rice, yogurt, salt, honey, and chicken liver) helped him stay the course. He tells another, "I'm really not that competitive, but I saw I had the opportunity to win, so I thought, Why not?" He mentions that he ran about 60 of the 100 miles — "the flats and downhills, and I ran a few uphills, too."

The reporter from Durango has one last question.

"What interesting things happened in the race?" she asks.

Interesting things? Mr. Mellow grins.

"The flowers were just amazing."

SKIP HOLLANDSWORTH

The Killing of Alydar

FROM TEXAS MONTHLY

HE WAS A BEAUTIFUL, proud Thoroughbred, headstrong and demanding, the kind of horse who would snort impatiently if he decided the grooms were not paying him enough attention. Each day, his oak-paneled stall was swept, mopped, and replenished with fresh straw. His richly colored chestnut coat was constantly brushed. For his daily exercise sessions, he was taken to his own three-acre paddock, where he could frolic alone in perfectly tended bluegrass.

His name was Alydar. To sports fans, he was known for the thrilling duels he staged with his rival, Affirmed, for the 1978 Triple Crown. But to the world's wealthiest horse breeders, he was revered for a different reason altogether. Alydar was one of the greatest sires in Thoroughbred history — a 1,200-pound genetic wonder whose offspring often became champion racehorses themselves. Each spring, the breeders would come with their convoys of horse trailers to Kentucky's Calumet Farm, one of the country's premier horse-racing operations, willing to pay hundreds of thousands of dollars to have Alydar mount their finest mares. Day after day, more than two hundred times a year, he would strut into the breeding shed, eye his latest prize, rise up on his hind legs, and begin to dance forward. Within seconds, his tail would swoosh up, signaling the end of his encounter, and he would be washed and then led away, back to the stall with his name emblazoned on the brass doorplate.

But on a chilly November night in 1990, the great stallion was found in shock in his stall, his coat glistening with sweat, his right hind leg hanging by tendons, a shaft of white bone jutting through his skin. J. T. Lundy, the rotund, blustery head of the farm, told veterinarians that Alydar had shattered his leg by kicking his own stall door. He had kicked it so hard, Lundy said, that he had knocked loose a heavy metal roller that had been bolted into the floor just outside Alydar's sliding door.

In emergency surgery, veterinarians were able to set the bone and put a cast on his leg. But within twenty-four hours, Alydar, hearing the whinnying of some mares in a nearby pasture, turned to look out a window in the Calumet clinic, put too much weight on the leg, and this time broke his femur. The sound of the break was like a gunshot. As he lay on the floor, an uncomprehending look in his eyes, Alydar was put down, and his body was taken to the Calumet cemetery, where he was buried with the farm's other racing champions. Eight months later, Calumet itself unraveled, forced to declare bankruptcy with more than $127 million in debts. According to the stories splashed on the sports pages of almost every newspaper in the country, the farm could not begin to pay its immense bills and bank loans without the millions of dollars it had been deriving from Alydar's stud fees. Calumet was so broke that its horses and equipment were going to be sold at public auction.

It was difficult for Kentucky horse people to believe that such a calamity could have happened. A few of them quietly said they were haunted by the strange circumstances of Alydar's death. A foreman from the stallion barn, for instance, couldn't remember Alydar having ever kicked anything hard enough to do any damage to his leg. And it was difficult to understand how even a powerful horse could have kicked that solid oak door with enough force to knock it off its hinges. Yet there was never an official investigation into the events of that night. No public accusations were made. As everyone in the horse business knew, horses could be unpredictable, and they could also be fragile. Alydar's death, no doubt, was one of those accidental, heartbreaking tragedies that no one could have done anything about.

And that, by all accounts, was the end of the story — until one afternoon in 1996, when a young assistant U.S. attorney in Houston was sitting in her downtown office, flipping through some bank records. The attorney's name was Julia Hyman (she now goes by her married name, Julia Tomala), and she knew nothing about horse racing. She spent her days investigating one of the worst financial scandals in American history: the widespread failure of hundreds of Texas financial institutions. Her job was to unearth the most complicated of white-collar crimes, such as money-laundering schemes and check-kiting operations.

On that particular afternoon, Tomala was studying the documents of the defunct First City National Bank of Houston, looking for evidence of fraud. She paused when she came to a document that mentioned Calumet Farm. She paused again when she came to a document that mentioned Alydar.

At the time, Tomala, an elegant woman with thick dark hair and a fondness for stylish black pantsuits, had no idea who or what Alydar was. She had never even been to a horse race. But by the summer of 1997, she was on her way to Kentucky to ask questions about how that horse had lived and died. She was accompanied by a rookie FBI agent out of the Houston office, Rob Foster, a former college baseball player who had never conducted a field investigation and who also knew nothing about horse racing.

Quickly, the word spread among the Bluegrass aristocracy that a couple of outsiders intended to pry into their private business. Tomala and Foster had been seen in Alydar's stall at Calumet, at a veterinary clinic, even at a construction site, where a former Calumet groom had gone to work as a laborer.

What, people wondered, did this prosecutor think she was going to learn about Alydar that wasn't already known? And why, after all this time, did it matter?

It would not be until October 2000, almost ten years after Alydar's death, that Tomala would finally reveal what she had been doing. At a little-publicized hearing in a nearly empty federal courtroom in Houston, she stood before a judge and said that the death of Alydar was no accidental tragedy. Alydar, she proclaimed, had been murdered.

It is a blockbuster of a story, a sweeping saga of greed, fraud, and almost unimaginable cruelty that could have been lifted straight from a best-selling Dick Francis horse-racing novel. The settings range from the raucous pageantry of the Kentucky Derby to the hushed, baronial offices of Lloyd's of London in England, and even the minor characters — from an uneducated, chain-smoking Kentucky farmhand tormented by a secret to a corrupt Texas banker living in luxury at Houston's Four Seasons Hotel — seem right out of central casting. "This story has got blood and money, scandal and intrigue, and one hell of a beautiful horse," says Allen Goodling of Houston, one of the many lawyers who became involved in the case. "What more does anybody want?"

The story begins at the fabled Calumet Farm just outside Lexington, Kentucky — a picture postcard of a place consisting of some eight hundred acres of lavish pastureland crisscrossed with pristine white fences. Horse-racing fans once regarded Calumet the same way baseball fans view the New York Yankees — as an almost sacred institution, its horses having won eight Kentucky Derbies, two Triple Crowns, and more than five hundred stakes races. Founded in 1924 by William Wright, who made his fortune as the head of the Calumet Baking Powder Company, and later run by his son Warren Wright, it was already a racing dynasty by the early forties, producing such champions as Whirlaway, Citation, and Tim Tam. In 1950, after Warren's death, the farm was taken over by his widow, Lucille, an imperious grande dame who, like all proper Bluegrass ladies, wore white gloves to the track on racing day. She was devoted to the horses. She was not, however, devoted to her only child, Warren Wright, Jr., the sole heir to the farm. A likable but scatterbrained young man, he apparently forgot to pay his income taxes for a couple of years and was sent to prison. What earned him his mother's deepest wrath, however, was his lack of interest in the horse business. When he died before she did, she mostly ignored his widow and his four children — the new heirs to the farm — because they, too, showed little interest in working at Calumet. They seemed more interested in the farm's dividends.

But in the early sixties, one of Lucille's grandchildren, her own namesake, Lucille "Cindy" Wright, made a decision that would have an enormous impact on Calumet's future. She decided, at the mere age of sixteen, to marry a rambunctious good old boy who liked racing his souped-up car down the narrow two-lane roads that ran past the horse farms. J. T. Lundy, the twenty-one-year-old son of a tenant farmer who worked a piece of land in an adjoining county, was to the Kentucky horse gentry what Jett Rink was to the Texas ranchers in the movie *Giant* — the classic outsider who dressed in old work clothes and usually couldn't get through a conversation without letting loose a few choice cusswords. With a head the size of a gasoline can and a nose that looked as if it had been busted and reset by a plumber, he looked like a country bumpkin. As one disgusted Kentucky blue-blood would later tell Austin journalist Carol Flake, who wrote an absorbing profile of Calumet Farm in 1992 for the now-defunct *Connoisseur* magazine, a big night for Lundy was "sitting in front of the TV with a bucket of buffalo wings watching reruns of *The Dukes of Hazzard.*"

Yet underneath that salt-of-the-earth personality lay a surprisingly fierce ambition. Lundy often told his friends that his dream was to run Calumet. Some of those friends even remember him boasting that he was going to marry young Cindy Wright just so he could get into Calumet's founding family. If so, he made the right choice. Those who know Cindy say she was never much of a society girl — "She didn't like those parties where people sipped mint juleps," says a Lundy relative — and that she always preferred the company of plain-spoken rural boys rather than the college-bound sons of Lexington's aristocrats. To her, the down-home Lundy was ideal.

After their marriage, Lundy bought a small farm and started a breeding program to produce racehorses, perhaps to show Cindy and her family that he was serious about his desire to head Calumet. Throughout the sixties and seventies, however, the farm remained firmly in the hands of its matriarch, who by then had married a dashing retired U.S. Navy admiral named Gene Markey. Though approaching eighty, Lucille Wright Markey had not lost her resolve to produce one more Kentucky Derby winner. In 1976 she hired a brilliant young trainer, John Veitch, who began watching a horse named Alydar that had been born at Calumet the year before. At the Blue Grass Stakes in the early spring of 1978, Lucille Markey stood next to the outside rail, gripping it with her white gloves, as Alydar introduced himself to the world, sweeping around the final turn and racing victoriously to the wire. Then, at the Kentucky Derby, the Preakness, and the Belmont — the races that make up the Triple Crown — Alydar and another Kentucky Thoroughbred, Affirmed, staged what turf writers still describe as the greatest duel in horse-racing history. They literally raced side by side, eyeball to eyeball, their hooves pounding like cannon fire as they hit the home stretch. In their fight to the finish at Belmont, they ran dead even for the final seven furlongs.

To Lucille Markey's deep disappointment, it was always Affirmed who got to the wire just ahead of Alydar. Yet once the two horses were retired to their stallion barns back on the farms where they were born, it was Alydar that everyone wanted to see. In the Thoroughbred-breeding business, there is no way to tell which stallion, regardless of its own pedigree, will be able to produce a new generation of winners at the track. The business is a crapshoot, based almost purely on luck. So when Alydar's initial progeny turned out to be strong, fleet-footed foals, the word quickly spread that the most famous second-place finisher in the Triple Crown had semen as valuable as gold.

Initially Alydar's stud fee was $40,000. J. T. Lundy told his in-laws that Calumet's management team was forfeiting the chance to make millions off Alydar. His message to the heirs was clear: Calumet needed a new leader. And who better than Lundy himself? There was no question that he was a hard worker who knew how to make money in the horse business. At the time, Lundy's farm was said to be worth several million dollars.

According to a history of Calumet, *Wild Ride* by Ann Hagedorn Auerbach, Lucille Markey despised the overly ambitious tenant farmer's son. She refused to let Lundy breed his horses with Calumet horses, and she even tried to keep him from visiting the farm — which only reinforced Lundy's resolve to take over her kingdom. One story that circulated through Bluegrass circles was that Lundy had taken up jogging to stay in good enough shape just to outlive her. "Here was somebody who may have felt inferior his entire life," says Gary Matthews, Calumet's former chief financial officer. "And he wanted to get to the top just to show everybody he could do it."

He got his chance on July 24, 1982, when Lucille Markey died at the age of eighty-five. Soon afterward, the Calumet heirs announced an agreement with forty-one-year-old J. T. Lundy, granting him "full discretionary management powers" over the farm. The country bumpkin was now the lord of Calumet Farm.

Almost immediately, Lundy began a multimillion-dollar restoration of Calumet. He had workers install iron gates across the main entrance, as if to signify to the world that a new man was in charge, and he had the farm's twenty-three miles of fence repainted. He ordered the construction of a state-of-the-art veterinary clinic, complete with a treadmill and an equine swimming pool, which alone cost $1 million. He added new freeze-proof water troughs and a five-eighths-mile turf track, and he bought new stallions and racehorses, all in the hope that Calumet would regain the glory of its early days.

Lundy was in such a hurry to get his projects under way that in 1983 he took out a $13.2 million loan. His bankers could not possibly have been worried about Lundy's paying it back. The farm was then debt-free. What's more, Lundy soon raised Alydar's stud fee to $250,000. He also did something never before heard of in the Thoroughbred business: he started selling what he called lifetime breeding rights to the stallion. For $2.5 million, an owner could send one mare to Alydar's breeding shed each year for as long as Alydar was able to breed.

Lundy's timing couldn't have been better. In the early eighties the Bluegrass world was awash in money. Multimillionaire bidders — from Saudi sheiks to Japanese industrial titans and American oil barons such as Dallas' Nelson Bunker Hunt — attended yearling auctions at Keeneland Park, waving their hands to push the prices higher and higher. And whenever a son or daughter of Alydar was led into the ring, the bidding occasionally topped $2 million — for a single, unproven young horse. In 1983 Alydar was the industry's champion first-year sire: his offspring sold for an average of $760,000 each, at that time a record for a first crop.

Horse breeders who once rolled their eyes at J. T. Lundy were now slapping him on the back — hoping that he would look favorably on them when it came time to pick the new mares who would get to visit Alydar's breeding shed. Lundy even found himself the object of adulation by a respected columnist for the industry's journal, *The Blood-Horse,* who wrote, "While there has been some criticism of the methods of Lundy in his direction of Calumet, it seems to be based more on envy than fact. Lundy, in my opinion, is doing a great job in rebuilding a grand heritage."

But Lundy didn't just want to rebuild a heritage. He wanted to create a Thoroughbred empire unlike any other. He, too, joined the bidding frenzy for new horses — spending between $20 million and $30 million for a half-interest in a stallion named Secreto. He continued renovating the farm, installing a gazebo and a tennis court and a swimming pool (this one for humans). He renovated his office, adding a second story with a balcony from which he could survey the farm. Although he still wouldn't buy nice clothes for himself — he continued to wear open-collar shirts, corduroy pants, and Top-Siders to formal events at which every other horseman was dressed in a jacket and tie — he did spend $30,000 a month of Calumet money to lease a private jet, which he didn't hesitate to use for personal trips. (He once flew a group of friends to Maine for a lobster dinner.) He bought property for himself in the Florida Keys. In one of his most perplexing ventures, he made Calumet a sponsor of the Indy race car of A. J. Foyt, one of Lundy's longtime heroes.

Suddenly, J. T. Lundy was a jet-setting wheeler-dealer, sitting in the finest boxes at the nation's finest racetracks, cutting deals with other horse farm owners for horses and breeding rights, and paying himself a reported 10 percent sales commission on every deal he made. Perhaps because Lundy's wife, Cindy, had realized that she would never be able to compete with her husband's obsession with the farm, she began spending most of her time in the Virgin Islands, Scotland, and Colorado — which apparently was just fine with Lundy. He soon had a girlfriend, a young woman he had hired to work in the main office at the farm.

To pay for his newest ventures, Lundy took out a $20 million mortgage on the farm and received another $15 million line of credit from a Kentucky bank. Even in 1986, when the horse-racing industry went into a steep economic slump, due in large part to the collapse of the oil market and the restructuring of tax laws that eliminated one of the tax breaks for the purchase of horses, Lundy kept spending. He received an extra $10 million from the Kentucky bank that already had loaned him $15 million. And in 1988, just as the Thoroughbred market was really souring, Lundy got another bank loan for a staggering $50 million. It came from the flagship bank of Houston's First City Bancorporation, one of the state's largest bank holding companies, with more than sixty banks and $12 billion in assets.

Kentucky horse breeders who were scrambling to stay afloat were baffled. How did Lundy get a loan from a bank in Texas, where no one knew anything about horse racing? What bank officer did he find to approve that deal?

Actually, it was no ordinary bank officer. The banker behind the Calumet loan was none other than the powerful vice chairman of First City, a big, burly cannonball of a man named Frank C. Cihak.

According to stories Frank Cihak has told his friends, he was raised in an orphanage on the South Side of Chicago and became an amateur boxer. He must have been a formidable opponent: a *Wall Street Journal* reporter once wrote that Cihak was built like a Chicago Bears lineman. After college he entered banking, worked his way up the ladder at First Chicago Corporation, and in 1976 took control of a string of smaller banks, where he developed a reputation for his relentless pursuit of profits.

In 1988 his old boss, A. Robert Abboud, the freewheeling former chairman at First Chicago, made a deal with the FDIC to take over First City in Houston, which then was on the verge of collapse because of hundreds of millions of dollars of bad real estate and energy loans. (FDIC officials, thrilled someone wanted the bank, agreed to spend nearly $1 billion to bail out First City if Abboud would raise $500 million in new capital.) Abboud asked Cihak, then forty-five years old, to go to Texas and be his "right hand." The two had a lot in common. Like Abboud, who once had been named one of the nation's "ten toughest bosses" by *Fortune* magazine, cigar-smoking Cihak was aggressive and abrasive — and he didn't like to be second-guessed. "His employees knew if they questioned what he was doing, they'd likely get fired," says an attorney who knew him. "His modus operandi was to call in a loan officer to his office and say, 'You are going to make the following loan to this guy. I'm vouching for him.'"

Cihak came barreling into Texas. His salary, as vice chairman, was $450,000 a year (he also got a $1 million bonus for taking the job), and most of his expenses were paid for, including an apartment at the Four Seasons Hotel and his dinners and $200 bottles of wine at the pricey Cafe Annie. He hired various consultants, many of them old friends, to work on various bank projects. He also started looking to make very large loans. According to the deal Cihak had made with Abboud, he could authorize a loan of up to $120 million without having to go through a traditional loan committee. And one of the first loans he made, less than four months after First City was recapitalized, was for almost $50 million to Calumet.

When Cihak told the First City loan officers not to check Calumet's credit reference at the Kentucky bank where it already had a loan, they didn't consider the demand unusual. First City certainly didn't want to tip off the bank that it was trying to lure away a big client. But they were perplexed that he told them not to audit the financial statements or appraisals of the farm presented by Lundy and Gary Matthews, Calumet's chief financial officer. Nevertheless, when the deal was completed, in July 1988, Cihak was treated as a hero by Abboud and the other executives. Texas had just legalized pari-mutuel betting, and First City officials believed the Calumet loan would bring them a host of new horse-racing clients. They even took out an advertisement in the *Wall Street Journal* trumpeting the bank's addition of Calumet to its loan portfolio.

But within weeks, First City loan officers received a phone call from Matthews, asking for even more money. The officers couldn't believe what they were hearing. Matthews was telling them that Calumet was already unable to make its loan payments. Cihak suddenly stepped in, signed off on the larger Calumet loans, and said the farm just needed more time to weather the depressed horse market. Cihak also said he was going to transfer the Calumet loan to Structured Financing, a bank section created by Cihak and headed by one of his handpicked associates.

And that seemed to take care of that. For the next two years, the loan was handled by Cihak himself. As for Calumet, no one could have imagined that it was already veering toward bankruptcy. As 1990 rolled around, the farm had new white fences and more than one hundred Calumet horses at racetracks all over the country. One of the horses, a son of Alydar named Criminal Type, was on his way to winning seven times in eleven starts that year, earning $2.2 million for the farm. Meanwhile, Alydar remained indefatigable in the breeding shed. Lundy had his great stallion serving one hundred mares a year, which meant Alydar went to the shed about two hundred times; it took him an average of two mounts per mare to get her pregnant. A normal stallion goes through only fifty to seventy mares a year. Alydar was known around Kentucky as J. T. Lundy's ATM, a constant source of cash. The Calumet grooms called him the "cock of the walk." Ironically, his old rival, Affirmed, was also at Calumet in 1990, leased by the farm to be one of its stallions. When the two chestnut-colored horses were out in their paddocks, they would stare at each other, their manes flicking in the breeze. Occasionally, Affirmed would start running on his side of the fence, and Alydar would take off after him on the other side. Even then, twelve years after their races, they remained competitors.

It was hard to imagine that anything could have shattered such an idyllic scene, certainly not the little piece of news that came out of Houston in October 1990 that one Frank C. Cihak had resigned as vice chairman of the First City Bancorporation. In the twenty-nine months since First City had been restructured, the bank's pool of bad loans had grown from nothing to $433 million. According to stories in the Houston newspapers, the bad loans had been generated by Cihak. Although he was being given a graceful exit — the bank would continue to pay him $450,000 a year as a consultant — other officers would be taking control of the loans he had made.

But Cihak's resignation was to have immediate and catastrophic effects on Calumet. Lundy and Matthews were contacted by a First City vice president who told them their loan was being restructured. The time had come for Calumet to pay, he said. If Calumet didn't come up with $15 million by February 28, 1991, then First City would foreclose, taking all the farm's horses and assets.

That conversation took place on October 25, 1990. Less than three weeks later, Alydar was dead.

Julia Hyman Tomala missed the news that Alydar was dead. She also missed the news, eight months later, that Calumet Farm was declaring bankruptcy and that its president, J. T. Lundy, had resigned. She was then thirty, consumed with her career as a white-collar-crime prosecutor for the U.S. attorney's office in Tampa, Florida, where she had been born and raised. In late 1991 she moved to the U.S. attorney's office in Houston, which desperately needed prosecutors to deal with numerous criminal allegations that were flooding into the office regarding the huge number of Texas bank failures. For her, Texas was where the action was: from 1986 through 1992, 485 banks and 238 savings and loans in Texas went under, including First City Bancorporation. And the first case she was handed concerned the activities of the infamous Frank Cihak.

Tomala began investigating the transactions between Cihak and his cronies whom he had hired as bank "consultants." Within months, she had bank documents not only piled up on her desk but also stacked in the hallway outside her office. "What's required in this kind of work is a tenacity to follow very complex paper trails," says Jim Powers, a chief prosecutor at the U.S. attorney's Houston office who initially supervised her First City work. "And Julia was about as tenacious as they come."

Tomala discovered that Cihak had set up a complex scheme to steer more than $4 million in First City loans and fees to his consultants, who then gave Cihak part of the money as kickbacks. At Cihak's 1993 trial she told the jury that he had come down to Texas to use First City as his "personal piggy bank," which in turn helped lead to First City's own failure, putting thousands of people out of work. Although the once-swaggering Cihak, wearing a gray suit, royal blue tie, and unlaced white athletic shoes, offered a rambling courtroom plea for leniency, even mentioning that he had made a halfhearted suicide attempt, an unsympathetic federal judge sentenced him to prison for twelve years and seven months. Tomala immediately went back to work investigating Cihak, and in 1995 she had him indicted again for another series of multimillion-dollar kickback schemes with other "consultants." This time, he got a twenty-two-year sentence. Cihak was probably going to prison for the rest of his life.

Still, Tomala wasn't finished. After Cihak's second trial, she decided to find out why Cihak, a racehorse investor himself and a Kentucky Derby fan, had been so determined to get the bank into the equine-lending business. She knew that a few months after the First City loan to Calumet was funded, Cihak had received a personal $1.1 million loan from a Kentucky entity called Equine Capital Corporation (ECC). Curious, she started retracing the money coming in and out of the ECC and learned that the money had not come from the ECC at all. Through a series of convoluted check-kiting maneuvers, Lundy and Gary Matthews had provided the $1.1 million to the ECC, which was run by Lundy associates, and the ECC had then passed on the money to Cihak, which he wasn't asked to repay. Cihak then used that money to lease two Calumet mares and pay for them to get into the breeding shed with Alydar. He also had arranged a deal with Lundy to buy one-time breeding rights to another Calumet stallion, Secreto, which were worth $125,000 on the open market, for a mere $1.

In return for access to Calumet's best horses — and the possibility of getting a foal of his own that might someday be a successful racehorse — Cihak agreed to become J. T. Lundy's financial patron, pushing through the $50 million loan at First City and then protecting Lundy when loan officers became anxious about Calumet's financial condition. To Cihak, it must not have seemed like a particularly perilous deal. He no doubt assumed, as everyone else did in the horse business, that Alydar's stud fees would generate the money necessary to pay back any bank loan. Calumet itself had drawn up a document showing that Alydar's "stud fee revenue potential" could be nearly $25 million a year.

Actually, it was journalist Carol Flake who first learned that Alydar's earnings were not even close to what Lundy suggested they were. After poring over Jockey Club records, she discovered that Alydar was often performing on mares for free. Either the mares' owners had already paid for the trips to the breeding shed years earlier through one of the lifetime breeding rights that Lundy had been selling, or they had received free breeding rights from Lundy in exchange for something Lundy wanted. To pay for a stallion, for instance, Lundy offered that stallion's owner a series of visits to Alydar's breeding shed. In other instances, Lundy simply gave his closest buddies free passes to Alydar. By 1990 the free passes to Alydar were outnumbering the ones that were paid for with stud fees.

In her 1992 *Connoisseur* story, Flake hinted that Alydar's death might not have been accidental. After learning that the farm's insurance policies on Alydar totaled $36.5 million, making him the most heavily insured horse in history, she went so far as to suggest that Alydar might have been worth more dead than alive. Yet no law enforcement official had shown any interest in pursuing the issue — until Tomala began flipping through records about Calumet in 1996.

What she realized was that Lundy had to have been frantic in the months before Alydar's death. There was no way he was going to be able to come up with that $15 million payment to First City by February 1991. An accountant who had studied Calumet's records told Tomala that the farm was then losing almost $1 million a month. Lundy was unable to find new bankers to loan him money, and he was equally unsuccessful in persuading investors from as far away as Japan to purchase a minor interest in Calumet. What's more, Lundy couldn't get any more income out of Alydar, who was already being bred so often that, according to one veterinarian, the muscles of his hind end were constantly sore. And Lundy suffered another blow in 1990 when his best horse that year, Criminal Type, who was favored to win the Breeders' Cup, the most lucrative purse in horse racing, was injured just before the race, depriving a clearly distraught Lundy of the chance to receive millions.

Tomala also verified that Lundy had a big problem with the insurance companies that held multimillion-dollar "equine mortality" policies on Alydar. In 1990 they were threatening to cancel those policies because of Calumet's slowness in paying its premiums. Lundy had been forced to send Matthews and his own sister, who handled the insurance on Calumet's horses, to London to beg exasperated Lloyd's representatives to give them one more chance — which they did. But the head of another equine insurance company, Golden Eagle Insurance out of California, told Lundy's sister in the early fall of 1990 that he had reached the end of his patience with Calumet's delinquent payments. He said the company's policy on Alydar would not be renewed when it expired in December.

Tomala realized that if there was a perfect time for Alydar to die, it was precisely in November 1990, just after Frank Cihak's resignation and just before one of Alydar's insurance policies expired. She looked at another record. Calumet had indeed used Alydar's insurance proceeds to make its payment to First City Bancorporation and staved off foreclosure for a few more months.

For Tomala, there was only one person who could have had Alydar killed: J. T. Lundy. And she was determined to prove it.

The question was, how could anyone prove, seven years after the fact, that a racehorse had been murdered? Tomala had no experience investigating murders. Neither did Rob Foster, the young FBI agent assigned to work with her. Yet here they were in Kentucky, and it didn't take them long to understand that they were not welcome. Few people wanted to speak to them. Those who did said that Lundy couldn't possibly be a horse killer. They pointed out that on the night of Alydar's injury, November 13, 1990, Lundy got on the phone and begged the best veterinary orthopedic surgeon in Kentucky, Larry Bramlage, to try to save Alydar's life.

One of the first people Tomala and Foster interviewed was Tom Dixon, a mild-mannered, churchgoing Lexington insurance adjuster who had been hired by Lloyd's of London to handle its equine claims. Dixon was one of the first non-Calumet employees to arrive the night Alydar was injured, and according to the notes he took, it was Lundy who told him that Alydar was known to kick his stall violently and that he had no doubt broken his leg kicking the stall. Dixon had taken some photos and had conducted a few interviews, including one with the night watchman, Alton Stone, a muscular farm-worker with shaggy blond hair. Sitting in on that interview was one of Lundy's assistants, Susan McGee, who occasionally interrupted Stone to explain to Dixon what Stone meant to say. Dixon asked few follow-up questions of Stone or anyone else. He was a sympathetic man who felt bad for what had happened to the horse. He quickly filed a report saying the death was accidental, and he had Lloyd's of London's money to Calumet within thirty days. "The fastest payoff in history," he later said proudly.

There was another Lexington insurance adjuster who had tried to get into the farm the night of the injury, but he was prevented from getting past the front gates by a security guard, who said he was not allowed to let anyone in. When Terry McVey, representing Golden Eagle (the company that was not renewing its coverage of Alydar), was finally allowed in the stallion barn the next afternoon, he was amazed to find that Alydar's stall had been mopped and swept and that the heavy roller outside the door, the one that supposedly had been knocked loose from Alydar's kicks, had already been repaired and rebolted to the floor.

Why, he wanted to know, would Calumet employees so quickly clean up the evidence that suggested how Alydar had died? And why, if Alydar had been such a kicker as Lundy had said, were there no marks on the stall door consistent with heavy kicking? All horse farms would regularly add padding to the stalls of horses that kicked. Surely if the prized Alydar had been a kicker, Lundy would have had pads on Alydar's walls for his own protection.

Yet in the end, Golden Eagle officials decided not to challenge the circumstances regarding Alydar's death, and they too paid off the claim. "It was as if those who made a living off the big horse farms — like the insurance adjusters and the veterinarians — realized it was not in their best interests to rock the boat," Tomala says now. "Why risk losing any future business by asking too many questions?" Even breeders from competing farms were hesitant to talk about an event they knew could make the entire industry look bad. "There was this fear that a scandal about Alydar would deeply hurt the public's perception of horse racing," says Tomala. "So people started circling the wagons."

The veterinarians who had examined Alydar said they were firmly convinced that his injury was accidental: the horse had kicked the door, and the busted roller was proof. The roller was contained in a heavy metal bracket, about six inches long, that was bolted to the floor just outside Alydar's sliding stall door. The roller kept the stall door on its track. Because Alydar's fracture was the "torquing" type that happens when a horse twists its leg, the veterinarians theorized that when he knocked the roller loose with his kick, the stall door moved outward, thus opening a gap between the dislodged door and the wall of the stall. Alydar must have caught his leg in that gap, and in his struggle to get free, twisted his leg until it broke.

When Tomala and Foster asked to see an x-ray of Alydar's fracture, Lynda Rhodes Stewart, a former veterinarian at Calumet, told them it had mysteriously disappeared from her files less than a year after Alydar's death. They asked her if she remembered anything else about that night that seemed unusual. Well, she said, when Alton Stone had called her to say that something was wrong with Alydar, he had never indicated that Alydar's condition was serious. He told her only to come up when she had a chance.

On June 4, 1997, when Foster and Tomala finally tracked down Stone at a construction site where he was working, he nervously recounted for them the same story he had told insurance adjuster Tom Dixon. He said the regular night watchman, Harold "Cowboy" Kipp, had asked him to work for him that evening so he could have a night off. Between eight-thirty and nine-thirty in the evening, Stone said, he was sitting on a turned-over, five-gallon bucket in an office of the stallion barn, talking to a security guard whose job it was to drive the perimeter of the farm. Around nine-thirty, they drove over to the canteen to buy some sodas and returned ten to fifteen minutes later. Stone went back inside the stallion barn while the security guard returned to his rounds. It was then that he saw Alydar.

To verify Stone's story, Foster interviewed the security guard, Keed Highley, who told him he had never been interviewed by anyone about Alydar's death. Foster was stunned when Highley told him that he had not sat in that office with Stone but that he had stopped by the stallion barn at about ten to call his wife from a telephone there. When he approached the barn, he said, he saw Stone leaving. Highley noticed that the lights were on in the farm office — Lundy's office — which was attached to the barn. As he spoke to his wife on the phone, Highley heard the stallion whinny. He investigated, saw the horse's leg dangling, and then radioed Stone to call a veterinarian. For the first time, Foster realized there was a cover-up going on. It was Highley, not Stone, who had found Alydar.

Foster also found the original night watchman, Cowboy Kipp. Kipp's primary job was to take care of the stallions, specifically Alydar, and he had rarely missed a night of work since starting at the farm. He loved his job so much that he wouldn't even take vacations. In fact, when Foster found him, Kipp was still working as a night watchman at Calumet. (After filing for bankruptcy, the farm had been sold at auction for a mere $17 million to a Polish-born investor named Henryk deKwiatkowski, who lived there only part-time and who maintained a skeletal staff.)

Once again, no one — no insurance adjuster or reporter — had talked to Kipp. If they had, they would have been told a chilling story. About five days before Alydar's injury, Kipp said, he was at work on the farm when a dark blue Ford Crown Victoria with tinted windows drove up. A large man got out of the car. Kipp said he had seen the man in the main office a couple of times, but he didn't know his name or what he did for Calumet. The man told Kipp that the farm's management was worried he was getting burned out. Kipp needed to take a day off. "How about Tuesday, November 13?" the man said. Although Kipp didn't think he needed a break, he was the kind of employee who followed orders and didn't cause trouble. He did take that evening off, but he insisted to Foster that he never asked Stone to substitute for him.

Throughout 1997, Tomala had several of the witnesses — including Alton Stone, Keed Highley, and Cowboy Kipp — flown separately to Houston to tell their stories to a federal grand jury that had been secretly convened just to hear evidence about Alydar. In January 1998 that grand jury indicted Stone for perjury for telling numerous false stories to federal agents and to the grand jury itself. Obviously Tomala's strategy was to squeeze Stone (few people are indicted for perjury in federal court) to see if he would reveal what else he knew. Stone's court-appointed defense attorney said Tomala had become obsessed with conspiracy theories about Alydar's death. It was a charge Tomala could not deny. In a trial brief, she said that Stone was part of a plot to harm the horse.

As for Lundy, he had kept a low profile since his resignation from Calumet, staying mostly in Florida, where he was training horses at a small farm. Although he had declared personal bankruptcy in 1992, few people imagined he was really broke. An accountant who had studied the Calumet books said Lundy had paid himself nearly $6 million during his tenure. He did show up at a Lexington lawyer's office for a deposition regarding his bankruptcy. He took the Fifth Amendment more than two hundred times while fidgeting, rubbing his eyes, and chewing on his fingernails. Irritated, an attorney asked Lundy if he would just tell him the color of the shirt he was wearing. "I think it's red," Lundy said after consulting with his attorney.

Lundy had been subpoenaed by the defense to testify at Alton Stone's perjury trial, but U.S. marshals couldn't find him. Still, he was hardly ignored during the trial. Outside the presence of the jury, Marsha Matthews, who was married to Lundy's chief financial officer at the time of the horse's death, took the stand to say that she had overheard Lundy say during a conversation at the Matthewses' home about Calumet's deep debts, "There are ways to get rid of the horse." The judge ruled the testimony was inadmissible. But he did allow writer Carol Flake to testify that Alton Stone, whom she went to see again in 1992 after her magazine story was completed, suddenly had become very emotional in her presence and blurted out that J. T. Lundy "knew something was going to happen to Alydar."

Yet Tomala didn't get what she really wanted from that trial. Stone didn't cooperate with her, and he didn't testify. He decided to take his lumps, which weren't that bad: he received only five months in prison and five months of home confinement.

By 1999, it seemed, Tomala's investigation had run out of gas. After more than two years of interrogations and grand jury hearings, she hadn't been able to prove Alydar had been murdered. She had been able to prove only that Alton Stone couldn't keep his stories straight.

But she still had one more card to play.

In March 1999 Tomala persuaded a Houston federal grand jury to indict Lundy, who was finally found in Florida, and Gary Matthews, who was working as a lawyer in Lexington since his resignation from Calumet, on charges of bank fraud, conspiracy, bribery, and lying about the $1.1 million bribe they had offered to Frank Cihak. When the trial finally got under way, in February 2000, the most interesting case for Lundy's innocence was made by Dan Cogdell, one of Houston's most colorful defense attorneys. During his closing argument, he told Lundy, who was sucking on candy, to stand up and face the jury. Cogdell then asked jurors if they thought this man looked smart enough to pull off a massive fraud. The jurors did. They took less than three hours to find Lundy and Matthews guilty.

The story was barely covered by the press. By then the financial shenanigans involving Cihak, Calumet, and Lundy were old news. At Lundy's sentencing this past October, only a handful of spectators were in the courtroom gallery. But Tomala suddenly called FBI agent Foster to the stand to recount the questions and suspicious stories regarding Alydar's death. Then she called a surprise witness: a tall, silver-haired man with a deep Bostonian accent.

His name was George Pratt, and he was a full professor of electrical engineering and computer science at the Massachusetts Institute of Technology. He also was an avid horseman and the chairman of the National Association of Thoroughbred Owners Racetrack Safety Committee. Pratt testified that he had been contacted by Foster about a year earlier asking if he would analyze some evidence. Soon, a large box arrived at Pratt's cluttered MIT office. Inside was a section of concrete, about one square foot in size. It was a piece of the floor that had been cut out from the front of Alydar's stall.

Foster and Tomala had always been bothered by the busted roller story. There had been two bolts that had connected the roller to the floor, which a Calumet maintenance supervisor had told Foster were broken in half from the force of the kick. The supervisor said he threw the top half of the bolts away, then he had simply moved the roller over from its original location, drilled new holes in the floor, and installed new bolts. He told Foster that the bottom portions of the broken bolts were still embedded in the floor.

Foster noticed later that Tom Dixon, the insurance adjuster, had taken a photo of that roller while it was still lying on the floor. Clearly visible in the photo were the top halves of the bolts. It occurred to Foster that the upper part of the bolts should match the bottom part of the bolts. If they didn't, then there was finally physical evidence that the bracket had been removed before Alydar's accident, with the intention that it later be found to serve as an explanation of how Alydar broke his leg. With other agents, Foster cut out the section of the floor that included the original bolts, and he sent it to Pratt along with Dixon's enlarged photograph.

Almost immediately, Pratt noticed that the bottom half of the bolts were cut off evenly at the same height, while one of the top bolts was a little long and the other a little short. Then he noticed that the top parts of the bolts in the photograph were rusty and heavily corroded, while the bottom parts of the bolts had little or no corrosion. There was no way the upper and bottom halves of those bolts matched. He also noticed that if the concrete block was put back in its proper place in the floor, the shear on the bottom part of the bolts was parallel not perpendicular to the stall door — which meant the force applied to them had to have come from somewhere outside the stall, not from inside.

Then Pratt flew to Calumet, studied the stall, took measurements, and went back to MIT to devise an equation to determine how much force would be required from a horse to kick that roller off its hinges. He determined that 6,600 pounds of force would have to hit the stall door exactly three feet off the floor. The strongest stallion, Pratt concluded, could generate only 1,000 to 2,000 pounds with a kick.

Alydar, Pratt said in his Houston testimony, had to have been killed. He speculated that someone had tied the end of a rope around Alydar's leg and attached the other end of the rope to a truck that could easily have been driven into the stallion barn. The truck then took off, pulling Alydar's leg from underneath him until it snapped.

There was a long, long silence when Pratt finished. At the defense table, Lundy, who was wearing a poor-fitting sports coat, a thin tie, and soft brown walking shoes, kept his head down, writing on a notepad. From the government's table, Tomala, in her black Prada pantsuit, gave Lundy a lingering look, her eyes squinting in disgust. She had presented the evidence hoping the federal judge would rack a much larger sentence to Lundy's bribery conviction. In her summation, she said that only Lundy had "the motive and opportunity" to have the horse killed. He wanted the horse dead, she said, to collect the insurance windfall to forestall First City's takeover of the farm. And his false statements to the insurance adjusters, as well as the lies told by Stone, only confirmed that Lundy was responsible for the injury. "To believe otherwise, one would have to accept a string of coincidences that defy common sense," she declared.

There were still many unanswered questions. If Lundy had wanted Alydar dead, then wouldn't he have made sure the horse was killed that first night? And didn't the fact that Lundy was apparently so distraught throughout that night, begging doctors to operate on the horse, suggest that Lundy wanted Alydar to live? Tomala later said, "What was he supposed to do at that point — cheer?" It could also be assumed that Lundy had to have known from the extent of that first injury that it was unlikely Alydar would survive. Thus, he could pretend to be distraught to mislead others.

Still, the death of Alydar didn't accomplish anything for him in the long run. Calumet still went under. Lundy still lost his job. Yet as Gary Matthews himself says, Lundy had to have been terrified of going down in racehorse history as the man who ruined Calumet. "I can't imagine him doing something so drastic as to kill his best horse," Matthews told me after his trial. "J. T. loved animals. But he was in a desperate situation. I remember we discussed that if the First City debt was cut in half, the Japanese would be far more interested in investing. Maybe he thought this was the thing to do. I just don't know."

The federal judge overseeing the case eventually decided he didn't know either. He said he wasn't comfortable about a whole new criminal case being introduced at a sentencing hearing, and in his final ruling he said, "Although there is evidence Mr. Lundy had the motive and opportunity to injure Alydar, and although there is some physical evidence, I am not able to conclude by the preponderance of the evidence that Mr. Lundy is responsible for the death of Alydar." The judge sentenced Lundy to four years in prison for the bribery; Matthews received twenty-one months.

For more than an hour after the hearing, Tomala and Foster hung around the courtroom, packing up their exhibits and their files filled with a decade's worth of notes about Alydar's death. Although they hadn't won, they said they felt some satisfaction in getting their allegations into open court so that everyone would know that Alydar's death was no accident. I asked Tomala if she felt a sense of sadness that her long obsession with Alydar had come to an end. The statute of limitations on an insurance fraud case is ten years, which would make it unlikely that she'd ever be able to bring charges again regarding the horse's demise.

Tomala gave me a confident smile. "Actually, there are ways to expand that statute and keep the case going for a little longer," she said. "Somehow, someday, the whole truth is going to come out."

Meanwhile, Lundy, who had been given a few months to get his affairs in order before reporting to prison, headed out of the federal courthouse, saying he needed to get back to Florida to take care of horses and visit his sick mother. I saw him standing at the curb, his hands in his pockets, his shoulders hunched. For a moment I thought about the young Lundy from the sixties, the rambunctious, hot rod–driving son of a tenant farmer, dreaming of the day he would run Calumet. Nearly forty years later, the dream had turned his life into a shambles. "That Tomala knows she's full of bull——," he said. "All she wants to do is get her name in the paper."

"You didn't have anything to do with that horse's death?" I asked him.

Lundy looked at me, his face turning red. I realized it was the first time he publicly was going to answer a question about his alleged involvement. "Hell, no," he said. "I loved that horse. Loved him." He paused and shook his head, as if he couldn't believe he would be living for the rest of his life with the reputation as Alydar's killer. "I tell you, I'd give anything if Alydar was still at Calumet, heading off to his breeding shed," Lundy said. And then he jumped into a cab, and he was gone.

JOSHUA HARRIS PRAGER

Giants' 1951 Comeback Wasn't All It Seemed

FROM THE WALL STREET JOURNAL

BOBBY THOMSON, the New York Giants' third baseman, stands poised in the batter's box. In the bottom of the ninth inning in the final game of a playoff, his team trails the Brooklyn Dodgers 4–2, with two men on base. Dodgers pitcher Ralph Branca's fastball hurtles toward him. Mr. Thomson swings, he connects, and the ball sails over the left-field wall and into history.

That home run capped an unprecedented comeback by the Giants, propelled the team to the 1951 World Series, and secured Robert Brown Thomson's name in American lore.

Months shy of its fiftieth anniversary, Mr. Thomson's "Shot Heard Round the World" echoes ever louder. In recent years, the U.S. Postal Service honored it with a stamp. Author Don DeLillo threaded it through his 827-page novel *Underworld*. *The Sporting News* christened it the greatest moment in baseball history. *Sports Illustrated* ranked it the second-greatest sports moment of the twentieth century (after the U.S. hockey team's victory over the Soviet Union in the 1980 Olympics). And this year, among the many celebrations planned to mark the jubilee anniversary of the home run, there will be a reunion of the surviving Giants and Dodgers who met October 3, 1951, at the Polo Grounds below Coogan's Bluff in Harlem.

But in all the encomiums and analyses of that singular moment through half a century, one crucial element has been missing — unknown that afternoon even to the nine Dodgers on the field, the

34,320 paid spectators at the Polo Grounds, and the millions who followed the flight of the ball on radio and television. The Giants were stealing the Dodgers' signs, the finger signals transmitted from catcher to pitcher that determine the pitch to be thrown.

"Stealing signs is nothing to be proud of," says Mr. Thomson, now seventy-seven years old. "Of course, the question is, did I take the signs that day?"

Sixteen players and coaches who appeared on the 1951 Giants are dead. In interviews with all twenty-one surviving players and the one living coach, many are at last willing to confirm that they executed an elaborate scheme relying on an electrician and a spyglass. And, they say, they stole signs not only during their encounter with the Dodgers, but during home games all through the last ten weeks of the 1951 season, a period when the Giants appeared to summon mysterious resources of will and talent.

"Every hitter knew what was coming," says eighty-three-year-old Al Gettel, a pitcher on the 1951 Giants roster into August. "Made a big difference."

The Giants husbanded their secret well. Still, Mr. Thomson says, "it's reared its ugly head every once in a while." Indeed, a few times over fifty years, rumors that the 1951 Giants stole signs circulated in the press and sports literature. But they came to nothing. In the 1992 book *The Great Chase: The Dodgers-Giants Pennant Race of 1951*, author Harvey Rosenfeld devotes two pages to talk of sign stealing. He concludes the passage with a Dodgers official who said he "believes all this sign-stealing business is total fiction."

The secret was safe.

In 1958, the Giants left Harlem for San Francisco. The Polo Grounds later gave way to a housing complex. And as the remembered history of the 5–4 "Miracle at Coogan's Bluff" evolved into baseball legend, the keepers of the secret bore an ever heavier burden. "It was hard for any of us," says Al Corwin, seventy-four, a rookie pitcher on the 1951 Giants. "It's put a question mark as to what happened when and where."

The answer begins with a small leather case on a boy's desk in Westford, Massachusetts. Robert Henry Ehasz, sixteen, pops open a shiny steel snap engraved with the maker's name, Wollensak, and lifts out a telescope, "Papa used it to spy on the Germans," he says.

"No, not the Germans," corrects his mother, Susan. "An opposing baseball team."

"Papa," Robert Henry's grandfather, was Henry Leonard Schenz, a box of a man with a forty-eight-inch chest and sixty-eight-inch frame. Mr. Schenz was a utility infielder who played six middling seasons in the Major Leagues. In the middle of his last — on June 30, 1951 — the Pittsburgh Pirates put him on waivers, and the Giants snapped him up.

As a Giant, Mr. Schenz had no at-bats and no stolen bases and scored a lone run. Most of the time, the thirty-two-year-old ballplayer razzed opponents from the dugout.

He had other skills. Before his stint with the Pirates, Mr. Schenz spent four years with the Chicago Cubs and occasionally spied signals for his Cub teammates with a telescope. "This whole thing began when he was with Chicago," says his son Jerald Schenz, fifty-three. "They had a spot in the scoreboard at Wrigley. He was out there at times."

In the twenty or so seconds between every pitch of every baseball game, players and coaches communicate strategy in silence, tugging their ear lobes, for example, swiping their caps, or adjusting their pant legs. Likewise, scouts, coaches, and players keep close eyes on their opponents in hopes of glimpsing a pitcher's grip on the ball or deciphering a coach's body language. Runners on second base peer at the catcher's fingers as he signs to the pitcher whether to throw a fastball, curveball, or another type of pitch.

These tactics are accepted practice. More elaborate efforts are frowned on. In 1898, Cincinnati Red Tommy Corcoran got his spikes stuck in the dirt around the coaching box at third base in Philadelphia. When he tugged at what he thought was a root, he unearthed a telegraph wire that ran to the Phillies clubhouse (where a backup catcher sat with binoculars spying signals and communicating them to the third-base coach, presumably via vibrations from the wire). In the early 1960s, at Milwaukee's County Stadium, star pitcher Bob Buhl sat in street clothes among the fans in center field and peered through binoculars to spy and relay signs. In the 1980s, at Chicago's old Comiskey Park, White Sox batters looked to a flickering twenty-five-watt refrigerator bulb in the scoreboard for pitch tips.

Baseball has always been an ambiguous game. It has no clock. The strike zone is constantly reinterpreted. Official scorers can be notoriously loyal to the home team. Pitchers continued to rely on spitballs long after the pitch was banned in 1920, and groundskeepers still moisten base paths to slow fleet opponents. It wasn't until 1961 that Major League Baseball passed a rule banning sign stealing by way of a "mechanical device."

In theory, knowing the incoming pitch gives the batter an edge. But sign stealing, legitimate or otherwise, doesn't always help. Many batters don't even want to know what's coming. "Suppose he calls a curveball and throws a fastball," says Wes Westrum, the starting catcher on the 1951 Giants. "You could get ripped in two." And even with advance notice, a batter must still hit the pitch.

Mr. Schenz had been with the Giants eighteen days when, on July 18, 1951, the team lost for the sixth time in nine games, falling eight games behind the Dodgers. The team was in third place in the National League and heading south.

The next day, Leo Ernest Durocher, then the Giants' manager, called a team meeting. "He said, 'Goddammit!'" recalls Mr. Corwin, the rookie pitcher who joined the Giants that very day. "'We can't get first, but we got to get second!'"

Mr. Durocher, forty-six, and his new player Mr. Schenz were of like dispositions. Mr. Durocher is credited with coining the phrase "Nice guys finish last." Mr. Schenz, teammates recall, enjoyed sharpening his cleats in view of his opponents. No one recalls Mr. Schenz talking to Mr. Durocher about his telescope, but at that July 19 team meeting, players say, Mr. Durocher brought up sign stealing for the first time that year.

"He asked each person if he wanted the sign," says Monte Irvin, the Giants' star left fielder, now eighty-one. "I told him no. He said, 'You mean to tell me, if a fat fastball is coming, you don't want to know?'"

According to other surviving players, enough of the team *did* want to know. "I'd probably say fifty-fifty," Mr. Corwin says.

On July 19, the day of the Giants' meeting, rain washed out all major league games east of Cleveland, including a double-header scheduled at the Polo Grounds. Mr. Durocher told the press that the rainouts were a blessing — a chance to rest and align his tired pitching staff. And based on what the players say took place the following night, the rain gave Mr. Durocher time to put his plan to work.

The Giants' clubhouse looked out on the diamond from high above the center-field wall — 483 feet away from home plate in 1951, an absurdly long distance by major league standards. Mr. Durocher, who died in 1991, told his players that their clubhouse, directly aligned with home plate, was the perfect crow's nest for stealing signs.

The matter remained of somehow relaying the signs to the batter from behind a wire-mesh screen in the clubhouse. There were no lights in the scoreboard, so flashing a bulb was out of the question. However, the bullpens, where pitchers warmed up, were in fair territory along the outfield walls. When a batter stepped to the plate, he could look just to the right of the pitcher and see his teammates much farther beyond, on a bench in right-center field. Though they sat between 440 and 449 feet away, they could motion their signals unimpeded.

It fell to Abraham Chadwick to get the signals from clubhouse to bullpen.

The only thing Mr. Chadwick loved more than being an electrician was baseball. And when it came to baseball, he loved only the Brooklyn Dodgers. "His whole life was the Dodgers," says daughter Harriet Mesulam, sixty-six. "He would fight with anyone if they said anything about the Dodgers."

In May 1947, Mr. Chadwick's brother Nat, an official at Local 3 of the International Brotherhood of Electrical Workers in lower Manhattan, got a part-time job for Abe operating the lights at a ballpark. But it wasn't at Brooklyn's Ebbets Field. It was at the Polo Grounds.

Still, the forty-nine-year-old Mr. Chadwick was proud of his new gig. "He said, 'Without me, no game,'" Ms. Mesulam says.

Mr. Chadwick, since deceased, had only to turn the park's lights on before games and off afterward. The work lasted five minutes. The rest of the time, Mr. Chadwick sat in the stands in his fedora, smoking cigars and watching baseball. The Giants were no threat to his Dodgers. By July 1951, Brooklyn was comfortably ahead of New York for the seventh consecutive season.

According to electricians who knew him, Mr. Chadwick installed a bell-and-buzzer system in the clubhouse and connected it to the phones in the bullpen and the dugout. With the press of a button in the clubhouse — once for a fastball, twice for an off-speed pitch — the phones would buzz the sign.

Mr. Chadwick's nifty work was a hit at the Local 3. "The electricians were proud of him," says Walter Carberry, eighty-six, an electrician who knew Mr. Chadwick from union meetings. "They never let it get around."

The following day, July 20, the Giants hosted the Cincinnati Reds for the start of a four-game series. It was a night game, and, as always, Mr. Chadwick walked to the roof and flipped the park's circuit breakers. Players won't say whether they saw Mr. Schenz in the clubhouse spying, but they recall him talking about the duty. "The funny thing he said," recalls Davey Williams, a backup infielder on the 1951 Giants, "was that he couldn't hold [the telescope close] to his eye because it was so strong that it blurred everything."

Focused on an object 500 feet away, a 35-millimeter lens like the one in Mr. Schenz's telescope provides a resolution of about 0.2 inch. And so, peering through the spyglass from a perch in Mr. Durocher's locked office in the clubhouse, Mr. Schenz could have distinguished the tips of catchers' fingers spread at least 0.2 inch apart.

"The first time the buzzer went off, we fell off the bench," says Mr. Corwin, who was sitting in the bullpen. "We thought the whole ballpark could hear." But the crowd, which included General Douglas MacArthur, seemed oblivious.

The Giants beat the Reds, 11–5.

Mr. Chadwick fine-tuned his handiwork. "Whoever this guy was," Mr. Corwin says, "when we got out the next day, [the buzz] was softer."

The Giants took three of four games from the Reds and on July 23 left for Pittsburgh. Three days later, deep below the streets of New York on the Pelham Bay local, Mr. Chadwick grew faint. "He felt this weakness coming over him in the subway," recalls Helen Smith, seventy-four, Mr. Chadwick's daughter.

The news was bad. Mr. Chadwick had stomach cancer. After surgery, he returned home to the Bronx. In lieu of food, he drank vanilla malteds. He lay on a living-room couch in his pajamas and watched the Dodgers games on a television set his brother bought for him. Brooklyn closed out July with ten consecutive wins, and an electrician named Seymour Schmelzer replaced Mr. Chadwick at the Polo Grounds.

The Giants, meantime, were on their longest road trip of the season, a seventeen-game swing through Pittsburgh, Cincinnati, Chicago, St. Louis, and Brooklyn. They won nine of their first fourteen games. But heading into Brooklyn on August 8, they still trailed their rivals by nine and a half games. The Dodgers beat the Giants three straight. The gap between the teams ballooned to twelve and a half games. Proclaimed Dodgers manager Charlie Dressen: "The Giants is dead."

Home at last on August 11, the Giants hit rock bottom. They lost to Philadelphia 4–0, and Brooklyn beat Boston 8–1, pushing the Dodgers' lead to thirteen and a half games.

But then, everything changed.

The Dodgers' lead started to shrink a few hours later. Boston beat Brooklyn 8–4 in the second game of a double-header.

After losing the series opener, the Giants beat Philadelphia three straight. They beat the Dodgers three straight. They again swept three games from the Phillies. They took a pair from Cincinnati and a single game against St. Louis. They beat Chicago four straight.

When evening settled on August 27, the Giants had reeled off sixteen wins in a row, baseball's longest streak in sixteen years. Thirteen of their victories had come at home. They trailed the Dodgers by just five games.

By this time, relaying signs from the dugout, where chosen players could shout code words to batters, was deemed too conspicuous. The Giants were mainly relaying signals from the bullpen. The player relaying would sit closest to center field. After hearing the buzzer buzz, he might cross his legs to denote a fastball. He might toss a ball in the air. He might sit still. The method was based, Mr. Corwin says, on "what was easiest to see, what was the quickest."

Another change: Mr. Schenz was no longer the spy in the clubhouse. He had struggled to decode the opposing catcher's signs.

Herman Louis Franks, the Giants' third-base coach in 1951, had been a catcher. Like all catchers, he knew signs and how to mask them when runners led off second base. Mr. Franks, now eighty-seven, drops his fingers between his thighs and shoots numbers: two, one, two. "I varied them so much you could never tell what the hell they were," he says.

And so Mr. Franks took Mr. Schenz's spot in the clubhouse (and Mr. Durocher replaced Mr. Franks at third base). "I haven't talked about it in forty-nine years," Mr. Franks says. His voice rises. "If I'm ever asked about it, I'm denying everything."

Other players are more forthcoming. "Herman would sit in the clubhouse," says Mr. Irvin. "He's sitting there with a telescope, and he'd relay it to the bullpen."

Adds Salvadore Yvars, a backup catcher on the 1951 Giants, now seventy-six: "He knew how to get the signs. Catchers know what the hell they're doing."

Over the first two days of September, the Giants trounced the Dodgers by the combined score of 19–3. Mr. Dressen, the Dodgers' skipper, became suspicious.

"We took binoculars out on the bench to observe center field," Dodgers coach Cookie Lavagetto told author Peter Golenbock in his 1984 book *Bums.* Mr. Lavagetto, who died in 1990, continued: "The umpire spotted us. He ran over and grabbed those binoculars away from us. There was nothing we could do. We told the ump that we were just trying to observe center field. Whatever Durocher had out there, he had a good system."

The Dodgers investigated no further. And the Giants continued to win.

Winning streaks self-perpetuate. By the tune the Giants hit the road in early September, Giants batters had patient, level swings. Giants pitchers had rested arms. The team won fourteen of its final eighteen road games, including the last four games of the season. Incredibly, the Giants had overcome a thirteen-and-a-half-game deficit in just forty-eight days and finished the season tied with the Dodgers: ninety-six up, fifty-eight down.

The Yankees claimed the American League pennant, and for the first and last time, all three of New York's teams finished the season in first place. New York braced itself for a best-of-three playoff between the Dodgers and the Giants to determine which team would face the Yankees in the subway series.

The Giants won the first game, the Dodgers the second. And on the overcast afternoon of October 3, the Dodgers and Giants met for their deciding game at Coogan's Bluff.

"Twenty years from now, the fans will be talking about this afternoon's hero as yet unknown," intoned radio announcer Gordon McClendon of the Texas-based Liberty Broadcasting System. "And if there's a goat, his name will echo down the corridor of time."

Ralph Theodore Joseph Branca started warming up in the bottom of the ninth inning, with the Dodgers leading 4–1. Starting pitcher Don Newcombe gave up singles to Alvin Dark and Don Mueller and a one-out double to Whitey Lockman. The score was 4–2, with men on second and third.

Just twenty-five, Mr. Branca was a star. He already boasted seventy-six career wins. He was a veteran of three All-Star teams. Mr. Dressen pulled Mr. Newcombe and called on Mr. Branca to face the next batter, Mr. Thomson.

Mr. Dressen feared walking the potential winning run and instructed Mr. Branca to pitch to Mr. Thomson, even though Mr. Thomson had hit home runs off Mr. Branca in two of their previous three meetings. Mr. Thomson was hitting every one well. Since July 20, he had hit .353, with fifteen home runs, thirteen of them away from the Polo Grounds. (Before July 20, he had hit just .241, with sixteen home runs.)

Mr. Branca, nicknamed "the Hawk," eyed catcher Rube Walker for the sign. Mr. Walker changed his finger sequences to protect them from Mr. Lockman, the Giants runner who lurked off second base. It worked. "I didn't recognize the sequence," Mr. Lockman, now seventy-four, says. Mr. Lockman says he touched his belt buckle to let Mr. Thomson know that he couldn't read the sign.

But the Giants had other means. "My wife never likes me to talk about it," says Mr. Yvars, the backup catcher, talking as he chews a mouthful of muffin in a coffee shop. "She gets embarrassed."

The 1951 season was Mr. Yvars's first full year in the majors. He pinch-hit and occasionally started. But his chief duty was warming up pitchers. And as a bullpen fixture, he often relayed signs.

Now, as Mr. Branca pondered his first pitch to Mr. Thomson, Mr. Yvars, who had been busy warming up pitcher Larry Jansen in the previous inning, was in the hot seat. When the buzzer in the bullpen sounded just once, he knew what to do. "If I did nothing, it was a fastball," he says. "I did nothing."

It *was* a fastball, right over the plate. Mr. Thomson took it for strike one. Did he know that Mr. Franks was perched above center field? "Of course!" he says. Did Mr. Thomson take the signs earlier in the game? "I don't know why I wouldn't have."

Again, Mr. Branca recalls, Mr. Walker called for a fastball. Again, the buzzer sounded once. Again, Mr. Yvars says, he sat still. Russ Hodges, the Giants radio broadcaster, called the action at 3:57 P.M. on WMCA:

"Branca throws. There's a long drive. It's going to be — I believe! The Giants win the pennant! The Giants win the pennant! The Giants win the pennant! The Giants win the pennant! Bobby Thomson hits into the lower deck of the left-field stands. The Giants win the pennant! And they're going crazy! They're going crazy! Oohhh-oohhh!"

Mr. Thomson hopped around the bases. Mr. Schenz and his hollering teammates crowded around home plate. Mr. Yvars and his four bullpen mates sprinted toward the infield. Mr. Franks, No. 3, isn't visible in numerous extant photos and film footage of the scene.

At 1033 Elder Avenue in the Bronx, an electrician's heart broke. "He cried," remembers Ms. Mesulam, Mr. Chadwick's daughter, who was fifteen at the time. "He said, 'I can't believe it. I can't believe it. I can't believe it.'"

Mr. Branca walked slowly from the field, slumped face down on the clubhouse's concrete steps, and wept. "I guess we weren't meant to win it," he told reporters.

Within seconds of Mr. Thomson's shot, two spectators at the Polo Grounds suffered heart attacks. Within minutes, Dodgers fans hung effigies of Mr. Branca — complete with his No. 13 — from street lights and telephone poles. Within hours, *New York Daily Mirror* reporter Edwin Wilcox wrote: "There were those who thought of ending it all in a long leap from the Brooklyn Bridge or a deep dive into the Gowanus."

The Giants faced the Yankees in the World Series. Midway through the series, Mr. Chadwick checked into Flower Fifth Avenue Hospital. He didn't watch the Yankees triumph in six games. He died on November 3, a month to the day after Mr. Thomson's home run.

On December 5, the Giants sold Mr. Schenz to Oakland of the Pacific Coast League. He never returned to the major leagues and failed to qualify for its pension by forty-one days. His children say that for the rest of his life, until he died of a heart attack on May 12,

1988, he kept his telescope in its leather case, tucked away in a chifforobe in his bedroom.

Mr. Durocher managed the Giants to a championship in 1954 and left the team after the following season. He later managed the Cubs and the Houston Astros, and retired in 1973, after 2,008 career victories. Three years after he died, he was inducted into the National Baseball Hall of Fame.

Mr. Franks left the Giants in 1955. Eventually, he managed the San Francisco Giants and the Chicago Cubs to 605 victories. In 1980, after forty-one years in baseball, he retired to his hometown in the hills above Salt Lake City.

Mr. Yvars lined out to right field for the final out of the 1951 World Series. The Giants traded him to St. Louis in 1953. He retired the next year and has worked in finance since. In the 1980s, Mr. Yvars planned to publish dozens of tales from his baseball days in a book titled *How We Stole the Pennant.* But, he says, he lost his publishing deal when he refused to detail the personal peccadilloes of teammates.

Mr. Branca hurt his back during spring training of 1952 and won just twelve games the rest of his career. He retired at thirty and lives in Westchester County, New York. He has long been a partner at an insurance and financial-planning company and today is chairman of the Baseball Assistance Team, which supports indigent former major leaguers.

"What's it like to have to live with one awful moment?" wonders Mr. DeLillo in his novel. "Forever plodding across the outfield grass on your way to the clubhouse."

A few years after surrendering baseball's most famous home run, Mr. Branca heard talk that the Giants were stealing signs in 1951. "When I heard those rumors and innuendoes," says Mr. Branca, now seventy-five, "I made a decision not to speak about it." He adds, "I didn't want to look like I was crying over spilled milk."

In 1962, an Associated Press article reported that a spy in the clubhouse helped the Giants win the pennant in 1951, but the story relied on an anonymous source and was vague. Soon after the story appeared, sportscaster Howard Cosell asked Mr. Branca to comment on it, but the pitcher demurred.

Over the years, as Messrs. Branca and Thomson rubbed elbows at countless functions, posed together with President Nixon, and co-signed the sweet spots of baseball after baseball, the pitcher said nothing of sign stealing. "Bobby and I are really, really good friends," Mr. Branca says. "He still hit the pitch."

The Giants traded Mr. Thomson away in 1954. He left baseball in 1960, after fifteen years and 264 home runs, and worked more than thirty years as an executive at a paper-goods company.

Inside the one-story home in central New Jersey where Mr. Thomson has lived since 1958, there are few signs of a celebrated baseball career: a small horseshoe-shaped replica of the Polo Grounds, a signed copy of Mr. DeLillo's book, a mounted facsimile of the commemorative stamp.

"The Scots are very undemonstrative people," says Mr. Thomson, who was born in Glasgow, the youngest of six children. "We were brought up to be seen and not heard."

Mr. Thomson, now a widower, has never spoken publicly of sign stealing and has never raised the subject with Mr. Branca. "I guess I've been a jerk in a way," he says. "That I don't want to face the music. Maybe I've felt too sensitive, embarrassed maybe."

Mr. Thomson sits on his couch, wearing the tweed jacket and tie he wore to church that morning. Suddenly, he uncrosses his legs, squares his feet with his shoulders, and puts his fists together, right over left, as if gripping a bat. He hunches his torso forward and turns his head toward his left shoulder. He looks out of unblinking eyes into his fireplace.

Did he take the sign?

From the batter's box, "you could almost just do it with your eyes," Mr. Thomson says.

His hands relax. He drops his arms to his sides.

Did he take the sign?

"I'd have to say more no than yes," he says. "I don't like to think of something taking away from it."

Pressed further, Mr. Thomson later says, "I was just being too honest and too fair. I could easily have said, 'No, I didn't take the sign.'"

He says, "It would take a little away from me in my mind if I felt I got help on the pitch."

But *did* he take the sign?

"My answer is no," Mr. Thomson says.

He adds: "I was always proud of that swing."

JEANNE MARIE LASKAS

The Enlightened Man

FROM ESQUIRE

FIRST WE HAVE THE BULL. Yeah, that was his first piece. He's stretching his V-neck down to provide a view of that bull depicted on his splendid left breast. Yeah, he knows. It's the size of a pasta bowl, that breast. Yeah, it's a dark-brown hunk of human worthy of fear and awe and God's glory. It's a rock-solid, bulbous slab of man-flesh commanding adoration. Yeah. But what about the bull? Now, ain't that a good bull?

Tattoo-wise, the bull was an obvious first choice for a man whose body has always been the main event. A more or less 338-pound, six-foot-four body with a forty-six-inch waist and a size-fourteen foot, a body that could easily bring to mind thoughts of steak and hide and cowboys getting thrown off it. The kind of body that was always different, always extreme; you know, his mom would get so sick of having to take his birth certificate to T-ball games back home in Warren, Ohio, to prove that, in fact, her son really was only eight years old, even though he looked more or less like a sycamore tree.

He shrugs. This movement makes him sweat. Yeah, he almost always sweats, beads of liquid pooling and spilling, pooling and spilling down a deep brown brow. A thoughtful, earnest brow that seems to bear the weight of centuries but actually is topped by dreadlocks sprouting happily, joyfully, as if dancing maybe to the theme song from Wally Gator.

His cell phone rings. Doodle-loodle-leet. Doodle-loodle-leet. It's his dad on the cell phone. His dad is saying, How about I make liver and onions on the stove for when you come home to Warren,

Ohio, tomorrow? Korey feels a glow of happiness inside him. It's this whole situation, is what it is. Here in his roomy house in the fine Hillcrest Lakeview Farms development in suburban Minneapolis, with Kelci upstairs cooking chicken in the oven and their three-year-old boy, Kodie, watching Dipsy and Tinky Winky on the kitchen TV. And him, Korey Stringer, down here on the supersized black leather couch in front of the big-screen with the PlayStation on, and now with his dad calling about cooking liver and onions on the stove for when he comes home. Has there ever been a more perfect and comfortable intersection of time and space? This, he thinks, is what people long for. People don't really long to be rich or famous. Most people long to be comfortable. Comfortable with their families and comfortable with their houses and comfortable in themselves.

He realizes, okay, comfort differs from man to man. Because for him, comfort is also the feeling of being in like thirty car wrecks every Sunday afternoon. Yeah. Comfort is trying to knock the living shit out of some enormous, angry, bile-spewing brute snarling at you from across the line, over and over again, every play, like eighty times, banging your head into a wall of viciousness and barbarity. It really is. You know, football is a violent game. That's why you use words like destroy and crush and dominate and kill and all like that. Most people, like the average person, if you were an offensive lineman and you ached in the places that he aches after the game, after three hours of just heaving your entire body into men the size of side-by-side refrigerators, you would go to the hospital probably. You would go to the hospital and get yourself checked out.

But it makes him comfortable, so that's his gig. It makes him comfortable because he's an expert in controlled rage. He's twenty-seven years old, he's started all but three games at right tackle for the Minnesota Vikings since he entered the NFL seven years ago, he's been doing this since junior high school, so trust him, he's an expert. Football gets in your muscle memory, is where it gets. It gets to where the hard part is not doing it. That's where in the past he has always messed up. That's where, more or less, you could see his life falling apart. During the offseason. Never during the season, when he had the sweet, dependable rhythm of getting in thirty car wrecks every Sunday to count on.

This brings to mind his second tattoo. He pulls his sleeve up to provide the view. Yeah, they make belts for women that would be too small to fit around this upper arm. Yeah. But here on this upper arm, we have the initials "FTW" forming an arc over the planet earth, which is being cupped by a human hand supposedly intent on crushing it. This piece, inscribed on Korey's right arm when he was twenty-two years old, bears full and exact witness to the sum of his belief system at the time of its inscription: "Fuck the World." Yeah. That pretty much said it. He calls this period of time his FTW stage. It was his second year in the NFL. It was ugly. It was the culmination of everything. It was the dark cave into which the pilgrim retreats and, if it shall come to pass that he truly is to become the mythic hero, finds the way.

Which is damn convenient. Because now in his sizable square head, he has converted FTW from "Fuck the World" to "Find the Way." And when you really examine the tattoo, you have to note that the hand isn't really going to crush the earth at all; matter of fact, that hand is holding up the earth and all its people with all their problems and all their badness and all their goodness, whatever their gig may be.

His gig. Is he wandering too far off his original point? He's sorry, but this is the way his head works. He spends a lot of time alone with his head. That's like his most comfortable place probably in the world. He'll just sit there and talk to himself in his head, and of course when you're talking to yourself in your head, it doesn't matter how much you wander off your original point. It's funny. People don't automatically associate the word pensive with a giant football player such as him. Matter of fact, people don't expect anything they first get from Korey. Like, he's a clown. He's an entertainer. He can do impressions of anybody; he'll keep the crowd happy no matter what it takes. His perspective on it is, he has a duty to give you every opportunity to have the chance to like him. But people have no idea, like maybe only a couple people have an idea, that in his head he isn't funny, he's serious, he's thinking stuff through constantly.

He's sweating. He brings up a towel to wipe off the sweat. He almost always has a towel with him to wipe off the sweat. His position on it is, you've been blessed with an automatic sprinkler system, you should always bring a towel. He changes the big-screen from

PlayStation over to ESPN. He holds the remote gently, like it's a gerbil or a hamster maybe. His fingers are long and thin and still and tender, his forearm as thick as a car door.

His gig. Don't get him wrong, there are frustrations during the season. There are the ones you've probably heard of. Like a defensive lineman, that guy could be on the field for fifty plays in a game, but he gets two sacks, and, you know, he had a great game. He's player of the week. Then you take an offensive lineman who doesn't really get a break, doesn't get to rotate and stay fresh like the defensive linemen do, has to continually stand there and bash himself into guys, and he might be on the field for eighty plays in the game, but he gives up two sacks and he's a bum. He's trade bait. Regardless of whether the other seventy-eight plays were excellent. It's those two sacks that everybody is going to talk about. It's not a good position to play if your intent is glory.

But there is another frustration. There is this whole business of being cut off from where you just came from. From the past, you might say. When you think about it, his job as an offensive lineman is to move forward into a place that doesn't actually matter except to the people in the present, who haven't even gotten there yet — okay? Just stay with him on this. It's like once you break the huddle, you're thinking about the play, the snap count, the guy that's lined up over you, what the defensive alignment is. You're thinking about which way your man is going to go and how that's going to affect the play that you're running. You're blocking. You're attempting to move a 300-pound man in a direction he totally does not want to move in. This goes on and on; time is elongated, you might say. You're blocking so long — at least it feels so long because you've got your back to everything, to the action, to the quarterback, to the running back — on and on and on it seems like, because now all you're feeling, it's like you almost can't stop yourself, it's like you just gotta know, you want to turn your head around and look back and see what the hell is going on in the play, in the present, in everybody's whole reason for being here today. You get curious is what you get. But you can't ever look back. You are being paid almost $4 million a year to be a forward-headed bull, to use every available ounce of your God-given talents of explosive acceleration. You are among the best in the world at being a forward-headed bull. Even though looking back is basically 100 percent fundamental to who you are.

Looking back is Korey's way of understanding. Looking back at where he came from and how he got here. He spends a lot of time in his head doing this. Just in everyday life even, he spends a lot of time in his head going back to Warren, Ohio. You might say he spends a lot of time in his head gaining historical perspective.

It's funny to think about. He's just making this connection right now: his high school coach at Warren G. Harding High School was a history teacher. Maybe that's how he came to appreciate history so much. He loves to read. Mostly biographies. He loves to read how other people got where they got. And anyway, he's just thinking about this now: Do you know now they got a coach at Warren G. Harding who doesn't even teach — his whole entire job is to coach football? That can't be good for the kids. It certainly can't. How can it be good for a kid to idolize a man who is paid to think football is the center of the universe?

That's Korey's job with his rookies. He calls them his rookies. He thinks of it as his job. Keep the young guys reminded of the fact that there is more to life than football. Keep the vibe in the Vikings locker room loose. It's a high-pressure situation, but it's still the game you grew up playing as a kid. Oh, there's so many things to teach his rookies.

Like, earlier today, he drove his rookies back to their hotel. Oscar and Mo and Isaac. More than 1,300 pounds of human in one car. It was after a blazing-hot day of pushing the five-man sled around while offensive-line coach Mike Tice was riding on top, Tice all clean and perfect with his Bermuda shorts on and his skinny calves, yelling with that booming voice, you know how he does, Get your hands inside, there's a helmet there, I want your hands on each side of the helmet, I want the drill done perfectly, keep your hands on each side of the helmet, push the pad, if I see fingers outside the pad, you're gonna go again, I don't have anything else to do today. Set, thirty-eight, thirty-*hut!* We're not done yet, all right, here we go, all *set,* thirty-eight! Thirty-*hut!*

Oscar and Mo and Isaac, they were tired. They probably had headaches. They were stuffed like giant baked sweet potatoes in Korey's car, reminding you why General Motors invented a car as big as a Yukon. "Is there any particular music you'd like to listen to?" Korey said to them. "Okay, we got the oldies station. We got a little bit of every kinda CD, you know, I take requests: EPMD, Jackson 5, Bill Withers, Keith Sweat, Al Jarreau. . . ."

The guys didn't respond; they just sat there, smelling like a pine forest after rain. So Korey put in Al Jarreau, cranked it.

"Yo, Korey," Oscar shouted over the music. "I gotta get me some new pants. Where I'm gonna get me some new pants?"

"All right, okay," Korey said, pleased to oblige with the inside track on where a giant man might find clothes in Minneapolis. "I'm gonna write you down the directions. I'm gonna tell you how to get to the mall with the Big and Tall."

See, now, most guys, they don't pay any attention to the rookies, whereas Korey gives them directions to the Big and Tall. Korey routinely has them over to his house, throws some burgers on the grill. Hey, he believes every human being on this earth, no matter what their station in life, has the right to be comfortable.

He believes "Do unto others as you would have them do unto you." He mostly came to this belief when he was a rookie, wishing he was done unto better. He was barely twenty-one. He left Ohio State a year early to become a Minnesota Viking. Overnight he went from not being able to afford to pitch in for a pizza to making like a million dollars a year. He was supposed to be happy. He was supposed to be on top of the world. Instead he was sitting there all by himself in a Minneapolis hotel room with free soap and free shampoo, bored and afraid and soothing himself with TV and beer and calling home to his mom and his dad and his brother and his sister and Zig and Pap Pap and anybody else who would talk to him. They would say it's going to get better, they would say it's always hard starting out new somewhere, but of course what they couldn't know was that first it had to get a lot worse.

It always comes back to this. In his head it always comes back to FTW. In a thousand languages over thousands of years, this is the story of the enlightened man.

Okay, now, this right here is Southwest Boulevard. This is his street. It looks a lot smaller now. It was huge when he was coming up. He's crammed into the driver's seat of a bright-red Jeep Grand Cherokee rented from the Avis corporation, and he is dressed up fancy to come home here to Warren, Ohio. He's in his mustard-yellow velour warm-up suit and he's got on his big triangle diamond earrings and his big charm bracelet and a platinum necklace as thick as a copperhead snake.

This is the house he grew up in. His brother, Kevin, lives here now. He just had this garage built. It's kind of swampy back in that corner. But for the most part, this is it, you know. In Warren you could get a decent job, either at the GM plant or at Packard Electric. You got one of those jobs, you could afford a little house to raise your kids in. There were blacks and there were whites here in the Palmyra Heights section. You grew up knowing which you were, but you grew up wondering why it mattered, since everyone had more or less the same basic job and the same basic house.

Him and Kevin, they shared the room with that window right there. Kevin is two years older. Kevin had allergies. He was all brains, you could say. Korey was brains, too, but a different kind. Korey had a certain philosophicalness to his being. His main thing was, he just wanted to do what he wanted to do. This, you might say, was at the root of his philosophy.

Okay, Chris and Grady lived right here. And Shug and Shawn there. And Michael and Terrence. Clarence and Junie. Jermaine and Elbert. Clyde and Mitchell right there. Kevin and Toot. Popeye, Trevor, and CC. It seemed like every house had boys his age in it to play with. Baseball was Korey's main sport coming up. He was a natural athlete, good at anything he played, one of those kids who could hypnotize you with his power and rhythm and flow. His mom would not let him play football until he reached junior high school, which was kind of ridiculous when you consider football was everything in Warren, Ohio. Like in the old days when his father was born, like, if a baby boy was born, they'd give him a small miniature football at the hospital. Yeah. That tells the story right there.

But really, to Korey, any game was cool. Kickball, stickball — he'd compete at how many lightning bugs you could catch. His main thing was not losing. Just like he and his mom and Kevin would play Parcheesi or Trouble or something, every single night they played a board game, and if Korey came out the loser, it would be like something inside him was dying, like he was saying goodbye to a friend, having a damn funeral. Tears would start pouring out.

Korey was hungry all the time. No matter how much he ate, it was never enough. It was like he just needed constant fuel for a body on fire with growth. One time he was in the backseat on a family trip to Detroit, he was like in seventh grade, and he was like, this is ridiculous. He told his dad to pull over. His legs hurt. It was like his bones were just growing right there in the car. Eventually, the doctors gave him support sleeves for his legs to give the tendons a chance to catch up with his bones growing. By the time he was fourteen, he was six-foot-one, 210 pounds. Another kid might've gotten made fun of for being so big, but Korey had charm on top of his bigness. He knew how to use his bigness. He was the one to say, "Yo, this is stupid," to guys bashing each other up on the bus, and his bigness really helped the point be made.

He stops at the stop sign, leans in to see if anybody's at the Corner Store. All right. Yeah. Now. This is his other street. This is Fourth Street. This is the house he lived in when his mom and dad fell off for a while. They're together now. His Aunt Becky lives here now in this house. His father's parents still live next door. You want to go meet Pap Pap?

Pap Pap is waving out the window. Pap Pap is wiry thin with practically nothing on him but a belly and a smile. He sure is glad to see Korey. Grandma is upset because she didn't know anyone was coming or she would have made herself presentable. "You're still the most beautiful girl in the world to me," Korey tells her, and plops himself into the Barcalounger because Pap Pap took the couch in front of the big-screen, where Tim Conway and Don Knotts are starring in *The Apple Dumpling Gang Rides Again*. Pap Pap, he's complaining about the Troy-Bilt rototiller he got, it's so hard to switch the gears, he should have gotten the Honda.

"I guess you noticed all my teeth fell off the top," says Grandma, who is sitting out of view, in the dining room. "They just up and fell apart."

"They fell apart?" Korey says.

"Well, something happened," she says.

"Uh-huh," Pap Pap says.

"It just means you went through a lot of chewing, Grandma," Korey says. "Yeah."

"Unh-huh. All right."

An hour of afternoon goes by like this, Korey sweating and wiping off with a towel, until he heads out again in the car to make sure everything else is still in place. Like the Hot Dog Shoppe. Yeah, okay. He rolls down the window so as to smell the grandeur. They cook them on the grill, they don't boil them, and the superdogs are almost like a Polish sausage, but mostly what he gets is the two regular chili-and-cheese hot-dog special. Then this here is Eli's Barbecue. That's major. But at Eli's you gotta put the order in early. They take a little while, but it's gonna be right. And this is Carmen's Pizza, they've been slipping lately on the crust.

Coming up, Korey did dream of being a football star, but the dream wasn't about college or pro ball. His perspective on it was, it's the same game as they played in high school, so what was the difference? Coming up, he idolized the guys who played with Warren G. Harding and Western Reserve high schools. Those were the heroes of Friday nights, when pretty much all of Warren would drop everything and go watch one team or the other. Those guys were celebrities, just like Mean Joe Greene was a celebrity. Only those guys would talk to you.

As soon as he got to high school, Korey was put on varsity, unheard of for a freshman. So in a way he had achieved his life's dream right there. One day he got called into the coach's office. All the coaches were looking at videotapes of Korey, watching his nimble toes and his natural knee bend, how he could dance despite all that bulk. They were marveling at his power, which seemed otherworldly. They told him he was special, that he was not like other guys. They told him to be prepared for college recruiters, who indeed would start contacting Korey by his sophomore year. His coaches worked with him on how to hold on to his soul with everybody promising him the moon.

Whatever. The college thing didn't impress Korey much one way or the other. He just didn't want to have to go to like California or something like that. There was no way he'd go that far from Warren, where, by the way, a legend was being made: in 1990, the Warren G. Harding Raiders won the state championship, the biggest excitement to hit Warren in generations. Korey was a junior. By his senior year, he was two-time All-State and had been named to the All-American team.

Sitting here in this car thinking about this, Korey has regrets. He clicks the radio on, as if Destiny's Child might help drown out the grief. In his senior year, the Raiders didn't even make the playoffs. Didn't even get a chance to defend their title. He thinks about this all the time. It's his biggest regret in sports.

He ended up picking Ohio State, mainly because it was only two hours away. By his third college game, he was named a starter, and then Big Ten freshman of the year in 1992, then to the Associated Press All-American team in 1993 and 1994, and voted MVP of the Ohio State team. Yeah. By junior year he had accomplished all of that without a lot of headache, and, really, he was feeling done with the college gig. Just done. School was starting to feel like a bird pecking on his head. It was just like, stop it.

But, by the way, in college he did well with the ladies. Sure he did. He was Whatever Man. No, he was the Amazing Whatever Man. You want to be with him, you gotta just take whatever you get. And the girls would do it. No resistance whatsoever. All of them except for a certain girl named Kelci. She was Whatever Woman. No, she was I Got My Shit Together and No Guy Is Gonna Screw It Up Whatever Woman. He couldn't stay cool with her for more than one day at a time. They were always on-again, off-again.

The night of the NFL draft in 1995, Korey and Kelci were semi on-again. His mom was having a draft party, and Kelci was helping out, the two of them praying that Miami or someplace like that didn't pick Korey, because with the kind of temptation in a place like Miami, there was no way a gentle soul like Korey could survive. He wasn't what you'd call wise to the ways of the world. He was the kid who never had to work tremendously hard to get what he got, the football version of the straight-A student who never went to class, could just waltz in and ace the exam.

Korey himself was not at the draft party. He was over at his dad's. His mom and his dad were semi off. Korey and his dad and Kevin and Korey's best friend, Maceo, had a case of Bud Light, and they watched *The Lion King* and they watched *Raising Arizona*. They were Whatever Men. This draft thing was not going to matter. Korey was not going to get rattled by all the talk that had started: Korey was getting fat. Korey was out of shape. Korey needed to work out. Korey had to start caring more about a thing called a career. Whatever. For a while there, he'd been projected as a top-five draft pick. But now, with him not working out, with him putting on weight, with his attitude of not caring, well, put it this way: by the time he'd arrived at the NFL combine — late — he was tipping the scale at 348 pounds.

He ended up being the twenty-fourth pick in the first round. He was going to Minnesota, a place his mom and Kelci thought was good and cold and without a lot of temptation that might hinder a man's attempt to develop character.

When he got to Minneapolis, there was that whole rookie vibe to deal with, number one. And number two, he was coming from an Ohio State program built around running the ball, and he gets to the Vikings and it's all passing. So now he's pretty much blind on top of everything else, because he really doesn't know how to pass-block, and his coach at the time is basically telling him he sucks, telling him, you know, You're a first-round pick, we're paying you good money, figure it out. And he couldn't. And then in the newspapers, after the first year the newspapers were starting to make fun of him. He wasn't Korey Stringer, a fine example of what Warren, Ohio, could produce. No, he was "the blubbery kid from Ohio" who maybe couldn't survive the NFL. He was maybe the wasted draft pick. Yeah, he was putting on more weight. Matter of fact, the summer after his second season, he got up to 388 pounds. What do you expect of a man who has no routine, no, no, just nothing regular in his life, no schedule, no base, no foundation to his day or to his night? Alone. Like he would leave practice and go to his house and just sit with the lights out, sit there in the dark and think in his head. He'd think, Fuck the World is what he would think in his head. He was in the NFL. Everybody said it was supposed to be some kinda dream come true, and maybe for another man it would have been. But the NFL was never his dream. His dream was just being comfortable. And in his mind, being comfortable had always basically meant just doing what you wanted to do, and this right here is all he wanted to do: Fuck the World. He had his phone cut off because he didn't want anyone bothering him while he sat there thinking Fuck the World in his head. He would go down to the SuperAmerica and get on the pay phone and call his mom sometimes, but for the most part he would just sit there and eat and drink beer and think Fuck the World and pass out.

The Vikings sent him to a weight-loss clinic in North Carolina. Great. Now people were telling him what to eat and when to eat it. He skipped out and got himself two more tattoos — the Japanese character meaning courage on one arm, the Japanese character meaning strength on the other — etching words on his body the way a man putting on war paint prepares for battle.

He went back to Minneapolis and sat for more time in the dark, alone, in the belly of the whale as sure as Jonah, a cave, the only place he might be able to find Korey Stringer from Warren, Ohio, while at the same time do battle with Korey Stringer from Warren,

Ohio. Like Hiawatha and the monster Mishe-Nahma. Like Captain Ahab and the Great White Whale or Santiago and the Marlin or Luke Skywalker and Darth Vader, just any of those dudes throughout the history of the world who go through the trial, do the battle, either the dragon slays you or you slay the dragon, it doesn't really matter, one of you consumes the other, you emerge transformed into a brand-new powerful you.

The thinking, the cave, it led to a revelation, an epiphany as sure as hell. It was: hey, just doing everything you want to do doesn't make you comfortable. It makes you fat and miserable and hateful against the world because you hate what it has caused you to become. It was: hey, it ain't the world's fault. It ain't nobody but Korey Stringer's fault.

And another thing. Coach Tice came on board with the Vikings. He grabbed ahold of Korey. He had Korey's number. Like, the most important quality in a tackle is recoverability, being able to react without taking one false step. Most guys have to learn it, have to drill and drill and drill it until it's in their muscles. Korey was born with it. A combination of quickness, balance, and rhythm. But the thing with Korey, he didn't value it. He didn't care. He was throwing it away. Tice told Korey, he said, "You can take yourself from being labeled a fat man, a dud, a flop, just another wasted first-round pick, to being one of the premier athletes of the NFL. And you don't need to do anything except care."

Korey heard that.

And another thing. Kelci came up. Kelci got a job in Minneapolis. She and Korey had been off-again for quite some time. And now here was Kelci, slender and perfect in her innocence and hard as her long fingernails in her commitment to being the person she knew herself to be. She moved in. He wasn't alone anymore. It felt like . . . air. His first gasp of air. Then she said, "Uh-oh." She said, "I'm pregnant."

It could have gone a lot of ways. For another man, it might have gone differently. But the idea of a child, his child, it completed the man. It was like, you know, now it's something major. It was like, these past two years all you're doing is thinking of yourself, and the idea of a baby allows you to see it's bigger than that. It was like, "Let me figure out who I am so I can let my child know. Because if I don't know, he's gonna be lost."

Turbo. That's how it was. It wasn't like a diet or an exercise plan or anything like that. It was just waking up. It was sleep. It was caring. It was having so much to care about. It was getting to bed at a decent hour and going to work as a man goes to work, a man who thinks, Hey, I'm gonna make sure I'm hungry when I get home, because Kelci's cooking dinner and it's only right to make sure my stomach appreciates the beauty of that fact. He lost fifty pounds, got in the best shape of his life. In the newspapers they started to use the word *mauler* next to Korey Stringer. He could finish games like never before; he'd still have fuel in his tank for knockdowns in the fourth quarter.

Kodie was born in February 1998. Korey got himself a tattoo on his left shoulder; it says KODIE overtop a yin-yang symbol. Four months later, Korey and Kelci got married. Korey got a tattoo on his right breast; it says KELCI overtop a yin-yang symbol and a rose. Soon after, the Vikings locked him up long-term with a five-year, $18.4 million extension signed on Christmas Eve 1998, which included a $4 million signing bonus.

That's when he bought his mom the house. He said, Go pick out yourself a nice house to live in. It's a modest ranch on the east side of Warren with a much bigger yard than anything you'd ever see in Palmyra Heights. She has baskets of flowers outside. And inside, the hall to the kitchen is narrow, with the liver-and-onion smell spilling forth.

"All right, okay," says his dad, thin and wiry with an intelligent tilt to his head.

"Yeah, okay," says Korey, shoving his dad's shoulder.

His mom comes in, a Shrinky Dink version of Korey. She kisses him on the cheek but mostly is caught up in complaining about Scooter, her black cocker-spaniel dog that does everything wrong, everything bad a cocker-spaniel dog could ever do. And then Kevin, who looks like his dad, comes in with a pizza and gives a belly laugh and throws his arms around Korey like maybe Gumby throwing his arms around Barney, those arms can hardly reach. "All right, okay," Korey says. A cousin is here with chicken wings. Korey's little sister, Kim, comes in with french fries. Plus his mom had stopped and gotten two Caesar salads in those shaker mugs at McDonald's. There is no talk of football or the Minnesota Vikings or of last season, in which the Vikings came within one game of making it to the Super Bowl, or of how Korey and his offensive line helped Robert Smith break like a million team records, including most rushing yards in a season (1,521) and most 100-yard games in a season (eight). Or how the line gave quarterback Daunte Culpepper enough time to throw for 3,937 yards and 33 touchdowns in his first year at the helm. Or how Korey, the new and improved Korey, got himself named to the 2001 Pro Bowl.

No, the talk is all food and what shift you got put on and Kevin and Korey doing their Fat Albert routines. And his dad is concentrating on the liver and onions on the stove; he's saying it's gonna be good, it's gonna be so good you'll have to slap yourself and say, Is it for real? The TV trays are up and everyone sits and *Who Wants to Be a Millionaire* is on; it's a direction to stare in, like the ocean or a sunset or a fire, while you visit and while you eat and while you absorb the wondrous power of home.

In the morning, he shows up at 8:30 after a breakfast of grits with scrambled eggs and sugar all mixed together at the Empire Diner. He shows up here at Mollenkopf Stadium at Warren G. Harding High School. His mom had said, Would you do the event; he said, If it's for the kids, of course I will, Mom. The event is the eighteenth annual YWCA Olympics, and about 250 first- through sixth-graders are here to run and jump and throw.

"Now it's time to introduce our special guest, Korey Stringer!" says a blond lady with a microphone who is tickled pink Korey has agreed to do this. "Korey is an offensive tackle for the Minnesota Vikings. He grew up here in Warren, playing football right here on this very field. Korey?"

Korey takes the microphone. He's in a shiny blue warm-up suit spanning his giant chest with considerable stress. He's as broad as a billboard. The people in the stands cannot help but shake their heads in awe. "Good God!" and "Whoa!" and "Jeeezus, you could ski down that man."

"Thanks," he says. "Uh. It's good to be back here in Mollenkopf Stadium. Where it all kinda got started. And uh. I appreciate the people at the Y for getting me out here and letting me be a part of this. So uh. Good luck to the kids. And thank you, parents, for coming out."

He stands on the fifty-yard line, leading the children in their warm-up exercises; he's doing toe touches, squats, little bitty graceful jumping jacks that make you wonder what magical dimension of reality is absorbing the impact. He's thinking, Okay, this part is kinda stupid; he thought the whole point of kids was they had readymade muscles. He then takes his honored place next to the award platforms, one high for the gold-medal winner, and two lower for the silver and bronze. There will be three winners in each of five events for the first-grade boys and the first-grade girls and the second-grade boys and the second-grade girls, gold, silver, bronze, gold, silver, bronze, on and on like this through to the sixth-grade boys and the sixth-grade girls, and another man, his head might hurt thinking about standing here for all of this, and now it's starting to rain.

"Congratulations, man," Korey says, hanging the gold medal around Jason's skinny little chicken neck. "Good job," he says, hanging the silver on Justin. He tells Bryant to take his ball cap off before accepting the bronze. He handles the medals as if they were uncooked fish and he were preparing a sacred meal. There are cameras flashing. He leans into Jason and Justin and Bryant, whispers: "Look for your mom. Don't be looking at no cameras except at your mom's."

The juxtaposition is odd and beautiful and comical. Here is a man who makes his living practically bludgeoning men to death, and here he is on his day off and all you see is sweetness and love and tenderness. Here is a million-dollar man who thinks seriously about going back to college to get his damn college degree so that when football is done, he can go be a high school teacher, like a history teacher maybe, who can also coach football. But not a head coach, no. He wants to be one of the undercoaches, like a strength coach, because that's where the action is — that's the coach who gets to spend time with the kids and their heads.

He's putting medals on, gold, silver, and bronze; it goes on like this for hours and hours and hours in the rain. He is impervious to the rain. He stands here like the statue he has become. He is Father Time. He is Uncle Remus. He is a giant old dude on the bank of the Mississippi with a sax and a dog and a word or two of wisdom that is one half poetry, just language spilling out, and one half miracle. He is a bull. He is a big black sheep in spring before shearing. There is the enlightened man, and then there is the holy man. The enlightened man understands. The holy man brings the understanding out of the cave and disperses it as best he knows how.

Afterward, drenched, he is signing autographs. No, he will not sign autographs for adults. It's stupid and embarrassing and, think about it, stupid. But he will gladly sign autographs for kids.

"You would like me to sign your shirt, is that what I understand?" he says, coming down to a boy's eye level, bending at the knees because that's his natural way.

"Yeah," says the boy.

"All right. Is there something else?"

"Huh?"

"Well, you just heard the last two dudes go through the whole thing using the magic words and everything, and you forgot to put the magic in."

"Oh. Okay. Please?"

"All right. All right. Is there anything else?"

"Huh?"

"Dude, you gotta say thank you."

"Yeah. Thank you."

"All right. All right. Peace, my man. Peace."

At the snack bar, they give him a free lemon shake and also some nachos. He drinks the lemon shake and he eats the nachos and then he gets in the car and the cell phone rings. Doodle-loodle-leet. Doodle-loodle-leet. It's Kelci on the cell phone, Kelci calling from back home in Minneapolis, asking how it went. He says cool. He makes no mention of what maybe another man, especially a multimillionaire sports star, might regard in terms of discomfort, hours and hours standing there saying the same thing over and over again, "Congratulations" and "Good job," while water is pouring all over you, and that's not to mention the way the wind was blowing some of them signs they had into your face. He just says the kids seemed happy with the gig but he felt bad it had to rain on their heads.

Biographical Notes

MIKE BIANCHI, a graduate of the University of Florida, is a sports columnist who has covered sports in the state of Florida for the *Orlando Sentinel* for the last fifteen years. He has won numerous state and national writing awards. Bianchi's wife, Donna, is an attorney, and they have two daughters — Tess, six, and Jessica, two.

Sports Illustrated's senior contributing writer FRANK DEFORD is the author of a number of books, including *The Best of Frank Deford.*

STEVE FRIEDMAN is a freelance writer living in New York City. His work has appeared in *Outside, Esquire, GQ,* and many other publications, and he is co-author of *Loose Balls: Easy Money, Hard Fouls, Cheap Laughs, and True Love in the NBA*. This is Friedman's third appearance in *The Best American Sports Writing.*

ELIZABETH GILBERT is the author of the story collection *Pilgrims,* a finalist for the 1998 PEN/Hemingway Award. Her fiction has been published in *Esquire, Story, GQ,* and many other publications. Currently a writer-at-large for *GQ,* Gilbert's most recent book is *The Last American Man.*

KARL TARO GREENFELD is *Time Asia*'s deputy editor and the author of *Speed Tribes: Days and Nights with Japan's Next Generation.*

SKIP HOLLANDSWORTH was raised in Wichita Falls, Kansas, and graduated with a B.A. in English from Texas Christian University. He has worked as a reporter and columnist for the *Dallas Times Herald* and the *Dallas Morning News* and wrote for *D magazine* for two years. He has also worked as a producer and reporter for the televised version of *USA To-*

day, NBC's *Today Show, NBC Sports,* and the USA and ESPN cable networks. He joined the staff of *Texas Monthly* in 1989 and has been nominated for four National Magazine Awards.

STEVE HUMMER has been a columnist at the *Atlanta Journal-Constitution* since 1989 after stints at the *Fort Lauderdale Sun-Sentinel* and *Palm Beach Post.* He won a National Headliner Award in 1999, was named a top-ten columnist in the 2001 Associated Press Sports Editors awards, and has received several sportswriter/columnist of the year awards in Georgia.

MARK KRAM, JR., previously appeared in *The Best American Sports Writing 1994* ("The World Is Her Cloister"). A sportswriter for the *Philadelphia Daily News* since 1987, he worked prior to that for the *Detroit Free Press* and the *Baltimore News American.* He is also a contributing writer for *Philadelphia Magazine.* Kram lives in Haddonfield, New Jersey, with his wife and two daughters. His father, Mark Kram, the author of "Ghosts of Manila," has appeared in *The Best American Sports Writing* three times.

JEANNE MARIE LASKAS is a contributing writer at *Esquire* and the author of *Fifty Acres and a Poodle: A Story of Love, Livestock, and Finding Myself on a Farm.*

Washington Post staff writer MICHAEL LEAHY also appeared in *The Best American Sports Writing 2001.* His work has appeared in many national publications.

DAN LE BATARD, thirty-two, is a sports columnist for the *Miami Herald,* where he has worked since graduating from the University of Miami in 1990. He also serves as a regular contributor for ESPN television, radio, and magazine. He lives in south Florida.

MIKE LUPICA is a columnist for the *New York Daily News* and makes frequent appearances on ESPN. He is the author of many books, including *Full Court Press, Summer of '98,* and *Bump and Run.*

JULIET MACUR, a 1997 graduate of the Columbia University Graduate School of Journalism, joined the *Dallas Morning News* as a features writer in 2001. She had previously worked at the *Orlando Sentinel,* where she covered the NFL and NASCAR and wrote general sports features. She is a first-generation American, with Polish parents, and grew up in Bridgewater, New Jersey.

WILLIAM NACK'S 1975 classic *Secretariat: The Making of a Champion* has just been reissued. This is his sixth appearance in *The Best American Sports Writing.*

DAN NEIL is a freelance writer living in Raleigh, North Carolina. He is a contributing editor for *Car and Driver* magazine and a regular contributor to the *New York Times*. In 2000 he received the International Motor Press Association's Ken Purdy Award for Excellence in Automotive Journalism. In addition to automotive subjects, he writes about adventure travel, food, art history, and culture. He is married to Dr. Rebecca Schmorr and is the proud father of a sixteen-year-old son, Wally.

BOB NORMAN has been a staff writer for *New Times Broward–Palm Beach* since 1998. A recipient of numerous state and national reporting prizes, he was recently honored with a 2001 Livingston Award for Young Journalists for a September 11–related series titled "Admitting Terror." He lives in the Fort Lauderdale area with his wife, Brittany Wallman, and two children, Creed and Lily.

SCOTT OSTLER is a sports columnist for the *San Francisco Chronicle* and has a regular column on MSNBC.com. He previously wrote for the now-defunct *National Sports Daily* and the *Los Angeles Times*. He has been named California's sportswriter of the year seven times. Ostler has also contributed to magazines such as *Sports Illustrated* and *Reader's Digest*.

BILL PLASCHKE, forty-three, is a sports columnist for the *Los Angeles Times*. He has been named national sports columnist of the year by several organizations, including Associated Press Sports Editors (large newspapers division), National Headliners, Sigma Delta Chi, and the Association of Sunday and Features Editors. He began his career covering shuffleboard and bowling at the *Fort Lauderdale News*, moved to the *Seattle Post Intelligencer* to cover the Mariners, then moved to the *Los Angeles Times* to cover baseball in 1987. He was named columnist there in 1996. He made his big-screen debut in 2000 by playing a dedicated, probing sportswriter in *Ali*.

JOSHUA HARRIS PRAGER is a senior special writer at the *Wall Street Journal*. He was born in Eagle Butte, South Dakota, earned a B.A. degree in music theory from Columbia University in 1994, and is a huge fan of Bernie Williams. A book he is writing based on this article is due out in 2003.

PETER RICHMOND is a senior writer for *GQ* and formerly wrote for the *National Sports Daily*, the *Washington Post*, the *Miami Herald*, the *San Diego Union*, and the *New Haven Register*. He is the author of *My Father's War* and *Camden Yards and the Building of an American Dream*.

EUGENE ROBINSON, assistant editor of the *Washington Post*, is the author of *Coal to Cream: A Black Man's Journey Beyond Color to an Affirmation of Race*.

STEVE RUSHIN's popular "Air and Space" column appears in *Sports Illustrated*. He is the author of *Road Swing*.

ADAM SCHEFTER of the *Denver Post* co-authored *Think Like a Champion* with Mike Shanahan and *TD: Dreams in Motion* with Terrell Davis.

TOM SCOCCA wrote "Blood Sport" for *Baltimore City Paper,* where he produced the weekly sport column "8 Upper." He is now senior editor at *Washington City Paper.* He lives in Maryland with his wife, Christina Ho, to whom (and for whom) he is forever thankful.

GARY SMITH is a senior writer for *Sports Illustrated* and a past winner of the National Magazine Award for feature writing. This is his seventh appearance in *The Best American Sports Writing,* more than any other writer.

RICK TELANDER is a columnist for the *Chicago Sun-Times* and author of *The City Game: Basketball from the Garden to the Playgrounds, The Hundred Yard Lie,* and *Heaven Is a Playground.*

ART THIEL has been at the *Seattle Post-Intelligencer* for twenty-two years, the last fifteen as a columnist. He previously wrote for the *Bellevue Journal-American* and the *Tacoma News Tribune.* He is a graduate of Pacific Lutheran University in Tacoma. Art writes: "I have retired my jump shot, my fastball, and my willingness to engage in a crossing pattern over the middle, but I still can miss an Olympics media bus with the best of them."

GENE WOJCIECHOWSKI is a senior writer for *ESPN: The Magazine.* A graduate of the University of Tennessee, Wojciechowski has authored six books, including his recent novel, *About 80 Percent Luck.* He lives in Wheaton, Illinois.

Notable Sports Writing of 2001

COMPILED BY GLENN STOUT

ALAN ABRAHAMSON
Drive to Excel Brings Death to the Gridiron. *Los Angeles Times,* August 27, 2001
G. R. ANDERSON
Power Play. *City Pages,* March 21, 2001
KELLI ANDERSON
Losing to Win. *Sports Illustrated for Women,* May-June 2001
PAUL ATTNER
Heart of a Giant. *The Sporting News,* July 16, 2001

BILL BALLOU
Sox on Cusp of Being Freed. *Worcester Telegram & Gazette,* December 22, 2001
BRUCE BARCOTT
Dog Is My Co-Pilot. *Outside,* March 2001
BURKHARD BILGER
A Shot in the Ark. *The New Yorker,* March 5, 2001
BUZZ BISSINGER
A Darker Shade of Rose. *Vanity Fair,* September 2001
PETER BODO
The Player. *Tennis,* May 2001
BONES BOURCIER
Looking for Earnhardt. *Speedway Illustrated,* February 2002
JEFF BRADLEY
First Class. *ESPN: The Magazine,* April 2, 2001
ERIC BRANCH
Being Sportswriter Has Its Ups, Downs. *Town Talk,* July 28, 2001
HOWARD BRYANT
Yanks Are in Shock After Rivera Fails in Ninth. *Bergen Record,* November 5, 2001

SEAN COFFEY
The Man Who Rode to the Moon (and Back) (Twice). *Bicycling Magazine,* July 2001

RICHARD COHEN
Down and Out at Wrigley Field. *Harper's,* August 2001
TOM COTTER
NASCAR's 2001 Race Odyssey. *Road and Track,* May 2001

STEVE DEMEGLIO
Pieces of Cardboard, Pieces of History. *USA Today Baseball Weekly,* May 2, 2001
ERIC DEXHEIMER
Let Freedom and Gunshots Ring. *Westword,* September 20–26, 2001
SCOTT DICKENSHEETS
Roid Rage. *Playboy,* July 2001
CHRIS DUDLEY
Taming the Bull. *Honolulu Star-Bulletin,* July 2, 2001
BOB DUFFY
Men of Honor. *Boston Globe,* December 29, 2001

STEVE FAINARU
The Business of Building Ballplayers. *Washington Post,* June 17, 2001
BRUCE FELDMAN
Midnight Run. March 19, 2001
NATHAN FENNO
I Can Win. *Eastside Journal,* May 25, 2001
BILL FIELDS
The Man Who Loved Golf to Death. *Golf World,* March 30, 2001
SCOTT FOWLER
Last of a Generation Carries On. *Charlotte Observer,* June 10, 2001
TOM FRIEND
Tough Lie. *ESPN: The Magazine,* December 10, 2001

JUSTIN GEORGE
Heart of Gold. *Daily Camera,* May 6, 2001
PHILIP GERARD
Adventures in Celestial Navigation. *Creative Nonfiction,* #18, 2001
MALCOLM GLADWELL
Drugstore Athlete. *The New Yorker,* September 10, 2001
DOUG GORE
Too Dangerous? *Speedway Illustrated,* August 2001
SCOTT GORMAN
Take Me Out to the . . . Game. *Everett Herald,* October 14, 2001

ERIC HAGERMAN
He Ain't Your Sherpa. *Outside,* April 2001
DAVID HAUGH
Sarah Smile. *South Bend Tribune,* July 1, 2001
JOHN HAWKINS AND TIM ROSAFORTE
Inside Golf's Greatest Comeback. *Golf Digest,* September 2001

HAL HERRING
Silver Redhorse. *Creative Nonfiction,* #18, 2001
CATHERINE HOOPER
It's the Wild, Wild West in the Western Indian Ocean. *Fish & Fly,* Winter 2001
ROBERT HUBER
A Really Bad Call. *Philadelphia,* July 2001
MIKE HUDSON
Hard Times, Hard Driver. *Roanoke Times,* June 24, 2001
Restless Soul. *Regardie's Power,* January-February 2001
DAVE HYDE
Price of Perfection. *Fort Lauderdale Sun-Sentinel,* March 25, 2001

SCOOP JACKSON
All Out War. *Slam,* June 2001
JOHN JILOTY
Toe to Toe. *Inside Lacrosse,* November-December 2001

DAVID KAMP
Only the Ball Was Brown. *GQ,* October 2001
JESSE KATZ
Little Big Men. *Los Angeles,* May 2001
KING KAUFMAN
Backyard Boxing Is Back. *Salon.com,* September 7, 2001
A. L. KENNEDY
A Blow to the Head. *Paris Review,* 2001
STEVE KETTMANN
Baseball Boyfriend. *Salon.com,* May 26, 2001
MELISSA KING
Slammed. *Sports Illustrated for Women,* December-January 2002
JAY KIRK
Just Shoot Me. *Chicago Reader,* October 19, 2001
TED KLEINE
Army of One. *Chicago Reader,* February 23, 2001
ROBERT KURSON
The Greatest Athlete in Chicago. *Chicago Magazine,* April 2001

GREG LALAS
The Angel Lion. *Boston Magazine,* November 2001
PETER LAMEK
Ham I Am. *Milwaukee Magazine,* March 2001
GUY LAWSON
Bush League. *GQ,* October 2001

DAVID MCKAY
The Secret Life of a World Class Skateboarder. *Philadelphia,* August 2001

JIM MCMANUS
Feeling It on Man. *Pokerpages.com,* June 13, 2001
MANISH MEHTA
An Air of Uncertainty. *New York Post Sports Week,* February 15–21, 2001
SIG MEJDAL
Climbing the Stairway to Heaven. *Los Angeles Times,* August 5, 2001
ED MILLER
A Father, a Son, a Dynasty. *Virginian Pilot,* December 2–3, 2001
MICHAEL MORRISSEY
Out of the Shadows. *New York Post Sports Week,* January 25–31, 2001
MIKE MOSEDALE
Crappie Days. *City Pages,* December 5, 2001

ROBERT NELSON
ParTee On! *Phoenix New Times,* January 18–24, 2001
DAVID NEVARD AND DAVID MARASCO
Who Was Piper Davis? *A Red Sox Journal,* Winter 2001

JEFF O'CONNELL
Mister Universe. *Muscle & Fitness,* May 2001
TONY ORTEGA
Who Shot the Sheriff? *New Times Los Angeles,* July 19–25, 2001

KATIE PETTIBONE
To the "Hellish Depths." *Sailing,* April 2001
CHARLES P. PIERCE
The Stud. *GQ,* August 2001
RON POLLACK
Happily Ever After. *Pro Football Weekly,* August 2001
S. L. PRICE
Cross Road. *Sports Illustrated,* November 26, 2001
A Good Man in Africa. *Sports Illustrated,* April 16, 2001

SCOTT REID
Success, Sadness. *Orange County Register,* September 16, 2001
PETER RITTER
The Athletic Cup. *City Pages,* August 29, 2001
JIM RIZZUTO
2,000-lb. Marlin! *Sport Fishing,* August 2001
SELENA ROBERTS
In the Shadows. *New York Times,* June 17, 2001
LINDA ROBERTSON
The Man Who Lost It All. *Miami Herald,* December 23, 2001
STEPHEN RODRICK
Grappling with Redemption. *GQ,* August 2001

JULIAN RUBENSTEIN
Being John McEnroe. *ESPN.com,* September 19, 2001

DAVID SAMUELS
The Runner. *The New Yorker,* September 3, 2001
JOHN SCHULIAN
Against the Grain. *MSNBC.com,* October 29, 2001
ROBERT SCHULZ
Hardball. *Hudson Review,* Spring 2001
MARK SEAL
Still Afloat. *Golf Digest,* August 2001
DAN SHAUGHNESSY
Carrying On. *Boston Globe,* November 21, 2001
DAVID SHIELDS
Baseball Is Just Baseball. *McSweeney's Internet Tendency,* August 10, 2001
BILL SIMMONS
Still Haunted by Len Bias. *ESPN.com,* June 20, 2001
ALLEN ST. JOHN
Fall Classics. *Village Voice,* October 2, 2001
TIM STRUBY
Fighting Chance. *ESPN: The Magazine,* April 30, 2001

JOHN UPDIKE
Never to Sleep, Always to Dream. *Golf Digest,* March 2001

JAY WEINER
Warming Benches and Hearts. *Minneapolis Star-Tribune,* March 31, 2001
RON WHITTEN
The Ghost of Miracle Hill. *Golf Digest,* March 2001
RALPH WILEY
Death Is Like Joe Louis: We Can Run, but Can't Hide. *ESPN.com,* March 1, 2001
ALEC WILKINSON
A Game of Stitches. *GQ,* December 2001
GEOFF WILSON
Eighteen Is Enough. *Baseball America,* October 2001
BRAD WOLVERTON
Tennis Everyone. *Tennis,* September 2001
ALEXANDER WOOLF AND GEORGE DOHRMANN
A School for Scandal. *Sports Illustrated,* February 26, 2001

JERRY ZGODA
Desire and Ice. *Minneapolis Star Tribune,* February 25, 2001
WILLIAM ZINSSER
Field of Tin. *Atlantic Monthly,* July-August, 2001

THE BEST AMERICAN SERIES™

THE BEST AMERICAN SHORT STORIES® 2002

Sue Miller, guest editor • Katrina Kenison, series editor

"Story for story, readers can't beat the *Best American Short Stories* series" (*Chicago Tribune*). This year's most beloved short fiction anthology is edited by the best-selling novelist Sue Miller and includes stories by Edwidge Danticat, Jill McCorkle, E. L. Doctorow, and Akhil Sharma, among others.

0-618-13173-6 PA $13.00 / 0-618-11749-0 CL $27.50
0-618-13172-8 CASS $26.00 / 0-618-25816-7 CD $35.00

THE BEST AMERICAN ESSAYS® 2002

Stephen Jay Gould, guest editor • Robert Atwan, series editor

Since 1986, the *Best American Essays* series has gathered the best nonfiction writing of the year. Edited by Stephen Jay Gould, the eminent scientist and distinguished writer, this year's volume features writing by Jonathan Franzen, Sebastian Junger, Gore Vidal, Mario Vargas Llosa, and others.

0-618-04932-0 PA $13.00 / 0-618-21388-0 CL $27.50

THE BEST AMERICAN MYSTERY STORIES™ 2002

James Ellroy, guest editor • Otto Penzler, series editor

Our perennially popular anthology is a favorite of mystery buffs and general readers alike. This year's volume is edited by the internationally acclaimed author James Ellroy and offers pieces by Robert B. Parker, Joyce Carol Oates, Michael Connelly, Stuart M. Kaminsky, and others.

0-618-12493-4 PA $13.00 / 0-618-12494-2 CL $27.50
0-618-25807-8 CASS $26.00 / 0-618-25806-X CD $35.00

THE BEST AMERICAN SPORTS WRITING™ 2002

Rick Reilly, guest editor • Glenn Stout, series editor

This series has garnered wide acclaim for its stellar sports writing and top-notch editors. Now Rick Reilly, the best-selling author and "Life of Reilly" columnist for *Sports Illustrated,* continues that tradition with pieces by Frank Deford, Steve Rushin, Jeanne Marie Laskas, Mark Kram, Jr., and others.

0-618-08628-5 PA $13.00 / 0-618-08627-7 CL $27.50